"It's good to see Herb McCormick's saili
gether in hard-copy form. In *Gone to the*
the globe in the company of a sailor so en
humored, so infectious in his love of saili
even keep me glued to my seat with a des        ... a yacht race—an
activity that usually strikes me as less interesting than watching paint
dry. What I treasure most in the book are the warm portraits of friends
and friendships, McCormick's tender sketch of sailing with his young
daughter, and his exuberant ability to render on the page the life of a
veteran wharf rat and expert sailor."

—Jonathan Raban, author of *Passage to Juneau* and editor of *The Oxford Book of the Sea*


"Like the psalm that begins "They that go down to the sea in ships," this
book is about the people, more than the sea or the ships. All the great
sea stories, from the Bible through Conrad and beyond, are about what
happens to the human psyche when it answers the siren call of the sea;
wind, weather, boats are simply the dramatic props. People go to sea,
consciously or not, to meet their truest selves. What happens out there,
over the rim of the world, out of sight of everyday society, almost always
results in some kind of epic story of human aspiration, be it achievement or the tragic unraveling of a dream. No one now writing about the
sea and sailors appreciates this more acutely than Herb McCormick.
As for the props, few living sailors have as complete an experience as
McCormick of the truest nature of the sea in all its moods, in every far-
flung ocean."

—Peter Nichols, author of *Sea Change* and *A Voyage for Madmen*


"He seems to have sailed everywhere, with everybody, and here's the
thing I love most about this anthology. Sure, the stories are vintage Mc-
Cormick—hilarious, poignant, rollicking, absolutely beautifully written
about the people and events that have made up the sailing world as he's
covered it for three decades. But there's a new element. He front-loads
each with intimate behind-the-scenes revelations about getting the
story, and the famous people in the story. It's like sitting in a sailors'
bar, with your g                                            s about what
really happened                                            e closes the
place down.

—Bernadette B                                            ulting editor
*BoatU.S. Magaz*

# Gone to the Sea:

# Selected Stories, Voyages, and Profiles

BY

# Herb McCormick

Cover design by Rob Johnson, www.johnsondesign.org
Edit, book design by Linda Morehouse, www.webuildbooks.com

Cover and author photo by David Thoreson,
Around the Americas Expedition Photographer
www.oceanwatchdt@me.com

Printed in the United States of America
First Edition
ISBN:  978-0-939837-94-6

Published by Paradise Cay Publications, Inc.
P. O. Box 29
Arcata, CA 95518-0029
800-736-4509
707-822-9163 Fax
paracay@humboldt1.com

*For Maggie,*
*my Buddy*

# Contents

# Introduction

IF MY buddy Jack Mack hadn't broken his neck, you probably wouldn't be reading this. It was Labor Day weekend, 1979, and two of my best friends—Jack McKenna and Steve Cardoza—and I were hiking out of the woods after a three-day camping trip at a rock concert on the Vermont/New Hampshire border. We'd all grown up on Rhode Island's Aquidneck Island, spending many a summer day diving and leaping off the cliffs along Newport's Ocean Drive. Jack Mack and Steve were stupendous athletes, and they were also fearless. Tourists would pull over to snap pictures of them in mid-flight.

Thirteen months earlier, I'd earned my college diploma and more or less hit the road. I'd captained my high school and college football teams and always thought I'd end up coaching, but my desire to make a career of a game that had basically defined my existence to that point had suddenly waned. Instead, I hitchhiked through Mexico with a girlfriend; lost a week in New Orleans at Mardi Gras; took a very suspect job driving forklifts all night in a warehouse outside the West Palm Beach airport; and ended up back in Newport painting houses with Jack Mack and Steve. I had few plans and ambitions to match.

And then, at summer's end with my pals, we came to a rocky bend by a river, tossed our clothes in the bushes and jumped in. Jack saw a little sapling up on the ridge and shinnied up, swaying back and forth like Tarzan. We were all in stitches, right up to the moment that the tree cracked. Jack reacted instinctually, and tucked for the dive. He missed the water by about two feet.

In an instant, he was a quadriplegic. A week later, we were both living in Boston. Jack was in a rehab hospital at B.U.; most nights, the nurses let me crash on the mats in the physical therapy room down the hall. This lasted until November. It was time for both of us to move on with our lives. In some ways, Jack was better prepared than me.

A high-school buddy of mine, Ian Scott, was selling advertising for a new business in town, a sailing magazine called *Cruising World*. He needed a roommate. My mom, a local legend named Martha, ran a small employment agency that sometimes got calls from the publication. There was an opening at the front desk...the receptionist. It paid seven grand a year. My mother and Ian put their heads together and decided I was an ideal candidate for both the job and the spare bedroom. On November 26, 1979—precisely eighteen years, to the day, before the birth of my daughter, Maggie—I walked through the front door of the magazine's offices on lower Thames Street, ready for duty. Little did I know, and through very little forethought on my behalf, I'd stumbled into a career.

At Williams College—a fine institution to which I'd gained entrance solely for my ability to pluck pigskins out of autumn skies—I'd been a sorry student with one redeeming quality. At the end of almost every term, I resurrected a passing grade with a decent term paper. I had a knack, of sorts, for writing. I never in a million years thought I'd do it professionally.

But *Cruising World* was an incredibly nurturing place, and after spotting a typo on a press release I was delivering to the printer, I got kicked upstairs—literally—into the editorial department. Mostly, I proofread and handled correspondence. But I was surrounded by great writers and sailors: Dale Nouse,

George Day, Dan Spurr, Bernadette Bernon ("Brennan" at the time), Betsy Holman ("Hitz") and Danny Greene. I didn't realize it at the time, but I'd become an apprentice.

My first published article came a year later, about 700 words retelling the tale of running into an elderly family friend I'd stumbled into at a boat show right after taking her first sail. I'd scribbled it down, reworked it about a hundred times, and presented it to executive editor Dale Nouse, who called me into his office and went over it pretty much word for word. Then he gave me a thumb's up and my first actual assignment. I remember floating out his door.

The magazine's publishers, Murray and Barbara Davis, didn't, ahem, pay much, but the fringe benefits were terrific. If an opportunity for an interesting sailing trip came up, you almost always got the green light. My sailing experience to that point was mostly club racing on Narragansett Bay, but before long I was heading offshore to Bermuda and the Caribbean. And everything started to feed upon itself. The more I sailed, the farther I wanted to go. The more I wrote, the more obsessed I became with making it my craft. I was in the perfect place to advance both agendas.

A couple of years later, Murray sent me to South Africa to cover the first leg of the inaugural BOC Challenge solo round-the-world race, which ultimately led to a book deal with the "in-house" publishing arm of the Davis's ever-growing enterprise, Seven Seas Press. *Out There*, co-authored with George Day, was published in 1983. My half of it was dedicated to Jack Mack, who taught me lessons about grace and courage and friendship right up until his dying day.

*Out There* was my first and only book...until this one.

It's broken into about three equal sections: "Faces" recalls some of the interesting characters I've profiled; "Places" is a collection of voyaging and travel essays; and "Races" tells the tales of some of the competitive sailing I've covered, as both a sailor and a reporter. The chapter notes (in greyed boxes) that preface or follow each piece provide some of the back-stories surrounding the articles, and updates on some of the subjects. For someone who had no idea what he wanted to do with his life, I've obviously been a blessed and lucky lad.

The title, "Gone to the Sea," has a double meaning. It's one of the stories in the book, the tale of solo sailor Mike Plant's final voyage. But it's also an apt summation of my own journey as a sailing writer. For once I'd truly discovered the sea, in more ways than one, I was long gone.

# Part I

# Faces

*Bobby Grieser*

**The four-time America's Cup winner, Dennis Conner,
bears more than a few similarities
to the TV mob boss, Tony Soprano.**

# 1: The (Not Quite) Mellow Dude

## MR. AMERICA'S CUP: DENNIS CONNER

TONY SOPRANO. When I first laid eyes on Dennis Conner on a radiant Sunday morning at the San Diego Yacht Club in the spring of 2009, the image of the TV mob boss leapt immediately to mind. Both are outsized, imposing men, but that wasn't the only thing. Maybe it was because he was striding towards his big ol' Chevy Suburban (Tony's ride). Or because his happy black Lab, Benny, was dutifully at his side (Tony loved animals). Or perhaps it was the jaunty captain's cap he was sporting (Tony favored a similar chapeau whenever he was aboard his powerboat, *The Stugots,* a name that Dennis could surely relate to).

Whatever the reasons, I couldn't shake Tony from my thoughts. A larger-than-life character, it was the duality of his existence that made him fascinating. He was, by turns, charming yet scary, generous yet petty, insightful yet intimidating, genuinely funny yet bitingly sarcastic, incredibly successful yet vaguely dissatisfied, and remarkably intelligent yet continuously self-deprecating.

Only later, after hanging out for awhile with Dennis—still the only sailor universally known by his first name, sailing's equivalent to a Brazilian soccer star—would I connect the dots and come to the conclusion that, yes, he and Tony shared more than a few similar characteristics. But only one of them is real, and ongoing, and as puzzling and intriguing as ever.

Over the years, I've had the opportunity to interview Dennis on several occasions. Ours is strictly a professional relationship, and I'm well aware that on the best of days he considers people like me a necessary evil, and on most others, a royal pain in the ass. (In somewhat gentler terms, he reminded me of this several times during the course of our time together.) At 67, he rarely grants interviews anymore (more reminders), and did so this time as a favor to photographer Bobby Grieser, a mutual friend and fellow San Diegan who's covered his career and done occasional commercial shoots for him.

All that said, I was positively giddy when he agreed to spend a few hours with me. Everything else aside, I harbor deep respect for the man and consider him a worthy champion and a sporting hero (albeit a complicated one), as well as a towering symbol of loss and redemption. I believe he's an icon of sailing, a man going down in history for almost all the right reasons, a defining emblem of an entire era. But no matter what one thinks about Dennis—and it seems everyone has an opinion, not all of which are floral bouquets—there are certain salient facts that are utterly beyond reproach.

He is a four-time America's Cup winner and the only skipper to lose it and win it back. He's appeared on the covers of *Time* and *Sports Illustrated* and earned the sobriquet "Mr. America's Cup." He's won countless world championships and an Olympic medal. He can still raise hell in an Etchells. Many consider him the greatest racing sailor of all time, and one must be quick and stubborn to argue the point.

And there's this: These days, as either a partner or outright owner, he reigns over a fleet that would be the envy of any sailor. His San Diego business, Dennis Conner's America's Cup Experience, includes a pair of International America's Cup Class yachts and a stunning replica of the original Cup winner, the schooner *America*, the helm of which he loves to take. An East Coast enterprise based in Manhattan's North Cove Marina employs a pair of 52-foot Formula One's for charters and corporate team building. He owns four Etchells, two of which reside in New Zealand and Australia, respectively, and remains a fierce presence in the class, where these days he enjoys his most rewarding competitive sailing. He takes his Farr 60, *Stars & Stripes* (ex-*Numbers*), out for the SDYC Wednesday-night summer series and the annual jaunt to Ensenada.

Then there's *Brushfire*, the classic, impeccable Sparkman and Stephens-designed 51-foot woody that's tied up a stone's throw from the yacht club bar and that serves multiple roles as a race boat, office, and retreat (it's his second antique wooden boat in recent years, the first being the 1925 Q-Class yacht *Cotton Blossom II*, which he completely restored and then raced on the Mediterranean before selling it there).

I'd heard that Dennis spent loads of time aboard *Brushfire*, usually with Benny at his feet, sometimes baking cookies or making lunch in the comfortable galley for his crew and friends. As a warm, fuzzy picture in the mind's eye, it had a lot going for it, and before our meeting I'd begun imagining the vintage-2009 Dennis as a mellow dude chilling on the waterfront, the lion in winter kicking back on his wooden boat and finally finding peace and respite after all the long, countless, grueling campaigns.

This fantasy, in some (but not all) ways, proved to be as fictional as Tony Soprano. That was clear almost from the very moment he nodded toward the Suburban and said, "Get in."

THE NEXT couple of hours were incredible; he was as gracious a host, as interesting a companion, as any you'd hope to find.

We ate breakfast at a fine little diner in Ocean Beach where he ordered "the usual" and knew all the waitresses. We took a long drive through Point Loma, past the modest little house at sea level where he was raised and the much more substantial residence up the hill that he now calls home. We stopped at a headland where he urged me to get out and sniff the salt air. "The Pacific looks very pacific today," he said.

We drove up through Fort Rosecrans and pulled over to take in the wide vista of San Diego Bay and the downtown skyline. Dennis spoke knowledgably and even passionately about the city's geography and history, the voyage to its shores by European explorer Juan Rodriguez Cabrillo, the changes that had unfolded over the years. When it comes to San Diego, his beloved hometown, Dennis should run the Chamber of Commerce.

"It's the nicest place in the world to live," he said. "I've been around. You've been around. What's a better alternative, especially in America? New Zealand's nice, but it's too far away. This is the best place in the world."

Back at the yacht club, I thanked him for the tour, which had basically blown me away.

"It's all relative," he said, invoking an oft-repeated line. "Imagine what it would've been like if you were with someone who knew what they were talking about."

I thought he was kidding, though I don't know him well enough to be sure. Whatever the meaning, it certainly introduced a new tone to the conversation.

Over the next few days, I'd run into a couple of people who do know Dennis well. Troy Sears is his partner at Dennis Conner's America's Cup Experience. "He's very involved in the day-to-day operation but not hands on," he said in *America's* vast saloon, right before heading out on a whale-watching sail from a downtown pier.

"He's a very early riser. Typically I'll get up in the morning and I'll have an email from him, time-stamped at four or four-thirty a.m. He'll have a whole list of ideas, or questions, or things we could do better. Typically, they're all very good suggestions."

I asked Sears about Dennis's reputation as a stern taskmaster. "I've found that once you're inside his inner circle, he's very warm and he cares," he said. "Do I see him get stern? Yeah. But not typically to the people in his 'family,' if you will."

For nearly two decades Jack Sutphen got to see and know Dennis as few do, as his sparring partner and the skipper of his trial horses in one Cup campaign after another. Now 91, Sutphen remains witty and insightful, and his stories about life with Dennis, on a daily basis, are rich, warm, funny, and endless.

"What's disappointing is that Dennis does a lot of nice things and gets no credit for them," said Sutphen. "One day in Australia (in 1987) he comes down to the dock and he's got a little kid with him, all dressed up in (*Stars & Stripes*) foul-weather gear. I said, 'Who's this?' and Dennis says, 'It's my newspaper boy. He delivers my newspaper. And he's going to sail with me today.' And he had him out the whole day, sailing, this kid we'd never seen before.

"Everything he's done for me has been wonderful. So I have tremendous respect for Dennis and I like him tremendously. But he can turn around the next day and walk right by you and your wife and not say a thing. He's focused on something else. He has tunnel vision. But that's what people who don't know him remember about him.

"One of his great strengths is that he's a great guy to sail with," added Sutphen. "Anybody who sails with him wants to sail with him again. Look at the pictures of the old Cup teams. Year after year, the same guys. There's a lot of loyalty with Dennis on both sides. I can't make the point strongly enough."

AFTER THE drive, we stepped aboard *Brushfire*. The varnished cabin house was exquisite. The topsides gleamed. The entire boat was gorgeous, Bristol fashion, a work of art. The only thing that seemed out of place was the dish antenna mounted off the cockpit, feeding the satellite signal to the flat-screen TV below.

"I want to see what's happening with the NASCAR race," said Dennis, flipping it on.

The next hour or so, however, was more like a tennis match than a stockcar race. I'd serve up a question, and he'd volley back an answer, sometimes with a bit of pace, and others with a little spin.

On *Brushfire*'s PHRF rating for handicap racing: "Ever hear of the Tall Poppy Syndrome? That's why I get a rating that's six seconds a mile less than I should. If I can't win, who should? The boat's in perfect shape. The sails are perfect. I've got the best crew. So what do they do to level it? They give me a higher rating."

On wooden boats: "There's something about old wooden boats that have a certain cachet. It's hard to explain to people who've never experienced it, or don't have gray hair. They think fiberglass is the smell a boat should have. They don't understand the warmth and beauty of wood."

On the America's Cup: "I reckon old guys like me remember the old days, when it was a sport. It wasn't a business. It was a sport. That was then. And now is now. It's a big business now. It changed. Some people are having trouble grasping that change. That's their personal problem. These days it's all about litigation and power and juice. It's a game that plays to [the billionaire's] strengths. It's not about who's the best sailor. The best sailors aren't in the America's Cup."

On mellowing out: "Am I less competitive? I would think so. You still do the best you can. But it's not life and death. The other thing is, it's not as satisfying to beat someone who isn't putting the same amount of effort into it."

On the end of our interview: "How much longer is this going to take? This is all personal anyway. It's nobody's business. What good can it do me? I did this as a favor to Bobby. A good deed never goes unpunished."

As we walked down *Brushfire*'s dock back toward the club, a pair of very attractive women ("cougars" in the modern vernacular), dressed to the nines, hair perfectly coiffed, stopped Dennis cold. They introduced themselves and babbled at him for a moment—honestly, they seemed barely coherent—and after Dennis paid them a compliment and wished them a pleasant day, everyone carried on.

A moment later, as we parted ways, Dennis made an amusing comment about "desperate housewives" and I said that I had to hand it to him. Good-looking strangers, even crazy ones, rarely halt me in my tracks and flirt shamelessly.

"Man, it's good to be Dennis," I concluded.

He nodded pleasantly. Against long odds, I'd finally grasped the obvious.

"I told you it was," he said.

Photographer Bob Grieser, an old friend of Dennis Conner's from San Diego, arranged the interview with the America's Cup legend for a piece that originally appeared in *Sailing World* magazine.

Getting to San Diego was a story in itself. I was ultimately bound for Seattle to begin a 27,000-mile expedition called Around the Americas, a voyage that circled North and South America via the Northwest Passage and Cape Horn. With a pair of kayaks lashed to the racks of my Chevy Silverado, I made it from Rhode Island to California in 72 hours flat (counting the two hours I was stuck by the highway during a New Mexico dust storm), arriving the day before I was scheduled to meet with Dennis.

Knowing what I know now, I'm sure he wouldn't have rescheduled our meeting if I'd missed my appointment. I yawned my way through the whole thing.

# 2: *A Spaced Odyssey?*

## RECORD-SETTING VOYAGER REID STOWE

THINK ABOUT it: two straight weeks at sea. It's not an insignificant amount of time, but most of us could handle it, and even enjoy it. So let's up the ante: two straight months at sea. Hmmm: pushing it, no? But what about two straight years at sea? Honestly, think about it.

Food. Communications. Spares. Navigation. What if this went wrong or that broke? Ouch! What if we got hurt?

No new movies, books, music, or magazines. No ripe fruit, no fresh veggies. No family, friends, or nights out. No walks ashore, no drives to town, no long conversations, no moonlight kisses. Heck, not a single lovely evening anchored in a quiet cove: just the sea and the stars, the calms and the storms, the open ocean, the endless blue, you and your boat. Two. Long. Years.

We can all agree on this, right? Nada. No thanks. No way, José.

Unless, of course, you're the voyager, explorer, boat-builder, spiritualist, dreamer, sculptor, musician, father, and sometimes extremely controversial ex-convict named Reid Stowe. Two years? Ha! In his quest to spend a thousand (or more?) successive days at sea, on April 21st of 2009 Reid put two straight years, or 730 consecutive days, behind him. After well over a couple of years under way—and counting—and a full spin around the planet, things are really starting to get good. In fact, by Reid's measure, they're just about perfect.

How do you know this? Why, you call him up!

Reid answers his satellite phone after one ring, and when asked for a status report, the answer spills forth like a wave breaking on a beach.

"I don't know if you've seen my track on my website (www.1000days.net), but I just recently finished drawing a 2,600-mile heart in the ocean," he says, referring to his latest water-borne creation. Part navigator, part performance artist, Reid has a history of combining the two disciplines to render grand patterns with his wake, likening them to the constellations in the sky, but even better defined.

"It comes up," he adds, "very clear."

Later I'll go check out his recent course track. Yep, there it is: The connected dots of his route form a plump, round heart.

He continues: "That left me on the west side of the South Atlantic. I'm now almost up to the Equator. I can see the Southern Cross. I've just sailed through the biggest school of tuna I've ever seen in my life. When I finish this call I'm going to have another look at their phosphorescent bodies, swimming behind the schooner. So it's a beautiful night, I'm feeling good and strong, and things are looking real good."

Two years? Reid Stowe, now well into this third, laughs at your two short years.

A RELATIVELY short profile cannot do justice to the exuberant, eccentric Life and Times of the one-and-only William Reid Stowe, who set forth upon this celestial orb and began his epic stab at human existence on January 6, 1952. Fit, lean, and handsome at 57, Reid looks a good decade younger, which is a remarkable feat considering the never-ending adventures he's packed into his earthly travels thus far.

Reid was the eldest of six kids; his father was an Air Force pilot who kept the family moving throughout his formative years. It's almost too easy to surmise that the path Reid ultimately chose, one diametrically opposed to the strident regulation of a military career (even though he credits his dad for teaching him the virtues of routine, regimentation, and hard work, the core values of a diligent seaman), was in some ways an act of rebellion (though he also makes it very clear that the unconditional support of his parents has been instrumental in his endeavors).

Still, Reid, who came of age as a young artist in the Age of Aquarius studying Buddhism and other religions, and practicing yoga and meditation—in short, embracing your classic "alternative lifestyle"—was never destined for the Air Force Academy. Even now, Reid speaks in New Age platitudes, about being "in touch" and "connected" with various people, objects, beliefs, and philosophical doctrines. Once again, it's almost too easy to reject such discourse as the ramblings of an aging space cadet.

(In fact, having known Reid for several years, at times I've pled guilty to the above, though I've come to realize that his outlooks and views are considered and sincere. Even so, while writing this piece, on numerous occasions I forced myself to recall the straightforward question posed in the Elvis Costello song, "What's So Funny About Peace, Love And Understanding?" Even to dolts like me, the answer is obvious.)

The point is, it's tempting to write off Reid's earnest penchant to embrace his karma and consciousness. But if you dismiss his hard-earned credentials as a talented and tenacious sailor and mariner (albeit a very unconventional one), who earned his chops building and sailing his very sound but unusual

boats over a ton of demanding, difficult miles, you do so at the
risk of sounding very foolish yourself.

Reid cut his boat-building teeth molding fiberglass surf-
boards at a summer beach house in North Carolina owned by
his mother's family. Later, he built his first real boat there, a
27-foot Wharram-designed catamaran that weighed a mere 1,400
pounds.

Though Reid entered college to study art, he didn't last
long. On a surfing vacation to Hawaii, he met a young local sailor
who invited him to crew on a voyage across the South Pacific,
an invitation Reid happily accepted, and which gave him his
first taste of blue-water sailing. In New Zealand, he made the
acquaintance of another youthful cruiser, Dutchman Ivo Van
Laake, who'd recently sailed with the French legend, Bernard
Moitessier. Later, Reid met Moitessier personally, and says he
"had a great influence over me," though it would be Van Laake
who left the more lasting impression.

Returning to North Carolina, Van Laake soon joined him,
and the two crossed the Atlantic on Reid's 27-foot cat, *Tantra*.
After the double-handed passage to Portugal, Reid soloed to
Morocco. Once his Dutch friend returned after a visit home, the
two made a second Atlantic crossing, to Brazil, and then into the
Amazon River. Finally, having visited four continents, Reid concluded the journey with another solo sail back to North Carolina. In voyaging, he'd found a calling, and he was ready for more.
But he needed a boat large enough for his growing ambitions.

Once again, he decided to build it himself. Back on the
Carolina beach, with assorted family members and a cadre of
free-spirited volunteers, Reid began constructing a 70-foot
gaff-rigged schooner based on the old Gloucester fishing boats.
Originally called the *Tantra Schooner*—on breaks, the workers

enjoyed chanting the words aloud—Reid later changed the name to *Anne*, after his mother. The main hull was fashioned of a material called Ferri-lite, a two-part micro-balloon/polyester resin lay-up over steel mesh; the interior, with elaborate carvings and woodwork, of walnut, driftwood, and Caribbean hardwood; the ballast, 42,000 pounds of poured concrete.

With his first wife and his daughter, Reid took off for the Caribbean, and then later on his first truly intrepid offshore exploit aboard *Anne*, a five-month expedition to Antarctica. In subsequent years he was busted for helping unload a shipment of pot and served nine months in a medium-security penitentiary; was divorced and remarried; sailed to Manhattan, established a base at Pier 63, and became immersed in the Chelsea art and music scene; and with his second wife embarked on several significant sailing trips including a 200-day, nonstop Atlantic cruise he dubbed "The Voyage of the Sea Turtle" in honor of the tortoise track *Anne* "carved" through the seas.

He also kept thinking about a long sea journey of "extreme endurance" he'd originally envisioned on the voyage to Antarctica, one that was so unique the only thing he could equate it to was a passage to the heavens. He even had a name for it: "1,000 Days at Sea—The Mars Ocean Odyssey."

THE ORIGINAL idea was to land a major sponsor, and for years Reid searched for one, hoping he'd find a corporate backer who'd understand the value in a "space analogous" expedition that would take as long as a journey to Mars, and pose similar psychological challenges. But none ever materialized, and on April 21, 2007, with minor support from a handful of companies and individuals but little hard cash, Reid and his girlfriend, Soanya Ahmad (his second marriage had also ended in divorce), took off anyway.

The trip almost ended before it really even began.

Two weeks after departing from New Jersey, on Day 15, *Anne* collided with a freighter and lost her bowsprit and headstay, a harrowing incident, Reid says, that Soanya and he were lucky to survive. It took nearly a month to effect adequate repairs, and once completed, *Anne* resumed a slow course through the South Atlantic towards the Cape of Good Hope and the Roaring Forties.

Blown sails were problematic but paled in comparison to Soanya's chronic seasickness. Ultimately, the couple decided she'd abandon the voyage and Reid would continue alone, so on Day 306, off Western Australia, Soanya stepped aboard a Royal Perth Yacht Club launch piloted by none other than Aussie sailor Jon Sanders, who at the time held the record for the longest non-stop solo voyage ever, of 657 days.

As it turned out, Soanya was not only seasick: she was pregnant. Five months later, in July of 2008, she gave birth to a boy named Darshen Ahmad Stowe. By that time, the new father had experienced more broken sails off South Australia, as well as a busted desalinator, and he sailed north across the Equator and into the North Pacific to fill his water tanks. With that mission accomplished, and now well into this second year under way, he turned back towards Cape Horn to complete his first circumnavigation aboard *Anne*. In an email message, Reid described what happened next:

"After I filled my water tanks I decided to sail south back into the trade winds. I let nature dictate my course, continuing with my daily seamanship work as usual. At the bottom of the trades I got a wind shift and as it was much too early to head to Cape Horn, I followed the wind around and headed back up into warmer weather.

"Around October 2nd (of 2008) I got an email from an old sailing buddy saying, 'Congratulations Reid, you have drawn a whale with your course.' I looked at my map and sure enough, it was a (4,600 nautical mile) whale! This accidental art confirmed to me that I was in tune with the ocean with my style of sailing, having created an unbelievable but true spiritual and technical wonder. This gave me the freedom to go deeper into oceanic prayer and I slowed down and looked around in awe and wonder... My divine spirit swelled with love... This is where I am now, living out my lifelong dream close to the sea and the grace of the universe."

With that, Reid rounded the Horn and sailed back into the Atlantic, where he passed the two-year milestone on Day 730 and kept right on going.

IN EARLY August of 2009, a few months after I spoke to him via satellite phone, I sent Reid an email asking the exact date of his thousandth day, and where precisely he planned on concluding his journey in early 2010. (For an update on Reid's triumphant return home, see Chapter Notes on page 17.) A few days later came this reply:

"I still plan on arriving in (New York City, but) not on Day 1,000. It is no longer that to me. Nor is it the Mars Ocean Odyssey. Anyone who has been reading my story closely knows that. It is now The Love Voyage and I intend for The Love Voyage to go on. And when I do come back, The Love Voyage will continue and keep going and take on new direction and meaning."

Along the way, Reid has had his detractors, some of whom appear dangerously obsessive. One such critic, who hides behind the Internet pseudonym Regatta Dog, has gone so far as to build entire websites devoted to Reid's claims, deeds, and transgressions over the years.

"I am not a perfect sailor and they have found some flaws," Reid says of his denouncers. "They don't like my lifestyle, my philosophy, my woman, my personality, my boat, and perhaps the fact that I am following my dreams. But I can't see how any man who spends any amount of time at sea alone could hate me. At sea you learn respect, otherwise you couldn't do it."

Here's how Reid has described his quest: "I have come to see that my mission is to inspire the world while using love to adapt to living with the forces of the sea. The human society part of me says, 'You must go, set a course.' The divine searcher side of me says, 'Pray here for a while, this is your place, your moment...' I have always seen my journeys into the wilderness of the sea as a spiritual quest... The winds and seas and wildlife follow me saying, 'Save us.' I say, 'Take me where you will, I'm seaworthy.'"

Meanwhile, he sails on and on. "I am on the back side of the Atlantic Trades," he wrote in his last email to me, "sailing gently, having new experiences."

Where and how will this odyssey, this journey through space and time, ultimately end? Only Reid knows. Like Kurtz, the protagonist in Conrad's *Heart of Darkness,* he's ventured to the far side of his deep soul. But while Kurtz chose to dance with the darkness, Reid has tacked for the opposite shore, is flirting with different obsessions. Alone with his sea, he's bathing himself in the light.

*Reid Stowe*

**Reid Stowe's sweetheart, Soanya Ahman, spent 306 days aboard *Anne* before leaving the boat after discovering she was pregnant.**

On June 17, 2010 at Pier 81 on the Hudson River, Reid Stowe finished his epic marathon voyage after 1,152 consecutive days at sea. In the process, he shattered not only the record for the longest sailing trip ever, but also the mark for the longest solo voyage ever; his 846 days alone easily surpassed the former record of 658 days set by Aussie Jon Sanders on a triple-circumnavigation in the late 1980s. (The discrepancy in the numbers reflects the time his "sweetheart," Soanya Ahmad, spent aboard *Anne*.)

The story that appears here was published by *Cruising World* about two-thirds of the way through his amazing adventure. I've known Reid professionally for over fifteen years, and we've always gotten along well. But in a follow-up interview for another article once he was safely back ashore, he let me know in no uncertain terms that he was none too pleased with the title of this piece, which he felt was disrespectful.

I actually admire Reid as a seaman, and I think the story accurately reflects that fact.

Billy Black

**Before his untimely death in 2006,
Captain Bob Tiedemann was a familiar figure
at the helm of his beloved 12-Meter, *Gleam*.**

Putting together what was basically a eulogy for a man I'd known and admired for many years, Bob Tiedemann, was one of the hardest stories I've ever written. I did so at the urging of *Cruising World* deputy editor Elaine Lembo, who commissioned this piece.

Bob's disease progressed so rapidly that I never did get a chance to interview him before he passed away; both times we tried to get together, he had to cancel because of his advancing illness.

I owe Elizabeth Tiedemann a huge debt of gratitude for her full and gracious assistance—this story wouldn't have happened without her.

Everyone in Newport still thinks about Bob every time they see *Gleam, Northern Lights*, and his other boats, which still ply the waters of Narragansett Bay. Quite a legacy.

# 3: Requiem for a Mariner

## CLASSIC YACHT RESTORER BOB TIEDEMANN

IN SOME WAY, shape, or form, the beginning of the end will happen to all of us, and for Bob Tiedemann it happened on January 1, 2006, in a strange, surprising manner. Other than the novelty of the holiday, it was a routine winter's afternoon for Bob and his wife, Elizabeth, a statuesque brunette who'd been at his side for all sorts of adventures—on water and on land—for some 15 years. The Tiedemanns' daily exercise habit this day favored an hour-long walk, and midway through the stroll Bob made an announcement that stunned his bride.

"I need to sit down," he said.

The record suggests that it was probably the first time in his entire 56 years that he'd ever uttered those words, or anything remotely close to them. Just four days earlier, he'd been schussing down the steeps of Stowe, Vermont, which he'd been expertly tearing up since childhood. But though he knew the mountains and enjoyed playing in them, his calling, his life, was the sea.

If you've ever visited or sailed into the charmed harbor of Newport, R.I., there is little doubt that you saw something of the work of Bob Tiedemann; in fact, the chances are pretty fair that you laid eyes upon Captain Bob himself. For he was there almost every summer day, dressed in white, blue eyes twinkling, at the helm of his beloved 12-Meter, *Gleam*, in many observers' eyes the prettiest Twelve of them all. It's been estimated that Tiedemann spent over 13,000 hours at her helm—13,000 hours!—though longtime Newport wharf rats may insist that the figure seems low.

While Tiedemann rested and caught his breath on that January day, one wonders if he gave at least a passing thought to the upcoming summer, and all the work and fun and sailing that lay ahead. Like every year, it was going to be jam-packed: *Gleam* had to be extricated from her winter wraps and brought back to her spit-and-polished stateliness. So, too, did the handsome 12-Meter, *Northern Light*, and the 54-foot Alden-designed yawl, *Mariner*, the other remarkable wooden sailboats in the Tiedemann's bustling waterfront business, Seascope Yacht Charters, which introduced countless sailors (and first-timers) to the singular joys of classic yachts and yachting.

And let's not forget the powerboats—the 62-foot commuter vessel, *Pam*, built in 1921, and the 40-foot, 1911 harbor launch, *Fawan*—both of which offered a more genteel experience to their passengers. After decades of finding and restoring derelicts to their full potential and glory, Seascope had evolved into an enterprise that, from a nautical perspective, served as a full-service portal to a more elegant time.

Once the fleet was again Bristol, there would be all the regattas, and weddings, and corporate team-building events, a full slate of nonstop activity that allowed the Tiedemanns and their closely-knit workforce of skippers and crews to live and thrive by working on the water and doing what they loved. Oh, yes, there would be plenty to do, plenty to see.

As it turned out, however, Captain Bob was suffering from something far more drastic and sinister than the excesses of the season, and a roadside breather wasn't even close to being the answer. For his energy, it would soon become apparent, was being sapped by the tumor on his pancreas. And by early May, five short months later, just around the time *Gleam* usually takes her inaugural summer sail, Bob Tiedemann would be gone.

SAILBOATS were a big part of the boy's life. Okay, perhaps on most days they were the very center of his world. He was a Connecticut kid, his father a naval architect, his playground the shoreline and boatyards of Long Island Sound, the latter of which he haunted year round, always on the lookout for a forgotten treasure.

By 12, he was racing the family Lightning. At 16, he convinced his father that what the clan really needed was a certain Alden yawl—built in 1950 for the CEO of Bethlehem Steel by the German yard Abeking & Rasmussen—and furthermore, that they should occasionally charter the boat to cover her costs. And just who would skipper this big 54-footer called *Mariner*? Well, there happened to be a talented, precocious teenager, who already possessed an uncommon sense of order and seamanship, right under the same roof.

Who knows what they want to do with their life before high-school graduation? It appears Bob Tiedemann did, though he also got a kick out of fast cars and at least briefly contemplated the notion of a career as a test driver and mechanic. But by 1975, when he learned that a dilapidated 12-Meter called *Gleam* was languishing at a boatyard along the banks of New Jersey's Maurice River—and that she might be had for a very good price—it was clear that boats had trumped autos once and for all.

In a wonderful article called "The Tiedemann Collection" that appeared in WoodenBoat magazine (and which can be accessed on the Internet at www.seascopenewport.com), writer Bill Mayher recounts many of the trials and tribulations Tiedemann encountered in his early business days, including the purchase and subsequent delivery of *Gleam*, a 68-foot 12-Meter built in 1937, from an eccentric university physics professor.

"At first glance *Gleam*, for all her storied past, was no beauty," wrote Mayher. "Perhaps in the spirit of some holiday occasion, her decks had been painted Christmas green, all bronze hardware Santa Claus red. To deliver the boat along the Jersey Shore to New York, Tiedemann was obliged to rig a gas-powered generator on deck to force sufficient juice through her ancient circuitry to run her bilge pumps. It wasn't until *Gleam* arrived at City Island for serious hull work that he discovered the problem with her wiring: her 32-volt system was made up of a virtually infinite chain of 3-foot lengths of used wire that the thrifty professor had harvested from the lab benches of his Physics 101 students."

Because of the professor's highly suspect "practice of renewing worn-out bronze screws by jamming a bit of bronze wool into the hole, and then setting the old screw back with a daub of white glue," Tiedemann had a major refastening job in front of him as well. But he was nothing if not resourceful, and by the summer of 1976 he had a vintage 12-Meter ready for charter customers. Soon after, he decided to relocate to Newport, at that time still very much the home of the America's Cup. What could be more alluring to Cup aficionados than watching the competing 12-Meters from the deck of an authentic Twelve?

With hindsight, it seems like a logical, straightforward, even brilliant idea. Back then, for a 27-year-old sailor who lived aboard to make ends meet, it was a mighty risk. He still had *Mariner* to keep going, too. But Tiedemann's next move was even bolder. Reasoning that if one classic Twelve was good, two would be better—more than anything else, it would heighten the sensory appeal when the two powerful sloops sailed aggressively alongside—he went searching for a stablemate to *Gleam*. He knew exactly what he was looking for.

Of the countless number of brilliant yachting pictures captured through the lens of legendary marine photographer Morris Rosenfeld, perhaps his most famous was "Flying Spinnakers," a study in light, shadow, and symmetry that featured a pair of pre-World War II 12-Meters under full, blossoming sail, running before a galloping sea. One was *Gleam*. The other was a 70-foot Sparkman & Stephens design built by the famed Nevins yard in 1938. She was called *Northern Light*.

Like a dog scratching for a bone, Tiedemann dove into research and learned that *Northern Light* was surviving—barely—just below the surface of a foul slip on Michigan's Lake Macatawa. If bringing *Gleam* back to trim was something akin to writing an interesting screenplay, then rescuing and restoring *Northern Light* could be likened to producing an epic, far-reaching novel, full of twists and turns and obstacles.

The saga took two years, during which nearly every structural component, along with all the machinery, rigging, and electronics, needed to be addressed and overhauled. When the work was done, her deep blue hull, contrasted with her varnished wood spars, made for an object of exquisite, jaw-dropping beauty. Soon after, *Northern Light* and *Gleam* were swapping close-hauled tacks on Narragansett Bay on a daily basis, and no one needed a latter-day Morris Rosenfeld to hone the image into view.

For a moment, Bob Tiedemann could rest. He'd realized his vision and his fleet, at least the sailing half of it, was in.

ONE HAS to admit, if the story ended right there, it would seem pretty complete. But it didn't, not by a long shot.

If you visit Newport today, you'll see no fewer than a dozen 12-Meters plying the waters, plying the trade. The amazing collection of long, lean sloops has become its own cottage industry. They add grace to a waterfront that was victimized by one lame, poorly executed development project after another throughout the 1970s and, especially, the 1980s. No, it wasn't necessarily a gorgeous harbor before then, but it was an honest, working one. One can make the argument that the fleet of Twelves, constantly under sail, has helped return to the city an air of legitimacy, of heritage. They certainly have played no small part in bridging the town's rich, important yachting history between Then and Now.

Bob Tiedemann was the instigator. Others, following his strong lead, joined ranks with him and the whole, as they say, became so much greater than the sum of its parts. The America's Cup disappeared from Newport in 1983, spirited away by the Aussies and their quirky, effective wing keel. But, remarkably, the grandeur of the event somehow still remains, mostly because so many important Cup winners and contenders still sail its waters. Simply put, Captain Bob came to Newport and helped change it for the better, not in esoteric terms, but in real, tangible, visual ones that people can see, or sail, or just admire from afar. That's one powerful legacy to leave behind.

And yet there's another open end to the story that's more personal, for Tiedemann may have started out on his life's work essentially alone, but that's not at all how he finished it.

Elizabeth Tiedemann met her future husband in 1991 aboard—what else?—*Gleam*. She was working in corporate sales for a local hotel and had been invited out for a "familiarization" sail. "Bob called me afterwards and I thought he was looking for business from the hotel," she said. "It took me awhile to realize he was after my business."

Both Elizabeth and Bob were casualties of broken marriages, and they didn't rush anything. Eventually she came aboard *Gleam* as a hostess, a stint that lasted two years, where she literally learned the ropes. From there she took her corporate skills to the shoreside end of the Seascope operation, booking the charters, handling the payroll. Three years to the day from their first meeting, on July 10, 1994, they were married aboard *Gleam*. It's hard to imagine a more balanced union, her yin in perfect alignment to his yang, their lives together a whirlwind where it was impossible to demarcate where the business ended and the passion began, because they were all one and the same.

Still, at first, she was wary of one thing and one thing only. "When we first met I thought I'd come behind *Gleam*," she admits. "He was devoted to her. She was an extension of him and vice versa. He loved her. She enabled him to do what he loved to do. She was responsible for the restoration of *Northern Light*, for the maintenance of *Mariner*, which has been in the family for 40 years. *Pam* and *Fawan* never would've been restored without her. *Gleam* paid her way."

So, yes, as it turned out there was plenty of room in Tiedemann's heart for *Gleam*, and Elizabeth, and for the projects that would follow, that they took on together. The restoration of *Pam*, for example, is an excellent object lesson in how that process worked. "Bob always approached it like this," said Elizabeth. "First you find the boat, then you rescue and restore it, and then you find it a market."

As with *Gleam* and *Northern Light*, *Pam* was a certified mess when Tiedemann found her awash in a Fort Lauderdale canal. But he'd always reckoned that the Twelves could use their very own tender, and that it would have to be something special, something worthy of the role. Tiedemann took one look at the wreckage of the once-glamorous vessel—the caved-in foredeck, the seized engines—and, once more, saw something that others couldn't see.

"It was love at first sight," said Elizabeth. "He had to have her."

Tiedemann got the engines going, limped up the Intra-coastal Waterway, had a temporary shed built for her in James-town, R.I. Slowly, slowly, the couple put a bit of money into her, launched her, chartered her out at low rates until they had more cash to inject into her rebirth. Today, in her own way, the "rum runner" *Pam* is every bit the equal of the Twelves; she has found her market, and does active duty on cocktail cruises, ash scatterings, dinners, lunches. With her classic lines and abundant brightwork, she's a throwback to another time and place. Then again, so was the man who found and saved her.

"He was old-fashioned," said Elizabeth. "He was in this world but, really, he was a man of the 1920s and 1930s. When we first met he had little handlebars at the end of his moustache, which would definitely typify him as an old-world kind of guy. He was a gentleman, always a gentleman. Even when he was sailing, he always said 'please' and 'thank you.'

"I know exactly how I would've answered if, fifteen years ago, someone said to me, 'You can have your soul mate, but only for fifteen years. Would you still walk down that path?'

"The answer's simple: In a minute I would."

*Not of the sunlight,*
*Not of the moonlight,*
*Not of the starlight!*
*O young Mariner,*
*Down to the haven,*
*Call your companions,*
*Launch your vessel,*
*And crowd your canvas,*
*And, ere it vanishes*
*Over the margin,*
*After it, follow it,*
*Follow The Gleam.*

—Alfred Lord Tennyson
"Merlin And The Gleam"

MAY 12, 2006, was a stormy, rainy day in Newport, R.I. The weather was unsettled. Maybe the whole universe was unsettled. That's what it felt like. Four days earlier, Bob Tiedemann had passed away after losing his battle to pancreatic cancer, and on this miserable afternoon, several hundred mourners packed old Trinity Church on Spring Street to its very rafters to celebrate one mariner's remarkable life.

Bob's friends were eloquent, sad, and funny. Jeff Marlowe spoke about Tennyson's lyrical "Merlin And The Gleam," from which the revered Twelve got her name. He said how right it was that Bob was one of the founders of the Museum of Yachting, whose mission is the preservation of the sport. And he got a big laugh when he said, "Bob loved his crew and treated them like family. Perhaps it's more appropriate to say that Bob treated his family like crew!"

Old pal Amos Shepard said, "I think he's here, listening to me, his hand on a railing of wood close by, and wondering how many coats of paint or varnish it will take to make it look new again." Elizabeth's friend, Lydia Babich, spoke about how Bob was always an avid participant in the regular Girls Night Out, about how he pampered and looked after the ladies.

His mates and captains were the ushers, and one of them, Kyle Dufur—a Renaissance man like his boss—played a stirring rendition of "Ave Maria" on the violin. Soon it was over, and Bob's friends and colleagues, sailors all, disassembled in the rain, the community weakened, and strengthened, by the words and music.

One other thing happened that day. *Gleam* was launched, ready for yet another summer. Her true captain was nowhere in sight.

Herb McCormick

**After sailing with Don and Mark Street,
only one question remained:
How could two guys so different be so much alike?**

Sailing with Don Street was a joy, even though
for this anthology I've deleted the sidebar that
appeared in *Cruising World* when this story was
originally published about how we somehow mis-
placed a degree of longitude on our passage from
the Caribbean and missed Bermuda on the first try
by a mere, um, sixty miles. If you ever see me in a
waterfront tavern, that story will cost you one cold
beer. Maybe two.

# 4: *His Old Man and the Sea*

## CRUISING ICON DON STREET AND SON MARK

THE TAPPING'S what woke me. Persistent. Annoying. Click-click. Pause. Click- click-click-click-click. Pause. I squinted at my watch—Oh, joy: 0600—and then at my surroundings. Yes, having flown into Tortola the afternoon before, I was indeed in full horizontal splendor in a forward berth aboard the Oyster 49 *Nimrod of Orwell*. Glancing out the port, yup, we were still tied up at the Village Key Marina. But what in the world was that tapping?

A loose halyard? Iffy. A recycling pump? Possible. Whatever it was, it needed attention and there were no other volunteers. I stumbled from my bunk.

It was coming from the aft cabin, and its source proved a surprise. There, sitting before an ancient Olympia Traveller II portable typewriter, the pioneer Caribbean cruising sailor and author Don Street was pecking away for all he was worth. "The 'd' sticks," he said, as if I'd come searching for which was the problem letter. "Never have been able to get that fixed."

"Good morning" seemed an improper response and, considering that Street is one of the most prolific sailing and cruising-guide writers ever, even in my haze I did have a question: "Don, you don't have a laptop?"

He spun around, grabbed the tiny typewriter from the desk, and plopped it atop his skinny thighs. Shirtless and smirking, in the cackle for which he earned his nickname—"Squeaky"—he replied with what was clearly a well-rehearsed line. "Oh yeah," he said. "I've got a laptop."

It seemed a tad early to get played as a straight man, even to a legend, and my bed was still warm. Alas, there'd be no return to it. "Just want to finish typing up these ship's orders," Don rasped. "Need to get some coffee going. Lots to do. Where're the boys?"

Ah yes, the boys. I'd wandered into Don Street's world, but I wasn't alone. There were many miles ahead to be sailed, but there were others aboard with whom to sail them. To our veteran captain, Don, one of them was kin, far more than a casual shipmate. And if I was awake, well...

"Fellas," I called, moving forward. "Hey, fellas . . . ."

"YOU will PRAY for YOURSELVES!" the preacher bellowed to a thunderous lick from an electric guitar. "And I WILL pray for YOU!"

The tent revival had taken place aside a restaurant some hundred yards from our slip at Village Key. I'd been in Tortola about four hours, a quarter of which had been spent at the nearby bar with our floppy-hatted, much recognized skipper, knocking back several of his favorite green-bottled beverages. Downing Heinekens with Don Street in a Virgin Islands watering hole was fine entertainment. In passing, some people performed neck-twisting double takes, while others actually stopped to recall brief, long-ago meetings or to profess thanks for his books and articles.

Lounging in the cockpit after dinner, with Don retired below, the nearby prayer meeting had gathered steam. I must've looked shocked, or stunned, or something, but the three young sailors surrounding me were impassive. Bored, even. To varying degrees, though all in their early twenties, Mark Street, Ryan Dickerson , and Kim Carstarphen were all seasoned Caribbean hands. A rocking call to Jesus was not unfamiliar music to their ears.

"Don't worry," said Don's son, Mark, a lovely Irish lilt to his voice. "You'll sleep through it." And he'd been right.

The next morning, as Don typed, the toussle-haired lads emerged from their slumber, zombie-like, like unwilling extras in a B.V.I. revival of *Night of the Living Dead*. Their collective lassitude was in inverse proportion to Don's manic morning energy. "Okay," he said, bursting from his quarters and scattering paper across the saloon table. "These are the ship's orders. I want everyone to read them before we get going. If anything's unclear, ask me. Now, where's that coffee? And how about some bacon and eggs?"

In a universal gesture long employed by young sons to requests from pesky fathers, Mark's eyes rolled back in his head as if an anesthetic had just kicked in. He put the kettle on the stove and shuffled toward the icebox.

Over two decades ago, at the not-so-tender age of 50, Don became a parent for the fourth time. Now, some 20-odd years later, Mark was a big reason why we were preparing for blue water.

A talented, lifelong sailor with an ambition to skipper big, classic yachts, after several seasons as a paid schooner hand Mark needed to master celestial navigation to take the next step in his professional career. And so, when Don was offered the job of delivering *Nimrod of Orwell* across the Atlantic to England, it sounded like an all-around winning proposition. The father, a seasoned navigator, could teach his craft to an eager son; there was room to bring along a few friends for an ocean adventure; and there'd be a payday for the delivery.

Though time constraints would allow me to sail only to Bermuda, the first of three scheduled legs, when Don asked me aboard I leapt at the opportunity. After all, there's nothing like sailing with fine sailors and *Nimrod* was stacked with them. A laid-back Georgia boy, Ryan was Mark's best mate—the pair had spent the winter crewing aboard the 125-foot gaff schooner *Aello*. Kim was a family friend, the nephew of one of Don's old-time Caribbean sailing pals, being sent to sea to literally and figuratively learn the ropes.

And Don was, well, Don. "This is breakfast six days a week," he said, as Mark placed a steaming platter of cholesterol-laden protein before him. "Seven if the wife's not around. And six beers a day." This time it was Mark's eyebrows that went skyward. Apparently there was a discrepancy with the figure.

Don's point was, either despite or because of his dietary regimen, that he was in better shape than most fifty-year-olds, something his doctor told him after a recent physical. And he did bring to mind the old Mickey Mantle quote that if he'd known he was going to live so long he'd have taken better care of himself.

But to me, the truly fascinating part of that first morning together before getting under way was the subtle interplay—the gestures, glances, and words unspoken—between father and son. Something was going on between them, I just wasn't sure what. I'd have a better idea soon enough.

WHEN asked about his life in a quiet moment on our first night at sea, Don began with a nautical reference. Invoking the name of the famous J-class racer, he said, "My keel was laid in 1930, the same year as *Shamrock*'s." Remarkably, some seven decades on, he served as co-navigator aboard the regal yacht in the America's Cup Jubilee. And as his story unfolded, it became clear that "serendipitous" is not a poor word to describe Don's life journey.

The son of a successful New York investment banker, at 12 he began sailing at the Manhasset Bay Yacht Club on Long Island Sound. His mother was a fine sailor who came from a family of them, and the gift was passed to the next generation. Don didn't know it at the time, but he'd found his calling. His college years were interrupted by a volunteer stint in the Navy during the Korean War. Afterwards, he returned to school and earned a degree in American History at Catholic University. Then he went back to sea, for two years skippering race boats in Europe and making his first transatlantic passage.

Despite a growing interest in naval architecture, after returning home he declined a job offer from the prestigious yacht-design firm Sparkman and Stephens. It would've taken him into his despised "canyons of New York," those same dismal corridors that dispatched his father into retirement at 55 with a pair of heart attacks and three ulcers to show for it all.

Even so, Don almost succumbed to a similar path, going so far as to shave off his red beard after accepting a position with a downtown marine-insurance concern. Ultimately, he couldn't bring himself to do it. With a $45 ticket on a Pan-Am DC-6 "vomit comet" to San Juan, he headed for the Caribbean to seek his destiny. They'd said in New York that a man couldn't make a living on the water or in the islands—the idea was to get wealthy, then go sailing—but Don was out to prove them wrong.

In 1957, in the first of two life-changing events, Don purchased a 45-foot engineless cutter called *Iolaire*, built in 1905. Considering that the boat would in many ways define him for the rest of his natural days, it was a good deal: $3,000 down, and a grand a year for four more years.

Don used *Iolaire* to join the burgeoning Virgin Islands charter trade, which led to the second momentous incident. During a visit to Caneel Bay he met the vacationing author John Steinbeck who, over cocktails, urged Don to try his hand at writing. Don took him to heart and eventually published *The*

*Cruising Guide to the Lesser Antilles*, the first of seven books and hundreds of magazine articles. Later, to augment his earnings as a writer, he did deliveries, sold insurance, and started producing the Imray-Iolaire charts—anything for a buck.

IT WAS early the next evening when Mark popped on deck to take over the helm from his bearded dad, who was resplendent in a bright-red sailing frock. Mark, who bears a resemblance to the rock-star Sting in his younger days, couldn't contain himself. "Oh man," he laughed. "You look like Santa Claus on a summer holiday."

We'd been northbound from Tortola for two days and several things were becoming apparent. With its split, ketch rig and Don's penchant for pouring on canvas—we'd all become adept at hoisting and trimming his favorite sail, the mizzen spinnaker—*Nimrod of Orwell* was a quick, capable offshore sailboat that came alive in the fresh trade-wind easterlies. But the boat was also systems rich and maddeningly complicated, the over-engineered product of a tinkering owner who was an ocean away. It all probably made sense to him, but it didn't to us.

What did make sense, especially to Don, was establishing a clear sense of onboard order. As a sea-going creature of habit, a slave to underway routine, the successful execution of efficient, repetitive, well-reasoned tasks were to him the essence of good seamanship. And if the lads took nothing else from this voyage, this supreme lesson they would learn.

It started with "Nimrod's Standing Orders," the ship's papers he'd laid out for mandatory consumption the morning of our departure. The typed, single-spaced list—numbered 1 through 30—covered everything from man-overboard contingencies and watchkeeping to manners and etiquette. A fitting subtitle might have been, "Don's Unassailable Laws of the Sea."

As we ticked off steady miles towards Bermuda, Don underscored his written thesis with a steady commentary of advice, stories, and opinions. Of all three he had plenty, all gleaned from personal experience. Among them:

• On the four diapers you need to cruise with kids: "The dirty one's over the side, the fish handle the initial cleaning. The second's rinsing in freshwater. Third's on the lifelines. And the fourth is applied to the bottom of the little one."

• On retrieving a bucketful of seawater: "Always dip it from the windward side. If you slip you'll tumble into the cockpit, not overboard."

• On helming: "Steer small, no big rudder adjustments. But stay ahead of the compass."

• On the relative merits of thirst-quenching beverages: "I'll take beer. Ever see what water does to metal? Rust! What'll it do to a stomach?"

• On lifelines: "Give me lashings over turnbuckles. If someone goes over the side you can slash the lashings with a knife to retrieve them."

• On luffing headsails and maintaining a course when sailing to weather: "The minute the jib starts talking to you, you're too high."

• And, finally, on the wire halyards rattling in the mizzenmast: "Sounds like a pair of skeletons copulating."

Of course—and not surprisingly—Don's most pointed observations were aimed at Mark. At one stage at dusk, while holding course on a deep run and swapping stories with Ryan, for a brief, uncharacteristic instant Mark let the wheel drift, luffing the spinnaker and the genoa. The sails, and Don, responded noisily.

"Stop philosophizing and pay attention!" cried Don. "That's why helmsmen shouldn't talk during a race, it ruins their concentration."

Mark muttered something under his breath. Having witnessed similar exchanges at least a dozen times, Ryan cracked up. "I'm totally enjoying this," he said, looking up one Street and down the other. "You two guys are great. What a vacation."

Ryan was on to something. Like fathers and sons everywhere, one of them was pretty sure he knew everything. The other one probably did.


AS WE climbed the steps of latitude the weather, of course, became unsettled, and just after lunch on our fourth day at sea I was at the helm when the squall hit. The wind swung a good fifty degrees and I bore off with it, altering course from 360 to 050. It was blowing a steady 30 knots with fast, hard bullets to 40, and sheets of horizontal rain beat the angled waves into smooth, blue moguls of submission.

What happened next was equally impressive. In an instant Mark was on deck and bounding forward, harness on and tether clipped in. Quick as a point guard, he struck the preventer and took to the mainsheet. The breeze backed a bit and Mark trimmed perfectly as I came up on the wind. "How's the helm, how's the helm?" he called over the cacophony. The helm was just about perfect, thanks.

Another moment passed and the staysail was sheeted home and drawing, the mizzen doused and tightly furled. Mark went below. He wasn't even breathing hard. "Nice when that happens in the daylight," he concluded.

Uh, yeah.

All of us have formative memories from our youth, and Mark's came at the ripe old age of three, seated on the knee of a friend of his father's named Captain John Bardon in Antigua's Falmouth Harbor. Captain Bardon's charge at the time was a magnificent square-rigger, and Mark remembers the polished brass, the gleaming spars, and the respect he commanded from all the sailors in their crisp, full whites.

"From that moment on, whenever anyone asked me what I wanted to do when I grew up, my answer was always the same," Mark said during one wee morning's watch. "I want to be a skipper."

The path wouldn't necessarily be easy. He was a prodigy of sorts, just a speck of a thing when he started racing Dragons off the coast of Ireland with his dad, who later built him a little pram called *Mark's Ark* to refine his skills while living aboard *Iolaire* in the islands. But Don was a tough taskmaster. "If I went head to wind he'd go batty," Mark said. "I'd come in crying all the time. For a while I didn't want to go near the thing."

By 8, however, he'd started racing his own boats, without adults, and the thrill of beating kids a good five or six years older was very satisfying. "Winning silver, that was the business," he said. "That's what really got me enjoying sailing again, the racing. It's still my favorite thing to do on a boat."

Like his father, Mark sought his destiny on the water in the Caribbean. One day, working his way up the ranks as a deck hand aboard a classic schooner, he glanced up and damn near swallowed a bolt dropped from far aloft. Perhaps fittingly, like the yin-yang tattoo on his shoulder (an adornment his father finds less than appealing), even his chipped-tooth smile bears a souvenir of the life he's chosen.

Hours after the squall had passed, with all quiet down below, I described to Don the efficient, athletic grace which Mark had displayed in bringing sudden order to the potential chaos. Don's not the sort of person who dispenses praise liberally, but for the first time on the trip I caught a gleam in his eye as he spoke about his son.

"He's got a lot more confidence than I ever had at that age," he said. "Always has, really. When he was ten I nicknamed him 'Mr. O.C.' Mister Overconfident. But he does have tremendous confidence to go with his tremendous charm. He's going to go somewhere in this business."

I wouldn't disagree with him. But first we had to get to Bermuda.

THE LAST argument between the two-way Streets was a draw. Even at the time the details were hazy, something about who did or didn't turn the propane on or off. But the final exchange was memorable.

"Every time I've had to talk to you I've been absolutely right," said Don.

"Every time I've come back at you I've been absolutely right," countered Mark.

It was a Mexican standoff in the North Atlantic.

In all honesty, the end of the voyage was bizarre. We missed Bermuda on our first try because of an uncharacteristic navigational error by skipper Don, an unfortunate circumstance that added the better part of a long day to the trip. The lads had been despairing about the lack of female companionship (among other shoreside fantasies) and were ready for terra firma, but to their credit, they were magnanimous enough to let it pass (almost) without comment.

Then Don took a fairly nasty fall in the saloon and reiterated that this transatlantic crossing, his eleventh, would almost certainly be his last. With Mark in the midst of his first, I realized that I was witnessing first-hand the passing of a family torch. Among my many mixed emotions, I mostly felt privileged.

We finally made it, and the next day I gathered my things for the flight home. Before leaving, I asked Mark what it was like sailing with his father. "Well, the old man can suck some of the fun out of it; he doesn't really know when to take a break and chill," he said.

But then I glimpsed a sparkle not unlike the one Don had exhibited when talking about his boy's future prospects. "But you've got to hand it to him, he's a great teacher and always good to come back to. You can bitch about it but I don't know how many times on this trip I've thought, damn, I didn't know that. If I survive this, I'll be sorted."

Father and son. Young and old. Night and day. Yet they were both wonderful sailors, who lived to be at sea, with a shared love of traditional boats, sweet sheer lines, and night watches. Stubborn coots, yes, but cut from the same jib.

Still, even with hundreds of miles between and behind us, I hopped in the taxi for the airport with an unanswered question. How in creation could two guys so different be so much alike?

*Billy Black*

**Writer F. Scott Fitzgerald once said that there are no second acts in American life... but Fitzgerald never met Charlie Cary.**

A few years after my 2004 *Cruising World* profile of Charlie Cary, he passed away peacefully in Florida at the age of 89. By any measure, he had a hell of a run.

# 5:  Travels with Charlie

## CHARTER-YACHT PIONEER CHARLIE CARY

IT WAS a Saturday night in January at The Moorings' lavish base in Tortola, British Virgin Islands, and the place was hopping. The open-air, pool-side bar was crammed with visiting sailors eager to put the winter behind them and set sail for a week of charter cruising. A steel band had just started playing. And in the adjacent pavilion, the dining room had been transformed into a giant dance floor. A meeting of the B.V.I. Investment Club was about to commence. Dressed to the nines, the Tortolans had been arriving for the better part of an hour, and a handsome assemblage they made. One got the impression that the club and its members—the lawyers, bankers, politicians, and businessmen who ranked among the island's most influential citizens—were prospering. In a distant corner, lost in the hubbub but watching with great interest, sat a distinguished-looking gentleman who appeared to be some two decades shy of his actual 85 years. After an opening prayer and a pair of brief speeches, the evening's business was soon over. Very quickly, the dance floor was full.

The gray-haired man took much joy from all of this. Laughing, he rose from his chair and began to sway with the music. As the moon draws the tides, the beat tugged at him, drew him closer. He couldn't resist, and he began moving toward the throng. He danced by himself, slow and steady, until the song finished.

That's when he was recognized.

First one fellow came up, all handshakes and smiles, then another, and another still. They were moths to a flame. Now the word was out: Mr. Charlie was back in town, and it was time to pay respects, perhaps have a photo taken with the great, good man himself. For the islanders—the investors!—understood better than anyone. Yes, they knew that if it hadn't been for Charlie Cary and his wife, Ginny, this beautiful building, and the dozens of boats lining the gleaming docks, and the gaggle of well-heeled tourists, and the many jobs and opportunities that all this enterprise created, simply wouldn't be here.

So it was all very fitting that the quiet bystander—the founder of The Moorings, a pioneer of the giant bareboat chartering industry—had returned to his beloved B.V.I. on a night of celebration, and without even trying turned out to be the guest of honor.

WE SET sail the next morning aboard a spanking new Moorings 4200 catamaran—one of the 288 boats that constitute the company's vast Tortola armada—a vessel very unlike the six modest Pearson 35s that made up Charlie's entire fleet when he hung out The Moorings' shingle back in 1969. There were five of us aboard: current Moorings president Lex Raas and his wife, Carol, photographer Billy Black, me, and, of course, Charlie. Our itinerary was open-ended. The purpose of the trip was simple: We all wanted to spend some time cruising and reminiscing with Charlie.

Along with our fondness for sailing, it soon became apparent that Charlie and I shared an interest in football. That afternoon, my suddenly respectable New England Patriots were facing the Indianapolis Colts in a playoff game. Before striking out for the islands, Charlie had spent 25 years working in the mining and mineral industry based in New Orleans, and he was still aglow from the triumphant national collegiate championship season just wrapped up by the pride of Louisiana, the L.S.U. Tigers.

As snow fell in Massachusetts, the site of the contest, Charlie and I nestled up to the tiki bar at the Leverick Bay Resort on Virgin Gorda to catch the game on TV. Charlie favored the Colts and I the Pats, and a wager was struck—loser picks up the tab. As it turned out, I was the guy who drank for free, no small matter to Charlie, who for days thereafter vowed his revenge.

As we chatted about the past during breaks in the action, it became clear that Charlie's life journey had been about a lot of things: recognizing and seizing opportunity, cultivating a strong entrepreneurial spirit, heeding the call of adventure. But mostly, it was a love story. Charlie's partner in life and business, his wife of 59 years, Ginny, passed away some four years ago. Several times over the course of the afternoon I remarked about what an incredible thing he'd created from scratch. Each time, Charlie was quick to correct me: "It wouldn't have happened without Ginny," he said.

HIS DAD was a chemist, a winner of the Booker Prize for his role in discovering vitamin B12. Hers was a steelworker who'd left Pennsylvania for a job at the U.S. Navy Yard outside Washington, D.C. They met in junior high, and they soon realized they were meant to be together. By the mid-1940s, Charlie had earned a degree from the University of Maryland in industrial engineering and successfully completed his graduate work at the Harvard Business School. From Cambridge, he'd taken a job with a company called Freeport Sulphur and soon found himself heading up operations at a nickel plant in Cuba.

No less ambitious, Ginny had secured a job with the FBI. They'd already been married several years. In 1943, Charlie enlisted in the U.S. Navy and soon after was ordered to Bermuda. "At the time, I didn't even know where Bermuda was," he said. Charlie became the base's cargo officer, while Ginny—who'd deftly secured her release from the bureau—took a job assisting the officer in charge of welfare and recreation. In arranging the many parties and U.S.O. shows for which she was responsible, Ginny displayed a gift for organization that would come in very handy down the line.

In the meantime, during his off hours Charlie was acquiring a new skill that would prove to have life-altering consequences: He started sailing. In fact, he said, after his discharge from the Navy in 1946 and his subsequent return to the States, "We got a boat—a Lightning—before we bought a house."

Charlie returned to his job at Freeport (which later became Freeport-McMoran Copper and Gold Inc.) and began what would be a steady, 22-year climb up the corporate ladder. And Ginny continued to work for the Navy, landing a civilian position in New Orleans. As a sideline—after all, the Carys needed a place to live—Charlie headed up a group of investors who together purchased a thousand acres alongside Louisiana's Tchefuncte River and developed the tony Tchefuncte Estates, complete with golf course and marina, which became home to 250 of New Orleans' more prominent families (as well as to Charlie's boats).

Clearly, Charlie had a knack for business. But he was also becoming an accomplished sailor. From the Lightning, he graduated to a 28-foot Gulf one-design, then to a Knarr, then to a 40-foot, German-built wooden yawl called *Gung Ho*, so named by the young Marine who'd seized it as a war prize. Charlie, by then a member of New Orleans' active Southern Yacht Club, bought the boat in Florida and entered her in the prestigious Southern Ocean Racing Conference.

Later, having grown tired of maintaining a wooden boat, he embraced the simplicity of fiberglass in his next yacht, an Alberg 35 called *Flying Ginny*, which he campaigned not only in the SORC but in local regattas and regular races to Isla Mujeres, Mexico. And when not racing, Charlie and Ginny enjoyed many a cruise all along the Gulf Coast and to Florida. During one voyage to Miami in the late 1950s, on a lark they booked a cabin on a crewed charter to the Bahamas and had a fabulous time. They finished the trip envious of the skipper and his wife, whose lives appeared to be a perfect balance of business and pleasure. It was a portent of things to come.

Still, by the late 1960s, professionally and personally life couldn't have been much better. Then, upon the eve of his 50th birthday, Charlie came to a fork in the road.

In the dead of winter, he was summoned to company headquarters in Manhattan and offered a promotion to vice president, which would require relocating to the Northeast. From their hotel window, the Carys of Louisiana watched in frigid horror as a blizzard blanketed the city's streets. An ongoing commuter strike at the time did nothing to allay their sense of isolation. The decision about whether to take the job wasn't a tough one: No way.

"When I turned it down," said Charlie, "I knew it was the end of the line. That's when we decided to look into making our hobby our vocation."

Having made a good living, they had the financial wherewithal to do so, and now they had some free time. First, they met some friends on the Pacific side of the Panama Canal and spent the following six months aboard their 44-foot yawl wandering up the coastline of Central America and Mexico. Soon after, Charlie came across a photograph in a yachting magazine of sailing writer Carleton Mitchell's celebrated yawl *Finisterre*— the only boat ever to win the Bermuda Race three consecutive times—anchored in the British Virgin Islands.

He couldn't shake the image. "It left quite an impression," said Charlie. "So we decided to come down here to charter, which is exactly what we did."

Once in the Caribbean, the Carys almost immediately began searching for opportunities. Being American citizens, they started in St. Thomas—where Jack Van Ost was just getting his own chartering concern, CSY Charters, off the ground—but found they preferred the British Virgin Islands over its U.S. counterpart. They eventually leased some dock space on Tortola at Fort Burt, which conveniently came with a small hotel and restaurant. Charlie and Ginny were taking the plunge into the world of bareboat chartering. All they needed was a name for their company.

"The one that kept coming up was Virgin Anchorages," Charlie said. "But that name seemed too limiting. I said to Ginny, 'But what if some day we want to go someplace else, too?'"

To which Ginny replied, "Uh-oh."

His sailing sabbatical over, Charlie Cary was back in business. And that business was The Moorings.

IT WAS on a boisterous day at the famous Baths, the granite grottos on the southwest tip of Virgin Gorda, that we pretty much flattened Charlie. Until then, it had been, as Jimmy Buffett has crooned, a lovely cruise, and we'd settled into a daily routine. Billy would be up and off at the crack of dawn, the inflatable loaded with camera gear, in search of the perfect sunrise. The rest of us would enjoy a lazy breakfast and then I'd corner Charlie for a while with my tape recorder, eager to learn as much as I could about his early experiences in the Caribbean. Then we'd do precisely that which, over the years, has lured so many adventurous souls to these marvelous islands: hoist sail.

We'd had a terrific run out to Anegada under a colorful cruising kite, and Charlie treated us to lobsters at the Anegada Reef Hotel. The evening's special moment was a tableside visit by the hotel's youthful proprietor; like many young islanders, he'd once worked in Tortola for The Moorings, and Charlie was clearly pleased with his subsequent success.

"He's really done a wonderful job catering to people here," said Charlie, echoing the mantra so central to his own business philosophy. "It's so good to see."

From there we'd made for Jost Van Dyke, with short swim stops at Green Cay and Sandy Cay, before motoring to a slightly exposed but pleasant anchorage at White Bay. The following night, after the requisite snorkeling expedition at The Indians, we stopped at The Bight on Norman Island. Throughout our travels, we'd seen plenty of charter boats, and it was tempting to ask Charlie if things were better when there was a little less traffic, back in the "good old days."

"Well, the hills over Tortola were all black at night," he said. "No lights. No houses. There weren't even many cars there. My license plate was number 8. It certainly has developed a lot since we started here. But I have to say, it's still as pretty as ever." By the tone of his voice, it was clear he meant it.

From there, next morning, it was on to The Baths, and we hadn't really noticed how bouncy it was until Billy, Charlie, and I took the tender into shore and picked up a dinghy mooring right off the main beach. Still, Charlie was first over the side, and Billy and I watched as he confidently swam to within feet of the shoreline. At that point, we each rolled into the water with snorkel gear and headed in the opposite direction.

Only later did we hear about the ensuing drama.

As Charlie emerged from the surf, he was rolled by one breaking wave, and then another. Luckily, Lex was close by, having already paddled to shore on a kayak, and he soon had Charlie safely on his feet and up the beach. Recalling the story over drinks later that day, Charlie said he'd learned a lesson. "It's a pretty good reminder that I have to remember my limitations," he said.

Actually, we all took away something from the incident. First, of course, we understood that we needed to keep a closer eye on our senior crewmember. But more important, though midway through his ninth decade, we all realized Charlie had lulled us into complacency with his zest and vigor. And if that's not something to shoot for—denying the years and fooling the young 'uns by your sheer love of life— then what on Earth is?

WRITER F. Scott Fitzgerald once said that there are no second acts in American life. But Fitzgerald never met Charlie Cary.

With a pair of silent partners backing the enterprise, Charlie, as the sole active partner, had almost instantly become the real-life embodiment of Norman Paperman, the fictional protagonist of Herman Wouk's comic send-up of island escapism, *Don't Stop the Carnival*. The novel was published just four years earlier, in 1965, and the parallels weren't lost on Charlie. "Every single thing that happened in that book happened to us," he said. "And then some."

The very first client was an expatriate Brit named Roger Downing, a local architect who booked a boat to celebrate Commonwealth Day, the second Monday in March. But it would take a good two years for the business to turn a profit. Ironically, during that stretch Charlie found support from an unlikely ally in CSY Charters. On several occasions, CSY overbooked a vacation week and didn't have an available boat, whereupon they'd charter one from The Moorings.

"When it got to the point where we didn't have an extra one either," said Charlie, "they'd call and say, 'You know, Charlie, you're getting very undependable.'"

Unwittingly, CSY also played a major role in one of Charlie's most important early moves. CSY had been in negotiations with Canada's Grampian Yachts about building a new line of boats for their St. Thomas-based operation. But the Grampian deal fell through, so CSY approached Pearson Yachts in Rhode Island. Meanwhile, Charlie was also talking to Pearson about commissioning a new boat for The Moorings. He didn't learn about CSY's involvement until after CSY had taken orders for 21 new, Pearson-built charter boats.

Charlie was livid with Pearson over this perceived end run, and he said as much to yet another erstwhile player in the burgeoning industry, Bill Stevens, who was establishing his own charter business in the lower Caribbean. Remarkably, Stevens had had the same experience with Pearson. "We were both so put out that we decided to get together and try to develop a good cruising boat," said Charlie.

After interviewing several potential builders, the pair eventually got around to Florida's Charlie Morgan: "Up to that point, he'd been building mostly racing boats, but he was convinced that in order to get some volume off a mold, he'd have to go to cruising boats. So we hit him at the right time."

In 1972, the inspired product of this unusual collaboration—the shoal-draft, center-cockpit Morgan Out Island 41—was launched. Some 1,500 would be built over the next two decades. When Pearson was late in delivering their boats for CSY, it was a double victory for Charlie and The Moorings.

And thus began the start of an incredible roll. The year 1974 found the U.S. economy mired in a recession, but it didn't hurt The Moorings. "Sailors put first things first," said Charlie. "It was one of our best years."

In 1976, the firm acquired a prime parcel of waterfront property at the northern end of Tortola's Road Harbour, which to this day serves as its base in the B.V.I. Three years later, as the company celebrated its 10th anniversary in business, the government of Tortola conferred upon the Cary's the status of "Honorary Belongers," a rare entitlement indeed.

"From that point on, we didn't have to worry about work permits, which we appreciated very much," said Charlie.

As the years rolled on, the fleet evolved, too. There were Gulfstars from another Florida builder, Vince Lazarra, whom Charlie affectionately called "The Godfather."

And more Morgans, of course. In the early 1980s, in yet another watershed moment, The Moorings teamed up with Beneteau to produce a sleek 39-footer, followed shortly thereafter by a Bruce Farr-designed 44-footer. "That started us out as a performance-yacht charter outfit," said Charlie.

Around the same period, true to his word when the company was first launched, Charlie and his growing management team began seeking "offshore" opportunities, and it wasn't long before The Moorings had bases in St. Lucia, Grenada, Mexico, and the South Pacific. From a backwater outfit with a handful of boats, it had become the General Motors of the sailing-holiday sector.

As the years advanced, Charlie and Ginny slowly stepped down from the all day, every day workaday world. There were new owners, new bases, new trends. Even Charlie was intrigued by how well catamarans worked in the charter trade.

Ginny's death left a huge void in Charlie's life. But he's never been the sort to go backward. His new companion, Helen Craycraft, is actually an old family friend.

He's helping a foreign exchange student—one of two he and Ginny sponsored over the years, both of whom became like family—gain admittance to a Florida university. And boats, of course, are still a part of Charlie's life. He's wrapping up a project in New Zealand developing a fast, luxury power cat. On the dock adjoining his coastal Florida home is a McKinna 57 powerboat called *Sea Quest*, which suits his style just fine. "I hate airports and traffic, and this way, I just get aboard my boat right in my backyard and I'm off on my cruise," he said.

**CHARLIE CARY**

Yes, you could say Charlie Cary has come full circle. "It's funny, but now I'm trying to get back to where my boating's my hobby," he said. "Not my vocation."


ON OUR last night together we rolled into the lavish resort on Peter Island for supper; it was where Charlie used to bring Ginny for a night out, and it was a pleasure to be in his company in a setting that brought back such fond memories. Our travels with Charlie were coming to a close.

Before breakfast the next morning, we motored off the dock and around the corner and dropped the hook in Deadman's Bay, Peter Island's easternmost anchorage.

There'd been no advance plan to do so. It was quite simply the nearest quiet spot. But it turned out we'd come to a very special place.

Ashore, at one end of the beach, a big spa was under construction. Embedded in the cliff flanking the other end, a gigantic house was being erected. And in countless anchorages all around us, dozens and dozens of happy charterers were sipping coffee, setting sail, and getting down to the serious business of relaxing. This island, and all the others, had certainly evolved since 1969.

The one constant had been the palm trees, still rustling in the breeze. And it was upon those trees that Charlie leveled his gaze as he told our trip's last tale. Remarkably, and coincidentally, he'd mentioned this place in passing earlier on our cruise.

"Remember that picture of Carleton Mitchell's *Finisterre* I told you about?" Charlie asked. "It was anchored right here in Deadman's Bay. You could see those palm trees on the beach and the sun coming down and the shadow of the boat on the sand. It was quite an impressive photograph. It had a lot to do with our wanting to come here."

Imagine that, I thought, taking in the scene. Cutting short a lofty career, looking at life afresh at 50, leaving his home and hearth astern, he'd chanced it all on this very portrait of paradise. And, man, had it worked out in his favor.

It occurred to me that not only was the story inspirational, it was almost unbelievable, and I nearly said as much to Charlie. But I'm not sure he would've heard me. He seemed pretty intent on the sway of the fronds.

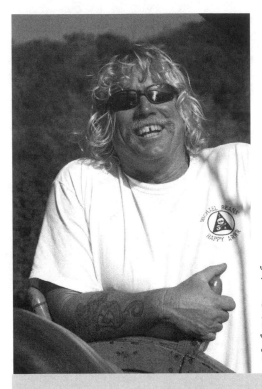

A jack-of-all-nautical-trades, Davis Murray's reputation as an all-around raiser of hell is firmly established throughout the Caribbean.

*Herb McCormick*

No one was ever more surprised by, well, anything, than I was when I learned my old sailing mate Davis Murray had not only picked up a guitar, but that he was good with it. "Researching" this story with Davis as we ambled through the Virgin Islands on his floating home was one of my more pleasurable *Cruising World* assignments ever. Davis, by the way, is still making great music. You can learn (and hear) more about his latest CD, released in late 2010, by visiting his website, www.barefootdavis. com.

# 6: The Master of Deviation

## CARIBBEAN CROONER DAVIS MURRAY

PINK. The audience is a resounding shade of pink, their collective tint suggestive of far too much tropical sun and several rounds of lunchtime drinks. "Damn," says a fellow in one of the more ridiculous floral shirts ever created, a ménage of colors that simply do not exist anywhere in the natural world. "We look like tourists."

"That's because," his pal says, a bit too glumly for a party animal on a rippin' trip to the islands, "we are."

It's 3:30 in the afternoon in an open-air courtyard at the exceptionally well-named Point of Sale Mall hard by the gleaming, downtown cruise-ship docks of St. Thomas, USVI. The assembled crowd, having spilled ashore from one of the bulbous white passenger liners nearby, represents the Atlanta chapter of what has become an international string of Parrothead Clubs, whose members worship at the altar of all things Jimmy Buffett. They're on their yearly swing through the islands (for which, it should be noted, they raise money for charity), and are more than ready to be entertained by an authentic island character.

They are not kept waiting.

For suddenly, there before them stands a rather strapping dude in dark shades and baggy Hawaiian shirt, his Harley-Davidson mug haloed by an unruly blond helmet, wearing a pair of khakis that look as if they were last washed and ironed during the Bush administration. The first one.

"I'm Barefoot Davis," the shoeless one says, strapping into his black, carbon-fiber guitar and nodding at the musicians who've assembled behind him. "And this is the Barefoot Davis Band. Welcome to St. Thomas. It takes an hour and a half to watch *60 Minutes* down here. Don't forget that." Then he launches into a song, the refrain of which poses a curious existential question: "How many lies are in that whiskey bottle?"

Truth be told, I met Davis Murray—the handle he was given when launched into life a little over five decades ago in Brookfield, Mass.—a long time ago. A jack-of-all-nautical-trades, his reputation as a top-notch compass adjustor, navigator, boatbuilder, mechanic, offshore sailor, beach-cat racer, and all-around raiser of hell is firmly established up and down the Eastern seaboard and throughout the Caribbean. And anyone who's ever done the annual Caribbean 1500 cruising rally knows him well; he's sailed all eighteen rallies to date and serves as the event's fleet captain, trouble-shooter, and general guiding light at its outset in the Chesapeake Bay, under way via the daily radio schedule, and at its conclusion in the Virgin Islands, which he's called home for over a decade.

Still, when I'd heard that Murray had picked up the guitar, formed a band, landed a record contract, and produced a CD, I was somewhat, shall we say, astonished. So when I found myself with some free time in the Caribbean one spring and he invited me to come hang out for a few days, I quickly accepted. Which is how I found myself swaying to his beat with a bunch of Parrotheads on a lazy weekday afternoon.

For as it turns out, Barefoot has written some pretty catchy tunes that he and his band—all of whom, he readily admits, are far more accomplished players than he—execute with more than a little skill and flair. When the gig ended, to solid applause, I clinked beers with him and admitted that I was quite pleasantly surprised.

"Yeah, well, someone came up and asked me to do some Buffett tunes," he said, sharply, sounding precisely like the Davis I've always known. "I figured they get enough of that on the ship. Hey, I like Buffett, but we're not a cover band. This is my island and this is our sound. If they don't like it, they can split."

He paused for an instant, the punch line briefly hanging, and smiled broadly. "But you didn't see too many leave, did you?"

HECTIC. When one spends several consecutive days in the company of Davis Murray—particularly when his wife, Margot, an accomplished sailor herself, takes off for a cruise of the Grenadines with some friends—the pace of life is hectic. It is most definitely not an exercise for the energy-impaired. Luckily, when we hop into his RIB the next morning and set forth from *Splinter Beach*, the 34-foot lobsterman-style motor launch the Murray's call home, the first stop is for caffeine at a place around the corner from his slip on the east end of St. Thomas, Lattes in Paradise.

"Davis!" cries a choir of coffee drinkers, in unison, as he enters the shop, where his first CD, *Daydreamin'*, is prominently on sale.

"You know who you remind me of, Davis?" wonders a jarringly attractive woman as we await our orders. "Norm, from *Cheers*. Nobody else gets a greeting like that."

"He's the mayor of St. Thomas," says Danny Silber, the classically trained keyboardist, jazzman, and prominent member of the Barefoot Davis Band, back at the Sapphire Beach Marina where he lives in a one-bedroom condo—the centerpiece of which is the giant grand piano plunked down right in the center of it—just a stone's throw away from *Splinter Beach*'s dock.

Murray has decided we should take a leisurely putter through the Virgins and while he's readying the boat I chat with Silber about the band and their music.

"Davis just has a knack for writing clever song material," says Silber, who left New York City for the islands years ago and never looked back. "Once he surrounded himself with quality musicians, he just blossomed. It's simple music, three or four chords. But there's an art to playing simple takes well. There's no place to hide. Miles Davis said that.

"He doesn't have a smooth voice, but neither does Bob Dylan. But he's totally in the moment. It gives the band great spontaneity. With Davis, you never know when the magic will come. That's the great thing about magic, about live music. I mean, you can't say, 'All right, let's put the magic in at 9:10.'

"And the other thing about Davis, he's a great self-promoter," concludes Silber. "Shameless. Is there any other kind of self-promotion? It's a show, and that's why they call it show business. But this is one of the most fun bands I've ever been a part of."

Moments later, we're off in Murray's beater old car on the day's errands, which are put on hold every time we're greeted by a grand, oceanic vista, at which point he immediately spins off the road to deeply drink it in. "You always have to keep in perspective what brought you down here in the first place," he says. "I know a lot of people who forget about that and don't take advantage of what we have here.

"I, fortunately, do."

The day is a whirlwind. We stop off at ISW, Murray's recording studio, while he lays down a guitar track over his pirate tune, "Dead Man's Grave," for an upcoming "Pirates of the Caribbean" compilation CD. "I like what's happening, Davis," says his producer, Dan McGuinness.

The pirate theme continues as we check in on *Carteza*, a converted Cheoy Lee Offshore 41 that Murray helped completely overhaul into a faux pirate ship/playground for the children of a wealthy Midwesterner who has a mansion on the island, and which he now oversees. Murray fiddles with the cannons and swings in the hammock, just another one of the kids.

Next, we're back on the water, where Murray pockets some change swinging the compass on a fast, twin-hulled inter-island ferry, the trade he plied from the mid-1970s through the mid-1980s on the Philadelphia waterfront after taking over his uncle's business. He reckons he's swung 10,000 compasses, and he's still knocking them off (his business card proclaims him the "Master of Deviation").

Finally, late in the day, we drop the dock lines and steam over to Cruz Bay, St. John. We're walking up the sidewalk when, without breaking stride, Murray bends over and picks up two crisp $20 bills lying in the street. "Look, beer!" he says, and moments later the currency is exchanged for a cold case of Dominica's finest, El Presidente.

Yes, it's hectic being the master. But it's also good. Very, very good.


COOL. Steve Black, the founder and director of the Caribbean 1500, says that when it comes to high-seas sailing, there are few cooler customers than Black's old Great Lakes racing buddy, Steve Pettengill—a veteran of the BOC Challenge solo around-the-world contest, and the current chief of offshore testing for Hunter Marine—and Davis Murray.

"They're just these warped guys who've never seen a day of bad weather," says Black. "They could be out there on the worst day imaginable and they'd describe it as 'fresh breeze.'"

Not surprisingly, Murray and Pettengill are also good pals who've knocked off a lot of miles together: over blue water and black pavement. Murray keeps his 1988 custom soft-tail Harley alongside Pettengill's collection of bikes in the latter's Florida garage. The pair has been known to drop everything and bolt for Daytona, despite the fact that Murray believes his ride has serious front-end issues. "When you go past a bar, it always turns that way," he insists.

Pettengill and Murray forged an alliance back in the late 1980s, when they helped deliver a mutual friend's Whitby 45 from Chesapeake Bay to Ft. Lauderdale. By that time Murray had left the family compass-adjusting business in Philly and his plans were, as they say, open-ended. So when Pettengill asked him to come up to Michigan to help him prepare his Hood 40, *Freedom*, for the 1988 singlehanded transatlantic race from Plymouth, England to Newport, R.I., Murray signed on.

It led to one adventure after another. Murray helped Pettengill deliver *Freedom* to the U.K. for the race start, then returned to Newport, which at the time was the growing U.S. hub of long-range solo sailing. He got to know Black, who'd raced his own Dick Newick-designed trimaran across the Atlantic, and started sailing with him on the New England multihull circuit. He also met an up-and-coming singlehander named Mike Plant, and became involved with Plant's *Duracell* campaign for the 1989 Vendée Globe nonstop sprint around the planet. Next up was another project with Pettengill, namely his successful assault on the New York-San Francisco Clipper Ship record aboard the tri *Great American*.

In 1990, Black got the notion to form a cruising rally from the U.S. East Coast to the Caribbean, an event not unlike the Atlantic Rally for Cruisers (ARC) that Jimmy Cornell had recently launched with resounding success across "the pond." One of the first people he enlisted to the cause was his handy, knowledge-able friend, Davis Murray.

"He's a wizard at problem solving, especially under way," said Black. "He's seen everything that can break on a boat."

Murray sailed that first 1500, and each subsequent one as well, a goodly fraction of the roughly 170,000 nautical miles he reckons he's accrued in his offshore career. Black usually pairs him up with a crew of fledgling voyagers on a paid gig that works out well for all concerned, especially considering that Murray handles the traffic on the morning SSB radio "sked" and has walked fellow rally participants through countless underway repairs, from wonky electronics to failed rudders.

There's no question that Murray has been a major asset to the rally, but the opposite is also true. For many years he "boat-sat" rally yachts at a marina in St. Thomas for owners who briefly returned home, picking up plenty of repair work as well. It was then that he decided to make a permanent move to St. Thomas, from which he's never looked back. More importantly to the telling of this tale, the Caribbean 1500 played no small role in in-troducing Murray to the guitar, a life-altering experience if ever there was one.

"A few years back, there was a guy from Colorado named Phil Robinson who did the rally," said Murray. "He had a guitar on his boat. I come to find out he's a pretty fine musician. One night we're on his boat drinking Heinekens and I happen to mention how I always wanted to learn how to play the guitar. He says, 'Grab a couple beers, I'll get mine and show you how.' So he starts me with a couple of chords, puts my fingers on the guitar and says, 'Strum.' He says, 'Davis, you got rhythm, and that's a good thing.'

"Next time I'm in the States, I buy my own guitar and start practicing. And practicing, and practicing, and practicing..."

FOXY'S. After a couple of crazy days in the Virgins, we end up, serendipitously, at Foxy's Tamarind Bar on Jost van Dyke on the very evening of the iconic watering hole's 40th birthday bash. There's music in the air, and more on the way.

To that point, the mini-cruise on *Splinter Beach*, fueled by that initial case of El Presidente and a steady string of reinforcements, had been a rather riotous affair. We pulled into Norman Island and scrambled up Spyglass Hill for a bit of treasure hunting at the site of an old pirate's lair, the inspiration for Murray's tune "Dead Man's Grave." We had a glance at the beach on Virgin Gorda where he was married before 250 of his closest friends, as well as several of the venues for the 75 or so weddings he's personally performed. (Yes, you may also call him Reverend Davis Murray, an online-ordained minister of the Universal Life Church, who...oh, let's just move on.)

But for many reasons, Foxy's is the perfect place to wind up the proceedings. For the little beachfront bar perfectly personifies the endless connection between sailors, cruising, the sea, islands, the tropics, rum, and the music that fuses them all into a glorious whole. It's a bond so strong and seamless that it's sometimes hard to tell where one thing ends and the next begins. Buffett, of course, has mined that vein for all it's worth with a spectacular collection of songs and ballads, but there's no end of talented, grass-roots performers—folks such as Eileen Quinn, Eric Stone, Derek Escher, Joe Colpitt, and now, Barefoot Davis and his talented right-hand man, Morgan "Steel Pan" Rael—who have taken his baton and are charting their own tuneful journeys along the watery way.

Colpitt, a singer and guitar player who sailed his trimaran, *Virgin Fire*, over from St. John, is on the venue at Foxy's for the momentous occasion, and during his set he calls Murray up from the crowd to do a few numbers. The barefoot biker, guitar in hand, does not require a second invitation.

Davis Murray calls his music "island country." As with any good songwriter, his tunes are derived from the path he's traveled, are picture windows unto his soul. "South Cakalacky" is an ode to Charleston, South Carolina, and the time he spent there building a custom catamaran. "Grape Jelly" hearkens back to his childhood in Massachusetts and the smells wafting from his mom's kitchen. "Rum Is the Answer—What Was the Question?" recalls the playful banter between a charter captain and crew on a day boat out of Red Hook. "Latitude 18" is a tribute to the St. Thomas gin-mill of the same name, where he began to find his way as a musician and still holds court every Monday evening as the house band.

But his most personal song may well be "One Eyed Dan," about a wandering soul who ends up in the Caribbean as a sailing troubadour, a mission he pursues right up to his dying day. Murray, of course, has two good peepers, but otherwise, the closing verse rings a familiar bell: "Though he lived his life with just one eye, he made it plain, you see; he seen twice as much as any man could ever see."

Landing an interview with Frank Butler was not an easy task. Public statements on the record to journalists are not his thing. But his associates at Catalina very much wanted to make this piece happen, as did the publisher of *Cruising World*, Sally Helme.

I flew to the Catalina factory in California and spent the better part of a long morning waiting for Frank to pay attention to me, which he was loath to do. I reckoned it was all a disaster and for the first time ever, I might fly home without a story, which really wasn't an option. When he realized I wasn't going to leave, he popped out of nowhere and suggested we take a drive. Sometimes it's better to be lucky than good; the story ended up writing itself.

By the way, three years later, Frank was still working, and at the 2010 U.S. Sailboat Show in Annapolis, Maryland, just about the entire marine industry showed up to wish him and wife Jeanne well at a "roast" attended by hundreds.

Only Frank could've gathered that crowd.

# 7: Cruising at 80

## BOATBUILDING LEGEND FRANK BUTLER

TRAFFIC IS moving briskly on California's famed Ventura Highway, flowing due west from Los Angeles, and Frank Butler is moving right along with it. Butler is the president of Catalina Yachts, but he's put that in the rear-view mirror for the day and he's heading out, bound for home. He's behind the wheel of his black 2002 Ford Thunderbird—"A piece of crap, really," he'll later say—dodging and darting, shifting lanes, chasing down the miles toward the afternoon sun.

When he sees a quick opening, he makes for it, with dispatch, and the needle on the speedometer tilts accordingly...65, 70, 75. There's only one problem, really. About three cars back, leaning on the gas in a whining, woeful, compact rental, someone is desperately trying to maintain contact, visual and otherwise, with the blazing T-bird.

That someone would be me.

Suddenly, almost without warning, Butler bolts right, across a couple of lanes and up an exit ramp, and I dutifully follow, grateful for the stoplights and congestion of suburban streets. The Thunderbird soon banks into a nondescript industrial park and Butler is already out its door when I wheel my pathetic little Chevy alongside.

"Come on," he says, impatiently. "I want to show you something."

We're at a small manufacturing facility, obviously, and Butler is waving at the electric pontoon boats strewn about the yard and saying something about how he designed these boats and owns this factory although, these days, it's not actually his operation, but all of it is clearly secondary to the mission at hand. This becomes abundantly evident when he flings open a garage door out back and there before us sit about a dozen vehicles nestled lovingly beneath soft, custom-fit covers.

They're cars, all right. Really cool, vintage, exquisite cars: a terrific 1920 Dodge Phaeton; a cherry-red '59 Ford Fairlane; a gorgeous '57 Caddy convertible; not one but two slick, mid-1950s-era Thunderbirds. And these aren't all of them, I'm told. There are a couple more similar garages in greater L.A., nearly forty automobiles in the collection.

In a boatbuilding career now spanning nearly five decades, Butler guesses he's manufactured some 75,000 vessels. During that time, he and his wife, Jean, also raised seven children. If you ask him about the former—as in, "Well, Frank, of all those boats, which is your favorite?"—he'll make a reference to the latter: "Do you have kids? Me too. Can you name your favorite? Me neither."

But cars are different, he says, and this becomes apparent when he uncovers what he unabashedly admits is the queen of his automotive fleet, a ragtop 1940 Lincoln Continental. "Now this is a beautiful car," he sighs. "I restored it right back to the original. Took five years.

"Cars are a lot of work," he continues. "You have to drive them, keep them up. They're just like boats. The more you use a boat, I think, the better it is."

With that, we're on the go, the autos back under their wraps, the garage door slammed. Moments later, we're again barreling down the freeway, revisiting Mr. Toad's Wild Ride. But in this brief interlude, I'm guessing, I've snatched a telling glimpse of the essential Frank Butler. A little contemplation, it seems—a pit stop on the road of life—is perfectly fine. But a whole lot of action is much, much better.

KNOCK, knock.

That's what you do when you desire an audience with Frank Butler. You stride down the hall to his corner office at Catalina's long-time headquarters on Victory Boulevard in Woodland Hills—the very facility he's occupied since 1974, when it was surrounded by corn fields and strawberry patches, long before the relentless advance of the malls, high-rises, and big-name hotels—and you rap twice. Then, one of two things happens. You're waved in (the usual response) or waved away (which means try again later). Thus order is maintained in the Catalina universe.

In January of 2008, on the very morning Frank Butler turned 80, Sharon Day knock-knocked and was granted entry, ostensibly to discuss lunch plans. Day and another long-time Catalina stalwart, Gerry Douglas, have each been at Butler's side for over thirty years and were made partners in the business in 1998; she handles corporate matters and oversees sales and deal-ers, he's in charge of design, engineering, and plant operations. Three or four times a week, the "Three Musketeers," in Day's words, meet for a bite and to cross notes on their respective areas of responsibility.

"We have a very shallow corporate pyramid," jokes Douglas.

It's important to know that Butler enjoys a chuckle, espe-cially at someone else's expense. Day recalls the time he fell un-characteristically ill during a big dealer's conference and begged to be excused. Soon after, a "dealer" came late to the meeting and began peppering Douglas and her with all manner of probing, uncomfortable questions about the company. It took a while before anyone realized it was Butler, all done up in a wig and phony beard.

So Day was fairly chuffed when the three amigos walked downstairs to the lobby on January 17th and Butler's chin dropped when the mariachi band began playing and the big gathering of workers, family, and friends yelled, "Surprise!" In honor of the milestone, everyone chugged another Butler favorite, a tall root-beer float.

There are changes afoot at Catalina, however, and the next party at the Woodland Hills location will probably be the last. In 1984, Catalina acquired Morgan Yachts in Largo, Florida, a smart strategic move that not only gave the company a second, well-known brand, but also served as a base to build the larger Catalina models that were becoming more and popular, and to develop new designs, as well. Plus, there was the not insignificant fact that the majority of Catalina customers, some seventy percent, in fact, lived east of the Rocky Mountains, which tacked on considerable shipping costs to every unit sold. "There's no resale value in freight," observes Douglas.

Now, the entire manufacturing end of the business is being shifted to Florida, a transition that's been ongoing for some time and which is scheduled to be completed by year's end. Though Butler and his team certainly have seen the writing on the wall for a while—face it, a factory utilizing fiberglass and resin looks, sounds, and smells a lot different than a Pier One, Best Buy, Marriott, or Hilton—the closing of the Woodland Hills operation signals the real and symbolic end of a grand era in American boatbuilding.

Southern California was once an epicenter during a revolution in production boatbuilding, the home to companies such as Cal, Ericson, Islander, Jensen, Columbia, and so many others that were once highly viable concerns, but which shut their doors long ago. "Hardly anybody is left," says Butler, in many ways The Last Man Standing.

"It's a wonderful business but it's not an easy business," he continues. "It's rough. You're with the economy. And it's not easy to be a manufacturer in California. It's not what you'd call a friendly state. There are so many rules and regulations, and they're always changing. They're right about some of them. But not all of them. Still, it's a fun business. But you better want to work. It's not like growing oranges. You don't just plant the tree and throw water on it."

WHEN HE was eight years old, Frank Butler went bird-hunting with his father, a plumber in the San Fernando Valley, and was taught a lesson that stayed with him forever. "If you shoot the wrong bird," his dad implored, "you still have to eat it. What you shoot, you eat."

"I've always remembered that," says Butler of a tale suggesting that several key, character-building principles were instilled at a very early age: There's a cause and effect to one's actions; you must respect and honor your decisions (even the lousy ones); and, when all is said and done, accept the consequences and move on.

Moving on was an apt theme in the early years of his career when he was honing several crafts, establishing his first businesses, and beginning to scratch what would become a strong entrepreneurial itch. "I've always liked problems," he says, tellingly. "I like solving them."

After graduating from high school, serving a two-year stint in the Navy, and attending college, Butler's inaugural foray into the business world was a machine shop called Wesco Tool that addressed his growing love of engineering and his affinity for hands-on labor. He didn't start sailing until his late twenties, when he bought a Sailfish and taught himself the ropes on Newport Harbor. He had no idea such a simple act would change his life.

With a growing family, it wasn't long before Butler was searching for a bigger boat, but he didn't have to look far. Just around the corner from his shop, a small yard was building a simple, sweet-sailing sloop called a Victory 21, and Butler decided it was just the ticket. He paid for the boat in full and waited for delivery. And waited, and waited, and waited.

On the morning the boat was supposed to be launched, a Saturday, Butler showed up at the factory, wife and four kids in tow, and learned that the Victory not only wasn't finished, it hadn't even been started. The builder, conveniently, was nowhere in sight. Off to the side, however, stood a completed hull and a new deck. So Butler chose an original response: Instead of jumping up and down and screaming bloody murder, he sent the family packing, commandeered the facility, and with the reluctant help of a handful of employees, began building his own boat.

"And I loved it," he said.

It was 1961. The remainder of the decade would be a whirlwind. The Victory guy went out of business and Butler assumed his operation, which he later named Coronado Yachts. He built several small boats, as well as the Victory, but he made his first big splash with his innovative Coronado 25. It was the first boat, he says, to be built with a pan liner that made for a light, rigid structure that also streamlined production, a trick he picked up from the plane manufacturer, Lockheed (and a sign of things to come). By 1967, Coronado was a tidy, profitable business, and Butler sold it to the Whittaker Corporation, a big conglomerate that also owned Columbia. Butler stayed on as a consultant for a year before tearing off a pointed letter to his employer that completely accomplished its purpose: He was fired.

"I didn't like the way they did things," he said. "I'm not a corporate type."

He was, however, an independent soul who'd amassed considerable knowledge about every single facet of the sailboat business, from designing and building them, to marketing and selling them. In 1969, he aimed all that hard-won experience towards a new enterprise. He founded Catalina Yachts.

THE STUNNING waterfront house that Frank and Jean Butler share in Westlake Village—the pleasant destination to which we ultimately repair after our escapade down Route 101—is made all the more comfortable by the fact that two of their daughters, and a nice representation of their twenty grandchildren, are right here in the neighborhood. There are two major constants in Butler's life—work and family—with the second underscored by the steady loop of images depicting birthdays, vacations, and other milestones that scroll continuously, all day long, across a flat-screen monitor on a kitchen counter.

"It was a gift from the kids," says Jean as Frank looks on. "They had all the old pictures scanned onto the computer. It's wonderful." For a long moment the proud parents gaze at the screen, transfixed.

They both, by the way, look great. For many years, they raced dinghies all over the West Coast. Eight years ago, they took up golf, which Butler says, "is like sailboat racing. If you make a mistake there's nobody to blame." But golf is a small part of his fitness regimen.  Upstairs, off the master bedroom, he shows me the set of well-used exercise equipment that augments his push-ups and stretching.  He asks about my back, guides me into the torturous machine that saved his, corrects my form as I gasp through a few crunches.

"It's not easy," he says of his daily routine.  "But you got to do it."

Back downstairs, on the sunny verandah, he soaks in the view of the distant, snow-capped Los Padres Mountains, and talks softly of this respite from the workaday world.  "You should see all the birds," he whispers.  "But watch out for the owls! They'll bite your fingers off!

"It's very peaceful here, though," he says.  "I really like it."

And he really earned it.

His first boat after hanging out the new shingle was the Catalina 22, a trailer-sailer he'd tried to convince Whittaker to build with no success.  "I believed in it," he says.  "I thought if I could sell 300 I'd be very happy."

To date, including the 22Sport version and the 22mkII, both of which remain in production, Catalina has built nearly 16,000 22s; at one stage, five a day went out the door.

Butler followed up quickly with the Catalina 27 and then the 30, the combined runs for which ultimately produced another 13,000 models sold.  But Catalina wasn't just amassing huge numbers; they were redefining how the game was played. First, nearly everything was done under the same roof at Woodland Hills, where Butler moved the company from North Hollywood in 1974.  Catalina had its own sail loft, made its own cushions, and even poured its own lead keels.  "If you need something and you own it yourself, you can get it right away," says Butler.

And if you bought a Catalina and called the company with any sort of issue, the man who picked up the phone was often its owner. "If there are problems, I want to know about them," he says. "Plus, anyone who buys a Catalina is part of the Catalina family. They can call me any time."

Butler's other against-the-grain strategy during Catalina's formidable years was eschewing advertising of any kind, a matter of considerable angst to magazine publishers and ad salesmen.

"Advertising was expensive, it added a lot to the cost of a boat," he recalls. "I always wanted my dealers to sell my competitors' boats, too. When people came in, they saw the other boats and they saw mine. If mine wasn't as good or better, for less money, that was fine. But that wasn't usually how it happened. So I was (effectively) using my competitors' ads. I did it that way for years, until we expanded into larger boats with a different clientele."

It's hard, he might've added, to argue with success.

THESE DAYS, Butler still puts in 50-plus hour weeks, still takes work home every night, still handles a ton of warranty claims. He has a computer at home but not in his office; instead, he dictates his letters via tape recorder and has a secretary type them up. It's safe to say he's a creature of habit.

When he looks back on his remarkable career, he has but one regret. "I wish when I started I took a picture of every employee," he says, reckoning the number would well exceed 5,000. "There have been so many good people."

With the major move and expansion to the Florida plant, that dynamic will continue to change and grow. One thing that will likely remain stable, however, is the staunchly loyal customer base that Catalina has enjoyed practically from the outset.

"When I go to a boat show," Butler says, "it's not unusual at all for someone to come up to me and say, 'I've had four of your boats.' Actually, quite a few people say they've had seven or eight."

"I think we've taken good care of those folks," seconds Douglas. "I think people got, in many ways, a better boat than they expected for the price. The more they came to learn, and the better sailors they became, the more they liked the boat, not the other way around. You give folks a good experience and they'll come back."

Today, Catalina remains one of the major builders of production sailboats, and is now as well known for its line of full-size, go-anywhere, systems-rich cruising yachts as it is for the entry-level boats that helped launch the brand. In recent years, the Catalina catalog listed 21 models, ranging in size from the tiny 8-foot Sabot dinghy to the ocean-going 47-foot Catalina 470, with a vast selection covering all the bases in between. Butler and Day have had major input, of course, but for many years the company's overall direction and philosophy have been dictated by Douglas, and that too will remain a constant as the company inevitably moves forward.

After all, at some point, Frank Butler has to retire, right?

Um, maybe not.

"No way," says Day. "You feel the energy of this place change when he walks into the building. He's the Energizer Bunny. He just keeps going and going."

Douglas concurs: "This is Frank's life. Besides," he laughs, "what fun is it being king if you have no kingdom?"

But Butler, surprisingly, sees retirement a bit differently. "It's coming," he says. "Like everything else in life. I know there aren't many people my age running a boat-building business.

But you see, I still enjoy it.  If it was work, that'd be one thing.
But it isn't.  I still like it.

"I do know one thing," he concludes.  "It went very fast.
When you enjoy things, they go fast.  Real fast."

Well, yes.  Fast.  That's the speed when you never take your
foot off the pedal.

**Not many men are still running boatyards
into their ninth decade, but few human beings
possess the energy of Frank Butler.**

After an illness left him depressed and discouraged, Jimmy Cornell decided to sell his boat...until a cruise with wife Gwenda changed his outlook.

*Herb McCormick*

Several years after the health crisis that almost caused him to sell his beloved *Aventura*, Jimmy Cornell was still going strong, spending summers wandering around the Med with wife, Gwenda.  In 2010, he published yet another outstanding voyaging guide, *World Cruising Destinations.*

# 8: An Anchor Un-Swallowed

## AUTHOR AND ENTREPRENEUR JIMMY CORNELL

LISTEN CAREFULLY, please, because it's not all that difficult. The secret to life, says Jimmy Cornell, isn't about landing in the right place at the right time. No, that's not it at all. Want proof? Try sailing, as he has, nearly 200,000 miles in all the world's oceans without a single serious problem. The secret, in fact, is on the coin's flip side, and is actually the underlying premise of his passage-planning bible, *World Cruising Routes*, a book that's guided countless voyagers on safe, globe-girdling journeys: Namely, avoid being in the wrong place at the wrong time.

Perhaps that's why the sudden, violent electrical storm was so annoying, so unnerving, for our timing, and placement, couldn't have been much worse.

It was a strange, gray, August morning in Croatia's Iski Canal, a narrow waterway beset by rocky islands and outcroppings and, on a busy summer day at the height of the season, literally dozens of charter boats zipping to and fro under wildly divergent levels of command. Jimmy, his wife, Gwenda, and I were under way aboard the couple's Ovni 43, *Aventura*, on a lazy southbound sojourn down the Croatian coast. It had been a mostly relaxing trip, right up to the moment that it all went to blazes.

The storm came, really, out of nowhere. One minute we were motorsailing in a zephyr of air, and the next we were scrambling to douse the main just ahead of a cold, 30-knot blast of breeze. The wind and rain came first, then the thunder and lightning, and finally the hail: big, nickel-sized pellets of ice.

You learn a lot about people when you go to sea with them, and though I'd known Jimmy for the better part of two decades, I'd never sailed with him before this cruise. It was no surprise to learn that, as a seaman, he was orderly and precise, and bound by routine. One flew the spinnaker off a pole triangulated with double downhauls and a topping lift; that way, you could set and douse it quickly, by yourself, leaving the pole in place in a passing squall for the quick re-hoist afterwards. There was never a need to wake the off-watch on a dark night. It was about self-sufficiency.

Likewise, when things broke, you fixed them, that very evening if not before. Never add the job to "a list": Lists are clutter, wastes of time, crutches for the procrastinator. The key was to have all the necessary tools and adhesives and spare parts stored properly and correctly, readily at hand. You slept easily when you knew the boat was shipshape and poised for strenuous activity. Just like the skipper.

Knowing Jimmy, having worked with him on stories and projects over the years, none of this was particularly surprising. He brought the same head-down, painstaking, no-stone-unturned style to his writing and journalism, and even to his role organizing rallies across the Atlantic and around the world.

What was more revealing—and this was a side of him I'd never seen—was his interaction with Gwenda, the mother of his children, the love of his life. And at no time was their intertwined partnership more revealing than at the height of the blow.

Despite what she says, Gwenda Cornell is a fine, intuitive sailor. It's just that, honestly, these days she'd prefer to be in her garden. She's a seasoned circumnavigator but, unlike her husband, the reward for her was never in the journey, but always in the destination, especially her beloved South Pacific.

So when the storm raged on for an hour, then a second, then a third, with thunder so loud it rang the ears, and with multiple lightning strikes a startling hundred yards away, it was abundantly clear that Gwenda would've preferred her sunny plot of earth with a spade in her hand. Yet even in the deluge, the Cornells were a team, trading places between the helm and the navigation station, piloting *Aventura* safely and efficiently through the hazardous waterway as the visibility closed down to nothing.

Was there a raised voice or two? Yes, there was, but always followed by a quiet word thereafter. Tellingly, Jimmy's greatest wrath was reserved for the things over which he had no control. "*There's* something for you to write about!" he hollered when a charter boat loomed out of the mist, a boat that provided no return target on his radar screen, though it was unclear exactly what should be written.

And then there was, well, the weather.

"I'm so tired of people telling me it's never like this around here," he sputtered, his still-black hair plastered to his skull, a clap of thunder punctuating his point. "This always happens to us in Croatia. Every time!" He shook his head at the indignity, the disorder. Wrong place. Wrong time.

WHEN Jimmy asked me why I'd decided to come sailing with him now, after the missed attempts and connections of the past, I looked him directly in the eye. And then I lied through my teeth.

"I always wanted to see Croatia," I said.

The real reason was that I'd learned that Jimmy was, as they say, "swallowing the anchor" and, unfathomably, selling *Aventura*. It was like hearing that Eric Clapton was burning his guitars, or that the Lone Ranger had told Tonto to shove off. There'd been a serious illness, apparently, the exact nature of which is irrelevant. What mattered was the aftermath, when Jimmy—on the path to full recovery but in a diminished state of mind and body—decided that the 43-footer that had taken him to the farthest corners of the planet had become a bundle of burdens and no longer the vehicle that nourished his soul. So I'd more or less invited myself aboard for the "last chance" farewell sail from Italy to Croatia's Kremik Marina, near Split, where she'd be put up for sale.

And that's how I ended up in Venice, sandwiched between Gwenda and Jimmy on their 10-foot Avon inflatable—she with the map, he at the controls of the 4 hp. outboard—as we wended our way through the maze of Venetian canals.

It was a comical journey. Gwenda, in her proper British accent, called out the instructions. Jimmy—though he's lived in the U.K. for many moons, he speaks with a distinct Eastern European inflection, a holdover from his boyhood in Romania— mostly followed her orders, though never silently.

"Turn here, Jimmy."

"We are going west. Look at the sun. This can't be right."

"Check the map, Jimmy. Here's the Grand Canal. We need to go right here, then left there."

"Okay, okay."

It was a fascinating, uneventful boondoggle until we found ourselves in the middle of a gondola traffic jam near the Bridge of Sighs. The fact that the outboard had no reverse was suddenly a distinct liability. Most of the gondoliers found us amusing. "Theees ees not the way to Australia," said one, pointing his finger. "Ees that way."

One, however, did not. He let loose with a verbal tirade in his native tongue which he finalized with a not-so-gentle tap to Jimmy's shoulder with the business end of his sweep. "He hit me!" said Jimmy, before extricating us successfully from the fray.

Alone again, finally, we took a collective deep breath. "He didn't need to be rude," said Jimmy, edgily. "Okay, Gwenda, where now?"

"Well," she said lightly, pointing at her map, completely nonplussed—apparently it wasn't the first time she'd watched her husband work in and out of a jam—"I think if we just go back here we'll be okay." It was the soothing voice of reason. She was right, of course.

"This is fine," said Jimmy, the tension gone, as he pointed his rubber boat down the corridor to open water. "Hey, it's an adventure!"

ANOTHER adventure. The Cornells have never lacked for another adventure. Ours began in earnest the next day, at dawn, when Jimmy deposited me in the dinghy off San Marco Square to snap some photos of *Aventura* under sail, reaching before the famous waterfront tower. His cruising friend, Arthur Beiser, supposedly had a picture of his boat powering along in the same spot, and Jimmy reckoned it would be good fun to reconstruct the scene, but with full sail flying.

He laughed when I was back aboard and showed him the digital images. "Ha," he said, pleased by the one-upmanship. "Arthur will never speak to either one of us again."

From there it was into the Adriatic Sea and the roughly 65-mile crossing to the ancient city of Rovinj. It was mid-afternoon before the breeze filled in properly from the northwest, but once it did, Jimmy hoisted his distinctive, broad-shouldered, slotted Parasailor spinnaker, and the boat—and its captain—came alive.

"Cruisers don't like spinnakers," he said, as *Aventura* surged along at seven knots in the puffs, a gleam in his eye. "They're my favorite sails."

*Aventura* is Jimmy's third boat, a hard-chine aluminum centerboard yacht built by the French yard Alubat that he's sailed from Antarctica to Alaska. To say that he has her *exactly* the way he wants her is a gross understatement.  He's shanghaied the former hanging locker in the forward cabin and lined it with Tupperware containers for his extensive inventory of spare parts. He carries two of most everything, including an extra prop and even a second dinghy and outboard.  He purchased the boat empty and customized it with Harken hardware, a Lofrans windlass, B&G instruments, a diesel heater, and on and on and on.

"Everything I bought was the best on the market," he said. "I did my homework. And it's paid.  It's really paid."

On passage, he strives to make an average speed of 6.5 knots, or a thousand miles a week.  It's all part of his orderly universe under way.  The world is a messy place; *Aventura*, most certainly, is not.  But don't, as I did, grab a pillow from the cabin to stretch out for a cockpit snooze.  "That belongs down below," he said, sternly, and I thought he was kidding until I met his stare.  Back went the pillow to its bunk.

Our night in Rovinj was enjoyable, and Jimmy, who has a firm grasp of history and abiding respect for it, was an excellent and enthusiastic tour guide.  The next day, he was hoping to make some serious miles south toward our destination, but ultimately changed his plans to lay over for a night in Pula, about 25 miles down the rugged coastline, so I could have a good wander through the remarkable Roman-era coliseum a short walk from the marina.  Sailing, to Jimmy, is always the main point of the cruising exercise, but it's also a means to an end.

Back on the boat after dinner that night, Jimmy laid his head in Gwenda's lap and she stroked his hair as they discussed the next day's itinerary.

"When are we going tomorrow?" asked Jimmy.  "What I mean is, how long from when I wake you up with coffee will you be ready to go?"

"Twenty-nine minutes," said Gwenda.

"Twenty-nine minutes," he repeated. "Really." His tone was of total disbelief.

"Well, maybe twenty-eight."

"I think," said Jimmy, "we will stick to twenty-nine."

THERE'S a saying in Jimmy Cornell's homeland of Romania that is difficult to translate, but it goes something like this: In life, it basically doesn't matter how stupid one is, as long as they're lucky. Intelligence plays no factor whatsoever, nor do connections, or good looks, or any other particular trait or skill. Sheer luck, baby. That's what matters.

"And I certainly had, and have, a lot of it," said Jimmy.

It's hard to disagree with him. At 67, he had two talented children, Ivan, a sailor and filmmaker, and Doina, who manages the informative cruising website (www.noonsite.com) that Jimmy launched several years ago. He's quenched his wanderlust and his endless passion for the sea through four decades of safe, fulfilling ocean voyages all around the world. He carved out not one but two successful careers, the first as a book author and a magazine and radio journalist, the second as an organizer of cruising rallies, a business he sold in 2000 that's afforded him the means to enjoy an active, comfortable retirement. Of course, one can argue that a person makes his or her own luck in this world, but one thing's for certain; whether he played a part in his own good fortune, or was randomly selected by a munificent Romanian god, fate has certainly smiled upon one Jimmy Cornell.

But of all those lucky moments in an existence that's been full of them, the luckiest of all was no doubt when he met a curious English traveller named Gwenda.

She was roaming through Europe with a small group of

fellow students, and the charming young Romanian that be-
friended them along the Hungarian border, with his grasp of
English and willingness to explain the mysteries of his commu-
nist country, was an interesting chap indeed. That winter she
returned home and they became pen pals. She returned the following year. "And that," said Gwenda, "is when it all blossomed
into different sorts of relations."

Heaven knows, life with Jimmy wasn't always easy, though
it was never, ever dull. Gwenda returned to Romania annually
for visits but it was 1969, six years after they first met, that Jimmy
received permission to emigrate to the U.K. By that time, Doina
was two years old; Ivan arrived a scant two months later. "I was
prepared to live in Romania if all else failed," said Gwenda. "I
knew we had a relationship worth fighting for."

It wasn't until Jimmy arrived in England, however, that
Gwenda fully realized why she'd been bringing her beau the
sailing magazines he always requested. He wanted to take his
young family to sea. "Well, yes, that took me a bit by surprise,"
said Gwenda, a self-professed "city girl" who'd never so much as
set a foot in a dinghy.

That would change. Boy, would it ever. She was there by
his side for the six-year circumnavigation aboard the first *Aventura*, a 36-footer aboard which they left England with a grubstake
of $100. By the time Jimmy was ready for his second spin around
the planet, Gwenda was too busy overseeing the shoreside operations for their fledgling business, the World Cruising Club—
which ran the ARC Rallies across the Atlantic and later expanded
to round-the-world jaunts such as the Millenium Odyssey—to
actually sail much of the voyage. These days, "Jimmy Cornell"
is a brand unto himself, a voyager, lecturer, and author known
by name to most every sailor. But make no mistake, without his

very silent partner assisting and enabling him in every project and passage, few if any would've actually come to pass.

Naturally, on our trip down the coast, at times I felt like the proverbial third wheel. I was with them morning, noon and night. But that's how I overheard this small exchange on the morning we pulled out of Pula. They were the closing remarks of what had obviously been a private, ongoing conversation.

"By the way," said Jimmy, standing behind the wheel, "I'm not selling the boat."

"That's firm?" asked Gwenda.

"That's firm."

WHEN WE finally got to Split several days later, I came clean about why I'd joined the cruise and what I'd heard. So I had to ask the question. What, Jimmy, made you change your mind?

"When you're sick, you start thinking differently," he said. "You never know what will happen, you're at home and all you think about are the problems. But once I was back aboard, in my normal life, I thought, 'What am I talking about?' Then Gwenda saw that I was quite happy and much more physically able than she expected me to be. So when I told her we weren't selling it, she quite agreed.

"I mean, this boat has grown around me. It's part of me. I can't sell this boat."

Amen.

We'll finish this tale where we started it, in the stormy waters of a rocky sea. At the height of the maelstrom, soaked and miserable, Gwenda made a simple statement. It was barely a whisper, but it also had the ring of authority, the stolidity of hard fact. There would be no arguing this matter.

"Next year," she said, almost to herself, her quiet voice strong and true. "We're going to Greece."

Between 2000-03, I wrote over 200 bylined stories for *The New York Times*, and this one, which appeared as a giant spread with a dramatic photo on the front page of the August 6, 2000, Sunday sports section, was easily my favorite.  (It was titled, not so succinctly, "For a Skipper, Smooth Sailing in the Wake of a Storm.") Sebastian Junger's *The Perfect Storm* was a small masterpiece, but he uncharacteristically botched the tale of a pretty cool guy, Ray Leonard, and I was very glad for the chance to set the record straight.

# 9:  A Character's Assassination

## RAY LEONARD, VICTIMIZED BY *THE PERFECT STORM*

ABOUT MIDWAY through *The Perfect Storm*, the film adaptation of Sebastian Junger's phenomenal bestseller, the skipper of the 32-foot sailboat *Mistral*, sporting a jaunty yachtsman's cap and a highbrow New England accent, makes an offhand remark about his vast offshore prowess.  It's a setup line.  He's silly, smug, and about to get walloped.

As readers of the book know, the character is based on Ray Leonard, the skipper of *Satori*, a Westsail 32 that was abandoned by her crew in a North Atlantic gale during a United States Coast Guard rescue operation in the fall of 1991.  Portrayed by Junger as a strange introvert with a fondness for the bottle, Leonard has now been skewered both in print and by Hollywood.

With each subsequent retelling of his story, the lines that define who Leonard is and what happened during that terrible, perfect storm become more blurred.  In fact, Leonard is a retired research ecologist for the United States Forest Service, a former college administrator, and an accomplished long-distance voyager with a Coast Guard license and tens of thousands of miles under his keel, and he does not fall within the neat, nasty boundaries of his depictions.

"I haven't seen the movie and I probably won't until I can borrow a copy of the video," Leonard said from the small home he is building for himself in western Vermont.  "But as for hats, I just wear a ball cap at sea.  It keeps the sun out of my eyes."

Junger, who did not speak to Leonard for his book, did not return a phone call seeking comment for this story. But in a 1997 interview about Leonard in *The New York Observer*, Junger said, "He didn't sound like the kind of guy I wanted to talk to."

That's a shame, because Junger, whose book focuses on the loss of the fishing vessel *Andrea Gail* and includes vivid writing about meteorology, long-line fishing, and Coast Guard heroics, missed a grand opportunity to capture the passion of a long-distance sailor.

Leonard, 72, bought his Westsail in 1974, the same year the rugged little double-ended yacht was featured on the cover of *Time* as the perfect vessel for folks to chuck it all and head for the South Seas.

"*Satori* is the Buddhist word for enlightenment," Leonard said. "I was at the midpoint of my career, and the boat gave me new insight into myself. Whenever I got into a bad fix with her, she always did better than I thought she would. She was very well suited for me."

From 1974 to '91, Leonard sailed *Satori* hard and often, mostly alone. The boat was well equipped with designated storm sails, and Leonard had plenty of chance to use them in roughly 60,000 miles of sailing. Divorced in 1985, he moved aboard *Satori* the same year. In October 1991, accompanied by Karen Stimson and Susan Bylander, two women he had spent the summer working with, Leonard and *Satori* set out from New Hampshire bound for Bermuda.

By all accounts, the voyage was a nightmare. Several days into the trip, after receiving a Mayday call relayed by a commercial vessel, a Coast Guard helicopter plucked *Satori*'s crew from a roiled sea. While that fact is indisputable, the events leading up to the rescue remain unclear; there are two very different versions of *Satori*'s fateful passage.

In Junger's book, which is based largely on interviews with Stimson, the sailors survive through the initiative of the women, who are forced to take action when Leonard, "sullen and silent, sneaking gulps off a whiskey bottle," refuses to do so. In what he describes as 30-foot seas, Junger wrote that *Satori* was "starting to lose the battle to stay afloat."

Leonard, however, dismisses much of Junger's account. "I'd guess the seas were 15 to 18 feet, tops," he said. "*Satori* had been in much worse. It was a very uncomfortable ride, but the boat was sound and we weren't taking on water, except for a few gallons that came through the hatch. And the drinking bit is just totally untrue."

Leonard was employing standard tactics for weathering extreme conditions: he had battened *Satori* down and was content to wait things out. "You never head towards shore in a heavy storm," he said. "It's too dangerous. And the weather forecast said a hurricane was heading towards Bermuda, so it didn't make sense to keep going that way."

Furthermore, Leonard said he did not authorize a Mayday call, though he did give the women permission to radio the Coast Guard to update *Satori*'s position. And when the chopper did arrive, he considered staying aboard the boat. Ultimately, when he was ordered to leave, he complied.

"When I knew the crew would have to jump in the water, I wasn't comfortable about having them go alone," he said. "Also, I knew if I disobeyed I wouldn't be able to land in a U.S. port for several years, and I've seen expatriates in foreign ports. I didn't want to be one."

Stimson, who was on vacation from her job in Maine (when this piece was written), was unavailable for comment. Interestingly, according to a friend of hers, she now owns a Westsail 32... just like *Satori*.

What transpired after the rescue supports Leonard's contention that *Satori* was still seaworthy when her crew leapt off her transom. Several days later, the boat washed up on a Maryland state beach. A bag of personal items that Leonard had mistakenly dropped when he jumped from *Satori* was still on the afterdeck. "A park ranger found my phone number in it," Leonard said. "He called me up and said come get your boat. It was fine. I went down and had her hauled off, cleaned her up, then sailed to Florida."

Leonard continued to sail *Satori* until this spring, when he sold the boat to a Texas couple. As for the fallout from Junger's book, which Leonard has read, he said: "People who don't know me who've read it have preconceived notions. I've only had one boat delivery job since, and I used to get plenty. I'm not bitter, but I don't think the book or movie explained what sailing's all about. Blue-water sailors are sharp, self-reliant, and proud."

And while Leonard no longer owns *Satori*, he is still drawn to the sea. Earlier this year, fulfilling a lifelong dream, he went to Alaska in search of the same work that took the lives of the crew of the *Andrea Gail*. Once there, he signed on aboard a salmon trawler. Of all things, the sailor became a fisherman.

# 10: Gone to the Sea

## SOLO SAILOR MIKE PLANT'S LAST VOYAGE

ON NOVEMBER 25, 1992, a team of French navy divers from the tug *Malabar* dropped into a frigid, storm-wracked North Atlantic seascape to inspect the overturned hull of Mike Plant's 60-foot ocean racer, *Coyote*. Plant, who had departed by himself from New York City in mid-October for the November 22nd start of the Vendée Globe Challenge, the singlehanded nonstop around-the-world race, in Les Sables d'Olonne, France, had last been heard from just over a month before; he'd radioed a passing freighter, informed the captain by way of handheld VHF that he'd lost all his shipboard electronics, and relayed his plans of pressing on to his destination.

A fortnight before the dive team dropped into the drink, on November 12th, authorities in Canada and the United States culled their records and learned that seventeen days earlier, on October 27th, a brief, incomplete transmission had been received from an unregistered EPIRB (an emergency satellite beacon) owned by Plant, thus initiating one of history's most intensive (and some would say misguided) airborne search-and-rescue operations, eventually covering some 200,000 nautical miles.

Yet it was a passing commercial ship that ultimately discovered *Coyote*'s inverted hull by accident on the same day that the Vendée fleet set off to begin the nonstop race around the world. Three days later, the French divers examined *Coyote*.

The 8,400-pound lead ballast bulb attached to the bottom of the boat's "straight razor" carbon-fiber keel was missing, as was the EPIRB and—as best could be determined—a survival suit. The 85-foot mast, though snapped off about four feet above deck level, remained in place, secured by intact rigging and hoisted sails. A partially inflated life raft was nestled up under the cockpit. The divers had held out hope that Plant might be alive and well, trapped in an air pocket of the overturned hull. It proved to be wishful thinking; of *Coyote*'s skipper, there was no sign. That day, all search efforts were suspended. Mike Plant was officially declared lost at sea.

THE *COYOTE* campaign was a microcosm for what Grand Prix, round-the-world, singlehanded ocean racing had become in the ten short years since Frenchman Philippe Jeantot won the inaugural 1982-83 BOC Challenge. In that race, Jeantot showed up at the starting line with the only boat truly designed and purpose-built for solo yacht racing. With the concept proven by victory, the water-ballasted, dual-steering station, twin-dagger board *Credit Agricole* became a benchmark boat that instantly defined the commitment necessary to win.

These days, as defined by the French—the acknowledged leaders in the sport—solo, long-distance racing is a pursuit fueled by corporate sponsorship that attracts a breed of talented, technology-driven sailors, designers, boatbuilders, and engineers. In the United States, nobody played the game on the same field with Mike Plant.

Born in 1950 and raised in the Minneapolis suburb of Wayzata, Minnesota, Plant learned to sail and race scows on nearby Lake Minnetonka; it was a natural pastime for a boy whose passion for the outdoors led to stints as an Outward Bound instructor, a trekker who hiked the length of South America, and a delivery skipper. Plant's true love may have been ice hockey, a game at which he excelled, but his career was cut short in his early teens after a string of concussions.

In some aspects, particularly in his younger years, Plant was the quintessential adrenaline junkie. He followed a wild star throughout his 20s, and in the early 1980s settled in the seaside community of Jamestown, Rhode Island. But it wasn't until after seeing a film on the first BOC Challenge—an event that circled the globe with three stops—that he discovered his true calling.

"He was a seeker," said Helen Davis, Plant's longtime companion and fiancée. "A lot of people are searching for the why; for Mike it was more the *how*: 'How can we do this?'"

Plant found the perfect outlet for his resourcefulness, wanderlust, and sense of adventure in singlehanded sailing. In the mid-80s, with much nerve and scant experience, he commissioned a design from Newport, Rhode Island-based naval architect Rodger Martin for a 50-foot, Class II BOC racer; built it himself with help from friends and partial financial assistance from the boat's namesake, *Airco Distributor*; and won his class in the second, 1986-87 BOC Challenge.

The taste of success whetted his appetite for more and he expanded his ambitions for both boat and venue. Once again on a shoestring budget, assuming the multiple roles of builder, project manager, and fund-raiser, Plant engaged Martin for a second design that became *Duracell*, partially backed by the battery company. An "open-class" 60-footer that Martin described as "fairly conservative," *Duracell* was conceived for a nonstop round-the-world race organized by Jeantot called the Vendée Globe Challenge.

Though rigging problems forced an unscheduled stop—and automatic disqualification—midway through the voyage, Plant finished the course to a hero's welcome and set an American record of 134 days for a solo circumnavigation. He was addicted to the pace of the event, where there were no layovers or distractions, and he could get down to the serious business of working a boat for weeks and months on end. Afterward, he went on to sail the boat in the 1990-91 BOC race, finishing fourth in Class I, but it was the nonstop race that had become his genuine passion.

By the time Plant began to ponder his second Vendée race, he was a seasoned professional who had earned his share of field promotions. He had repaired a holed boat at sea, survived a capsize, jury-rigged spars and generators in dire conditions. He had, in fact, climbed every mountain the sport had presented... with the exception of taking top overall prize in a major race. For Plant, it was not enough. He had yet to beat the French at their own game. *Coyote,* his third Martin design, would be his most radical attempt to correct that omission.

In Indian lore, Plant discovered, the coyote was a "trickster" who "traveled alone and ate sparingly." The temporary name was perfect, as Plant intended this boat to be the ultimate trick on the French competition. The name would change if a title sponsor came aboard.

*Coyote* was an extreme design with exaggerated dimensions. At 60 feet overall, she sported a plumb bow, a startling-looking 19-foot beam, and twin rudders. Her hull was a broad, Airex-cored, shallow dish with a displacement of only 21,500 pounds—5,000 pounds lighter than *Duracell.* With upwind and downwind sail areas of 2,600 and 4,700 square feet, respectively, she carried an impressive power plant. (For comparison, a Baltic 64 or Little Harbor 63, with about three times the displacement, would carry about 1,800 square feet of sail area.) It was a ton of sail, even for an experienced solo sailor.

Below deck, there were five watertight compartments and

tankage for 7,000 pounds of movable water ballast. The flat underbody was lanced by a 14-foot carbon-fiber keel, to the bottom of which was bolted an 8,400-pound lead ballast bulb.

"It was far different from *Duracell*," said Martin, "a big step forward, much more refined, and a lot more leading-edge. It was also a lot more sensitive and more of a handful to sail just because (the latest generation of Open 60) designs are more powerful, with a much higher righting moment, and stiffer, bigger rigs. At one stage during trials in 35-knots of breeze, she was sailing upwind at 13.5 knots as measured on the GPS."

"*Coyote* was stupidly fast," said Dan Neri of Shore Sails, who supplied the bulk of the boat's sail inventory. "Way faster than *Duracell*."

"It was probably the fastest 60-footer ever built in the States," added Steve Pettingill, a professional sailor who holds the record for fastest voyage from New York to San Francisco, and who was involved in *Coyote*'s commissioning and early work-up.

"We were trying to win," concluded Rodger Martin. "To do that, sometimes, you have to file down the edge."

IF PLANT HAD secured sponsorship early, *Coyote* would have been launched in the spring of 1992 and shaken down thrice across the Atlantic (a crewed delivery to England for the start of the singlehanded trans-Atlantic race; a solo return to Newport to do the race and qualify Plant for the Vendée; a return to France with crew in the Quebec-St. Malo race). That was the original plan. Instead, the boat was launched in Portsmouth, Rhode Island, on September 10, a mere seven weeks from the October 30 deadline for Vendée boats to report to Les Sables d'Olonne for the start.

It was a wicked schedule but not one to which Plant wasn't accustomed. At its base was money—a distinct lack thereof. "Mike was amazing in that he started these sorts of projects without the funding lined up," said Martin. "He was good about not committing to things that he didn't have the money to pay for, but he would start as much as he could handle at a time, and then let it grow as it could." Plant felt confident that he had a boat that could win the event, and that incentive would be able to attract a sponsor.

After discussing options, Plant and Martin chose Concordia Custom Yachts of South Dartmouth, Massachusetts, to build *Coyote*. "I think Concordia showed an interest in participating in the cost of the boat," said Martin; indeed, the project might have collapsed on more than one occasion without Concordia's strong commitment, financial and otherwise. And when construction commenced in October 1991—partly through the proceeds of the sale of Plant's previous boat—all parties believed that Plant's most recent corporate patron, Duracell, would ultimately become title sponsor. "He started the boat on that supposition," said Davis.

It wasn't to be. In December, with the basic hull nearly completed, Plant learned Duracell wouldn't be coming on board. Now the scramble began in earnest. "He (still) had some private sponsorship, and he was doing everything he could to raise money," said Bill Walker, general manager at Concordia. But securing cash for so esoteric a mission as singlehanded yacht racing has never been an easy sell in this country, and the state of the economy in the early '90s did little to entice fresh prospects.

The construction program went through fits and starts in early '92. Plant continued to hustle hard for gear, equipment, and in-kind contributions, but failed to secure the big hit that would ensure financial stability and a no-compromise program. Among other items on the wish list, a tungsten keel bulb—offering less bulk and wetted surface for the same weight—was specified in the original design writ. At a minimum cost of $100,000, it had to be scratched early on. This was not the last concession.

"There were cost issues associated with all sorts of things," said Walker. "For instance, should we build the (keel) fin out of steel or carbon fiber. Mike would say, 'Well, I want to save weight so I can win this thing, so let's go with carbon fiber.' But then something else would have to be sacrificed. It was a double-edge sword. He wanted to win the race and do it for nothing."

Even with the compromises, by springtime his money had run out and the building program was nearly dormant. There was talk of hauling the boat out of the building shed, effectively stamping a huge "On Hold" sign across its unfinished form. It was at this juncture that Concordia president Bill Steitz stepped in.

"Steitz was critical," said David Stevens, who was helping Plant with fundraising and public relations. "About this time he started writing checks. During the summer he started writing big checks."

"I don't know what transpired to have the boat finished," said photographer Billy Black, a friend of Plant's who chronicled the *Coyote* campaign from the outset. "I think it must have been Bill Steitz saying it will be finished. Concordia had made an investment that would only be productive to them if the boat got to the race."

In fact, Concordia agreed to lend Plant the money to complete the boat, the ultimate value of which ranged somewhere between $600,000 and $800,000. (In 2011, a budget for a similar

Vendée campaign runs in the millions of dollars.)

"It was basically a mortgage, similar to a bank mortgage," said Davis.

"Mike eventually took a loan from us, though it wasn't for the whole boat," concurred Walker.

The wheels of progress again began turning, but the program was terribly behind schedule. Serge Viviand, a close friend who had helped build *Duracell* and worked with Plant on other projects, called from his home in France and tried hard to convince Plant to sell the incomplete hull; he knew people who were interested and felt the program was too far behind to be successful. Other friends also advised Plant to forgo his plan to enter the Vendée, arguing that it was already too late and he could instead take a shot at the New York-San Francisco record or wait for the next BOC. But the nonstop race held too much allure and he was too far in. He pressed on.

The early sea trials surely gave Plant further grist to conjure bigger, French-slaying dreams. Here was a machine that provided the competitive speed that heretofore had been the sole domain of his rivals. To a racing sailor, boat speed is an addictive drug. Like any addiction, or obsession, it can falsely nullify other pressing concerns.

In *Coyote*'s case, the first was relatively straightforward. Of the "shortcuts" taken to complete the boat, at the top of the list was the triple-spreader, carbon-fiber spar. Designed and constructed by highly qualified engineers and builders (though not Plant's first choice if he'd had the luxury of unlimited funds), the spar was in and of itself a quality piece of equipment. In this instance, the cost cutting was further achieved by taking delivery of a disassembled spar and erecting it with a team of boatbuilders and sailors, including Plant, at the Concordia yard.

Because a carbon spar is lighter and more flexible than an aluminum mast, it requires more attention and tuning, but it also is more versatile from a sail trim standpoint and carries less weight aloft. On an extremely breezy day sail on September 29, just a month before Plant's scheduled arrival in France, it became evident that, when the spar was loaded up, the second panel or section down from the top of the mast—between the upper and middle sets of spreaders—would precariously "pop" out of column. According to sailmaker Neri, "Later that week they pulled the spar out of the boat, reinforced it with carbon (in the suspect areas), and put it back in. They did a great job." Evidently, it caused no further worry. The same could not be said of *Coyote*'s second trouble spot.

From almost the outset, *Coyote*'s electrical and, more specifically, battery-charging systems were a source of annoyance and difficulty. Plant's previous boat employed redundant 12-volt systems, but *Coyote* was specified with a 24-volt system—as were most of the top French boats—to more efficiently control the linear drive autopilots. Converters were installed to power gear dependent on 12 volts, particularly the SSB and VHF radios. There were twin gensets and alternators, and a complex network of relays, but the weak link might well have been the automatic "smart" regulators that may have tried to charge the system at too high a rate. It was a complicated setup that required near constant professional attention in the initial trials.

"Mike was never comfortable with it," said Davis. "He said it was too complex."

On October 4, in part due to a longstanding agreement with Concordia and partly to continue the chase for cash, *Coyote* departed Newport for a fully crewed run to Annapolis to take part in the U.S. Sailboat Show beginning on the 8th. In 18 hours, the boat covered the roughly 245 miles from the mouth of Narragansett Bay to the mouth of the Delaware Bay. After more than 12 hours of hard running under spinnaker, often hitting speeds up to 22 knots, Plant called to douse the chute. He was exhilarated.

The next day, however, while reaching across the Chesapeake Bay at nine knots to tune the rig while waiting for a tow into Annapolis Harbor, *Coyote* squished aground in soft muck off Maryland's Eastern Shore. "It was fairly gentle, not abrupt," said Billy Black, who was steering at the time. Still, they were solidly stuck. By back-winding the jib and holding the main to windward, the crew was able to pivot the boat a full 180 degrees, but remained parked. Next, they hailed a passing fishing boat that took a halyard and attempted to pull the boat out "sideways" from its masthead. Finally, the powerboat took a line from *Coyote*'s bow and tugged the boat again into deep water. The entire sequence, from grounding to freedom, had taken about half an hour.

A month and a half later, many people would speculate about what might've happened to the crucial bulb keel during those 30 minutes in the Chesapeake mud.

WITH A MORTGAGE on his boat, the clock ticking, and a deadline to be in France in just over three weeks, Mike Plant had one final hope of bagging a major, title sponsor. The Motorola company, and a recent South African emigrant named Tony McKeever, were his last best chance.

Experienced at the task of finding sponsors for solo sailors (two previous clients were countrymen Bertie Reed and John Martin, for whom McKeever had secured handsome packages in his homeland), McKeever was already trying to pitch Motorola on an intricate, multi-million-dollar four-year proposal for the

fully crewed Whitbread Round-the-World Race. As an entice-
ment, he wrapped Mike Plant's project into the package to show
Motorola an event in which they could, he said, "get their feet
wet." And Motorola, which offers a line of SSB radios and had
recently introduced a handheld GPS unit, seemed a natural corporate backer for marine-related events. They were interested.
After meetings with Plant and a test sail together, Motorola gave
McKeever a check for $50,000 to promote their relationship with
Plant and sailing, though at this point their only real involvement was as a limited product supplier.

McKeever showed a talent for spending money. He bought
a "Motorola"-emblazoned spinnaker from a sailmaker he was
trying to woo for his Whitbread campaign; alas, it was the wrong
size and cloth weight for Plant's purposes, a sin to a sailor desperate for inventory.

With the new chute, McKeever scheduled a photo shoot
for the day after the spar was repaired and re-stepped, a day
originally set up for rig tuning. With those photos, he made a
poster. At the Annapolis Boat Show, he hired boats, issued press
releases, hosted a Motorola dealer party. Meanwhile, aboard
*Coyote*, at least two electrical engineers tried to make sense of
the charging system.

Dave Weisz, Motorola's manager of sports marketing, liked
what he saw in Annapolis, though by the end of the show he said
there was "less and less" a chance that the company could take
on the role of title sponsor. Still, everyone in Plant's camp believed Motorola would show up in France with a check of some
denomination to partially sponsor *Coyote*. (Plant did secure one
significant deal with the marine communications division of
AT&T, receiving $50,000 up front with the promise of matching
funds later in the race.)

It was probably for this reason that Plant made one final detour before heading for France from Annapolis, as he had originally planned to do. Instead, he gathered a crew and pointed his bow north toward New York City, where McKeever had arranged for Plant to go on network TV in a final attempt to show Motorola the beneficial media exposure lavished on a solo adventurer. At McKeever's expense, the Motorola logo was secured to *Coyote*'s hull. The cameras rolled.

"Mike had a love/hate relationship with Tony," said Black. "He thought he would pull [a deal] together, so he thought it was worth putting the energy into it. The big concern at the time was the [cash] penalty late arrivals [would incur] in France. But Mike thought if a sponsor came in and was willing to absorb that [sum], it would be a small price to pay. But he did spend a lot of time schmoozing PR and that did sacrifice what could have been done on the boat." Plant had wondered aloud about hauling the boat to investigate the keel after the Chesapeake grounding. But it could wait until France. There was no time and no money.

On his last day in New York, Plant cruised lower Manhattan and purchased, among other items, a set of jumper cables, an extra pair of sunglasses, some hooks for foul weather gear, and an alarm clock. He had money for incidentals. Tony McKeever had cut him a check for $3,000, all that was left after McKeever paid his own commission and expenses from the fifty grand.

Then, on October 16, two weeks before his deadline in France, Plant took a tow out of New York Harbor, dropped his crew on the towboat, and set a course across the Atlantic. It was the first time he'd ever sailed *Coyote* alone.

THE FIRST THREE days were eventful, and Plant took care to keep his shore-side support crew informed by way of telephone hook-ups. "He told me it was [blowing] 35 knots on the nose," said David Stevens. "He said it was 'godawful,' a word I'd never heard him use. He also said he was having trouble steering in these seas, that the boat was 'laboring,' but that he'd get to know it."

Apparently Plant recovered quickly. "He called Friday, Saturday, and six times on Sunday [the 16, 17, and 18]," said Helen Davis. "Saturday was gorgeous. He said he'd slowed the boat down to 12 knots so he could sort things out. He was in a good mood, but lonely."

Then the airwaves went silent.

"When I didn't hear from him," said Davis, "I knew right away something was wrong."

On October 21, Davis received a collect call from the skipper of the freighter *SKS Trader* (these were the days before satellite phones), who was ringing on Plant's instructions. The skipper was in the middle of a three-way hook-up, having "patched" Plant's call through to Davis. Though she couldn't speak to him directly, she could hear Plant's voice quite clearly. "He told the captain that his power supply was out, he had some problems he was working on, his ETA was delayed, but he was pressing on. The captain asked him if there was anything else and Mike said, 'Yeah, tell Helen I love her and not to worry.' I can detect things in Mike's voice. He sounded fine."

It was, as best as can be determined, Plant's final conversation.

Later, several newspapers would report that during the transmission Plant said he would consider calling at Halifax, Nova Scotia, if he failed to regain power and get his autopilots operational. Davis heard no such comment.

At that juncture, *Coyote*'s position was 42°12'N, 53°30'W: 960 miles out of New York, and roughly 360 miles south of St. John's,

Newfoundland. Plant had averaged about 190 miles per day
at speeds of just under 8 knots. But without autopilots, there
was no way he could be expected to maintain that pace by hand
steering. He would need to take time to rest.

Now the airwaves truly went blank. Davis and other members of *Coyote*'s support team caught their previously scheduled
flights for France to await Plant's arrival. Days passed but, perhaps surprisingly, there was little tension. If Plant were in true
danger, his friends surmised, he would activate his brand new
Raytheon 406 MHz EPIRB.

The October 30 deadline came and went. Charts were
pulled out and scenarios imagined. Mark Schrader, who had
competed against Plant in the second BOC, arrived in France
to monitor the race in his official capacity as BOC race director.
Working on the assumption that it's better to laugh than cry, he
and Davis kidded about chartering a blimp, hovering out over
the Atlantic until they found *Coyote*, and flashing the message,
"It's insured, you can get off now." There was irony in the joke.
Plant's insurance for the boat hadn't come through until after
his last transmission on the 21st: He did not know *Coyote* was
covered.

All who knew Plant also maintained that it would take
more than an "inconvenience" such as a dismasting for him to
activate his EPIRB. He would've preferred to jump in the water
and swim the boat ashore than abandon it, they said, especially
considering he thought it was uninsured. And many did believe
that *Coyote* was dismasted and Plant was slowly making way
under jury rig.

On November 6, the Coast Guard issued an alert for all
North Atlantic vessels to be on the lookout for *Coyote*. There was
no sign of the boat and no response.

That same day, back home in Rhode Island, a group of local sailors and friends of Plant tracked down the identification number for Plant's 406 EPIRB and relayed the information to the Coast Guard, who in turn passed it on to the National Oceanic and Atmospheric Administration. Were a distress signal set off from a 406 unit, it would be received by a NOAA satellite and the information on the vessel's identity and position would then be passed along to the Coast Guard to begin search and rescue operations. But it seemed like another dead end: There was no word from NOAA or the Coast Guard.

However, on November 11th, Plant's increasingly concerned supporters again appealed to authorities to examine records and this time, both NOAA and the Canadian Coast Guard ran Plant's EPIRB I.D. number through their tracking computers. The news was devastating. Seventeen days earlier, on the evening of October 27, a Canadian tracking station in Goose Bay had received three weak transmission bursts from Plant's EPIRB. NOAA received two bursts from the same satellite pass; the information was downloaded to a ground station, but not retrieved until the next day.

For several reasons, the signal was not acted upon at the time: It did not meet the requisite four bursts deemed necessary for a positive, accurate fix; there was no registration record on file with NOAA or the Canadians; and the signal had been brief and singular, with no subsequent follow-up. Of the three, the primary reason the distress signal was ignored was that there was no record of Plant's EPIRB registration.

It begged the question: Had Plant attempted to register the EPIRB?

It's impossible to say. "Mike had a lot of paperwork on his chart table," said Stevens. "I guess he was going to do it in the North Atlantic and mail it in France. He wasn't dismissing the need for that kind of stuff, it was just at the bottom of a very long list."

On November 13th, the Coast Guard began an air search originating from a spot more than 300 miles due south of Plant's last known position at a coordinate that was "computer-guesstimated" by Canadian officials in Goose Bay based on the transmission bursts already acknowledged to be suspect. It did not jibe with Plant's announced intentions to continue eastward on the 21st.

Many shore-side followers still believed Plant had been dismasted, and that he may well have switched on his EPIRB briefly on the 27th, but turned it off after regaining confidence and control of the situation. But the search area, upwind and upcurrent from his earlier fix, continued to make little sense.

The original Coast Guard search lasted five days and ultimately involved six aircraft with support from both the Canadian Coast Guard and the U.S. Navy. The Coast Guard was convinced Plant had been run down by another ship and was primarily looking for a life raft, debris, or both. The first search was suspended on the 18th after scouring over 125,000 miles of ocean north of Bermuda and eventually northwest of the Azores.

Two days later (the day before what would have been Plant's 42nd birthday), after Plant's family secured data from weather and navigation experts on both sides of the Atlantic and convinced the Coast Guard that there was reason to believe *Coyote* was well east of the original search area, the hunt was resumed northeast of the Azores. It was the right place, but the Greek tanker *Protank Orinico* got there first. The French divers would soon follow. The search for Mike Plant was over.

IN THE WAKE of *Coyote*'s discovery, a host of questions regarding a number of significant issues begged for answers. What happened to *Coyote*'s keel bulb? Where was the 406 EPIRB and why was its transmission so brief? Did *Coyote* come to grief on October 27th? Did Plant continue on his easterly great circle course after his last radio transmission on the 21st—his stated intention—and if so, how far did he manage to sail? Why was the Coast Guard's initial search pattern so far off base from where the boat was actually found? Why was the life raft partially inflated?

The loss of the keel bulb was almost certainly Plant's undoing. Several observers who witnessed its construction described its rough specifications. Its carbon-fiber fin, or foil, measured approximately 17 feet and was molded in carbon layers in two symmetrical halves that were then glued together with two stringers down the center. The foil was built directly into the boat with strong connections at its upper end beneath the deck, and again where it passed through the hull.

The suspect point was the connection between the fin and the lead bulb. At the bottom of the fin, a stainless steel plate with nuts welded to its topside was bonded into the foil with carbon. The bulb had a flat top that matched the plate size. Six holes were then drilled up through the bottom of the bulb, and it was bolted flush to the bottom of the foil.

Though *Coyote* was later salvaged—and in fact, after a refit, completed the 1994-95 BOC Challenge under the command of American David Scully—an in-depth postmortem of the keel was never publicly revealed. But chief designer T.J. Perrotti of Pedrick Yacht Designs offered the following independent observations: "The vague area in my mind is how the plate was glassed into the carbon fiber. Everything up to that point is a mechanical bond; it's bolts and steel and lead. But anytime you bond a metal into a composite, it's something you want to address very carefully. Where do I see the weak link? It could be how that plate was glassed into the fin."

Another question: Did *Coyote*'s October grounding in the Chesapeake Bay ultimately lead to her demise? It will never be known, though designer Rodger Martin (who was joined by Dirk Kramers of Hall Engineering in the keel design, along with input from Plant) did provide this analysis of the potential ramifications of the mishap: "If you design a boat at this level to take a grounding like that you won't be [competitive]. They have to be treated more carefully around the shore. It's nobody's fault it went aground, the Chesapeake's shallow. I don't know if [ultimately] it had any effect on the keel, but it certainly wasn't the type of blow it was designed to take."

Two other remote possibilities exist. *Coyote* could have struck a whale or other debris at sea. Or, sailmaker Neri believes the boat may have capsized for reasons unrelated to the ballast bulb, and remained stable in the upside-down position. In that scenario, the keel bulb would have broken after the boat was inverted.

What happened to *Coyote*'s EPlRB is probably an even more unsolvable mystery. The unit was designed to "hydrostatically" float free of its mount when immersed in a meter or more of water. If the unit had been in its "automatic" rather than "off" mode, it would have spontaneously gone into operation at that time.

Offshore sailor Steve Pettengill had a unit similar to Plant's aboard a second, San Francisco-New York record run in 1989 when his trimaran *Great American* capsized near Cape Horn. He recalled that the EPIRB's external, whip-type antenna was bent 90 degrees during the episode, and that he had to straighten it out before turning it on. He believes Plant's EPIRB went off after *Coyote*'s capsize, the satellite captured the partial signal, and the unit was somehow damaged soon after in the melee. Kim Weeks of Raytheon acknowledged that a broken antenna would "substantially reduce the unit's ability to transmit a burst."

Most close observers believe Plant's capsize did occur on October 27 in the very general area that the boat was ultimately found. When the boat was first discovered on November 22nd, it had traveled approximately 1,130 miles since its last known position on October 21st, the day Plant hailed the freighter on VHF to report its loss of electrical power. Even without autopilots, in favorable conditions *Coyote* was definitely capable of covering several hundred miles in the five days between the 21st and the 27th. The French divers noted that sails were set, so the boat was certainly under way at the time of her capsize. Once inverted, the boat would make little progress with her rig serving as a sea anchor—about twelve miles a day if making half-a-knot, or roughly 300 miles in the 26 days that she may have been drifting. The figures are debatable, the logic basically sound.

So why did the Coast Guard begin its November 12 search in a location they later conceded was wrong? They acted on the only real information they had—the interpolated coordinates from the Canadian Coast Guard. Perhaps it says something about our times, and the willingness to follow electronic aids rather than human reasoning in the face of conflicting evidence. And at the time, they believed they were searching for a raft or the debris from a run-down vessel. In reality, knowing the distress signal was over two weeks old, they knew a successful mission was a long shot.

The life raft? It was a cockpit-mounted valise-type that required a tug on a tether, not a static-release model that would've inflated under water pressure. It's very possible that it was somehow washed open in the month of drifting; the broken rig was likely a victim of the same fate.

I WAS ABOARD *Coyote* on September 29th on that gusty sail that led to the decision to pull the spar out of the boat for reinforcement. *Coyote* met and surpassed her advance advertisement. She was the fastest, wildest, wettest monohull that I have ever sailed, before or since.

One of the great tragedies of Mike's passing was the awful timing. There he was, finally, after three solo circumnavigations, truly ready to contend for the crown. If all went well, if he had that mix of luck and execution required of all champions, he was ready to challenge the best on their own and his own terms. Despite all the trials and tribulations, the incredible pressure, the financial instability, the huge expectations, he was ready to live his biggest dream. It was within grasp.

At the end of our sail, after he'd secured *Coyote* to her mooring, Mike walked aft taking in his boat and said, "What have we created here..." It wasn't a question so much as an affirmation. Blue-eyed Mike was as handsome as he was focused, and he flashed a smile straight out of central casting. Amidst the undeniable chaos, there was true contentment. He had the gaze of a man on the verge of unlimited possibility.

When Mike Plant perished, my 6,000-word story about the tragedy, most of which is excerpted in this book, was the longest piece *Cruising World* had ever published, and I believe that's still the case. After it came out, the regional magazine *Rhode Island Monthly* commissioned another, more personal account that wasn't quite so technical. For this anthology, I considered weaving the two different pieces into a single chapter, but the tones were different and I decided against it. However, I think the lead of the *Rhode Island Monthly* piece does add some value and insight, so here it is:

THE FINAL IMAGE of Mike Plant's beautiful, terrible sixty-foot ocean racer *Coyote* was a November snapshot: the crippled hull was face down, whitecaps cascaded over it. The big keel bulb responsible for leveling the beast—its source of balance, its promise of stability—had vanished. So too had its forty-one-year-old captain.

Two months earlier, before the boat was discovered in the cold North Atlantic and Mike Plant was pronounced lost at sea, I dropped to all fours inside *Coyote*'s sparse interior to inspect the bulb and keel through a small window installed for that purpose in the bottom of the hull. Outside, under brilliant sunshine, the breeze clocked a steady, chilly thirty knots. The rig hummed in the gusts.

We were sailing upwind near the entrance to
Narragansett Bay on our way back to Jamestown after
a breathtaking run to Point Judith under spinnaker.
There were no other boats around, no outside witness-
es to the spectacle of the fastest sixty-foot monohull
ever built in America sailing hard and fast to weather
in the breeze she was designed to relish.

It was late September, the second day of the
season's first shrill three-day northwester.  *Coyote*
had been in the water less than three weeks; in a little
over a month it was due in France for the October 31
skippers' deadline for the Vendée Globe Challenge,
a nonstop singlehanded race around the world.  The
boat was far from ready for the trip.

No one knew this better than Plant.  Even on this
short shakedown sail, we'd had several problems.  A
mast-mounted winch, which had been secured with
screws that were too short, was wrenched loose under
load and had opened the chin of the sailor tending it.
Worse, an upper section of the boat's light, high-tech
mast swayed out of alignment.

Unchecked, the gyrations could lead to structural
failure, and a broken mast meant broken dreams.  A
plan to pull and reinforce it ashore was immediately
hatched, even though it meant a serious schedule
change.  Finally, reefing the mainsail to slow the boat
proved to be an arduous, painstaking task, even for our
large crew.  Clearly, the sheer force and weight of rig-

ging and sails were greater than any of Plant's earlier racing boats. *Coyote* carried a ton of sail, an enormous amount even for an experienced solo sailor. He needed to come to terms with his craft, and he needed to do so quickly.

But there was also much promise. Sailing upwind, we made a steady twelve-and-a-half to thirteen knots, speeds generally reserved for large trimarans, catamarans, and powerboats. Planing ahead through a running seaway, *Coyote*'s bow carved a deep wedge in the four-foot waves and parted the inevitable torrent before the thick spray settled. Remarkably, it didn't slow the boat whatsoever. There was not a dry spot on deck. The crew was drenched but seriously pumped, especially Plant. As he steered, his ever-present Ray-Bans caked with salt, water streamed from his face. Every so often he allowed a soaked grin that said the previous year's worth of endless setbacks had been worth it.

From my vantage point below deck, peering into the depths of the bay, the torpedo-shaped bulb creasing the shadowy, green water looked purposeful, efficient, rigid. The word *breakable* never once came to mind.

I first met Mike Plant in the early eighties while I was on the staff of *Cruising World* magazine. Plant was a new guy on the Newport waterfront and he had a crazy idea. He said he was going to build his own fifty-foot ocean racing yacht and then circumnavigate the

globe in the second BOC Challenge solo round-the-
world race.  One hitch:  he was neither a boatbuilder
nor a singlehanded sailor.  He also asked me to help
him write a sponsorship proposal aimed at corporate
America to entice a pile of money to make it happen.
He kept a straight face the entire time.  I took the job.
Like so many others who found themselves spinning
in Plant's orbit, I couldn't say no.

During the next several years, Plant would make
a career of laying outlandish plans, then living outrageous deeds.  Perhaps that's why, even after he was
missing and weeks overdue, all who knew him maintained a vigil of denial.  After all, he'd said he was sailing to France.  He did not abuse spoken promises.

Plant was an adopted Rhode Islander.  He grew
up in Minnesota and never betrayed his Midwest
respect for hard work and economy of language.  The
son of an affluent Minneapolis attorney, he learned
to sail scows on a nearby lake, drifted through school,
and nurtured thoughts of adventure.  He became an
Outward Bound instructor.  He hiked the length of
South America, a rite of passage that led to all sorts of
adventures and misadventures.  Bob Dylan once said,
to live outside the law, you have to be honest.  Plant
did, and was.  Much later, he moved to the island village of Jamestown.

Marathon singlehanded sailing became his passion and obsession.  Plant made good on that first

boatbuilding scheme in 1986, and entered his fifty-foot Rodger Martin-designed *Airco Distributor* (named after a partial sponsor, a manufacturer of industrial gases) in the BOC race. Midway through the event, he was locked in a duel with French sailor Jacques de Roux for top prize in Class II when tragedy struck.

Less than 250 miles from safe harbor in Sydney, Australia, de Roux's boat was discovered sailing erratically with her skipper missing. Neither his boat nor fate was ever discovered. It was devastating news to Plant, who had relished the competition with the accomplished Frenchman. Upon his winning arrival in Sydney, he announced his intention to quit the race. But he later realized it was not the way de Roux would have wanted it. He pressed on, completed the final two legs to Rio de Janeiro and Newport, and won his class, but the race had been a stern reality check. Plant now fully understood the boundaries of the game, and the penalty for crossing them.

Unwittingly, I was about to teach him a second lesson—that success breeds scrutiny, and scrutiny can stir unwanted memories. In my BOC race report, I described an incident that had almost prevented him from making the start of the race. After finishing his qualifying sail from Newport to the Azores, Plant had been detained when his name was discovered in a routine computer check of an Interpol fugitive list. (Some ten years earlier, he had reportedly been charged in

absentia with smuggling in Greece, where he owned
a charter boat used in an incident that resulted in
the conviction of two young Canadians.) Plant was
transferred from the Azores to a Lisbon jail and spent
thirty-five days, often in solitary confinement, before
his release; Greek authorities decided not to press for
extradition.

Plant was upset that I'd run the piece and he told
me so. Amazingly, the mainstream press had largely
ignored the episode, and Plant believed I should have,
too, as it was peripheral to the race itself. Plus, it was
not the kind of publicity he needed if he were to seek
more sponsorship for future races.

In Newport, Plant's past was sometimes alluded
to, but rarely directly addressed; gossip is no stranger
to this small island town. And, in fact, his past was
irrelevant to his accomplishments in his sport. But
perhaps it does shed a clue to character, especially
when speaking of an individual whose life's work was
devoted to a high-risk, dangerous endeavor where
flowing adrenaline is one of the rewards. Recently,
people who didn't know Plant have asked what he was
like; it's hard to answer because he wasn't a person
who let in many others. My own relationship with
him was generated largely by the jobs we had. We
were one another's necessary evils. Like all of us, he
had his good points and bad. Like most of us, he had
one big dream. His was winning the Vendée.

A postscript to this chapter: Mike's remarkable story, above and beyond the sailing bits, has never been fully told. It would make one amazing movie.

**On October 16, 1992, solo sailor Mike Plant set sail from New York bound for France aboard his 60-foot *Coyote*. He was never seen again.**

# Part II

# Places

This book is dedicated to the protagonist of this little tale, the light of my life, the one-and-only Margaret Martha McCormick.

*Bobby Grieser*

**On a trip to the islands with my daughter, Maggie, I got a clear glimpse at the coming attraction that all fathers of young ladies will inevitably face.**

# 11: Fathers and Daughters

## GLIMPSING THE FUTURE IN THE BVI

SO RIGHT before the trip I pick up a brand-new Red Sox cap—a white cotton one 'cause I know it's going to be hot in the islands—and as a lifelong fan of the Boston Nine I reckoned it was time to replace my ratty old blue one after the Sox finally "reversed the curse" and won the World Series the previous fall. You never know when and where the opportunity to yank the chain of a Yankees fan might present itself, right?

Now we're sitting in Trellis Bay near Tortola in the British Virgin Islands on our Moorings 4700 catamaran. I've just strolled back from the airport at Beef Island to meet the incoming flight of my old friend PK and his daughter, Helene. While I met the plane, another pal, who goes by the nickname Furbio, waited back on the boat with my daughter, Maggie, and his two daughters, Molly and Lauren. And yes, the trip did have a preconceived theme: After many years of idle chatter, we three dads were finally taking our rapidly growing "little girls" for a charter cruise.

As PK and Helene sort out their cabin in the forward port stateroom of our big cat, *Saturday Knight*, the rest of us slip over the side for a refreshing swim. Soon enough, everyone's in the drink.

We all come back aboard, and everyone's taking turns using the freshwater shower off the aft deck. Maggie yanks off her red bathing suit from beneath the towel wrapped around her and gives it a carefree toss before disappearing below to change.

A while later, we're all lounging around, getting the grill and the dogs and the burgers ready, when it occurs to me that I should be wearing my Sox cap. As I might've mentioned, you just never know who could be hanging out on the next boat over.

So I'm hunting everywhere for the cap and no one knows where it's gone to and I'm starting to wonder—egad!—if it might've blown overboard, when it finally appears. Under Maggie's red bathing suit. Maggie's brand-new, soaking-wet, red bathing suit!

My crisp white cap is now, well, damp pink, but I pull it on anyway. And later on I take it off and look at it. And as the evening unfolds I look at it quite a bit. And every time I do, I think of my beautiful little girl, and the pink hat starts to grow on me. I mean, really, really grow on me. By the way, isn't beer great?

So just before bed, I kiss my already snoozing daughter on the cheek and put the hat up on a shelf—the very same hat that just a few hours earlier I'd been planning to give a good scrub with hot, soapy water—and I go to sleep. As slumber comes, it occurs to me that I'm *never* going to wash that pink hat. Like, ever.


FROM THE very moment I learned that fatherhood was on my horizon, I wanted a daughter. My dad and I had ultimately weathered the slings and arrows of some outrageous father/son misfortunes—at times the outcome was seriously in doubt—but I'd had a good, hard look at that movie and was terrified by the thought of a sequel. Plus, I know precisely what happens to boys, and when. To paraphrase the comedian Paul Reiser, I went to high school with me.

Not that I didn't realize that raising a daughter would have its own tests, but all in all, I preferred my chances with the fairer sex. After all, my very own sister always seemed to be Daddy's Girl, even as he and I were at each other's throats. Would it be asking too much to have the same sort of relationship they shared?

There were, of course, early trials and tribulations. I was on a magazine assignment in New Zealand when I got the news that, back home in Rhode Island at the tender age of three, Maggie had plunged some 15 feet from the balcony of a health club, of all places. But she never lost consciousness and had a pithy comment to the ambulance attendants after they'd strapped her to the gurney for the ride to the hospital: "I'm stuck." She recovered fully and apparently inherited dad's hard head.

She hated loud noises—thunder, fireworks, roaring surf, the sunset report of a yacht-club cannon—which were all things I loved. She adored stuff—snakes, spiders, all the creepy-crawlies—which gave me the willies. But from her earliest days we undoubtedly shared a passion for several of the most important things: books, music, the water. Especially the water. By 7 she could swim nearly the length of a regulation pool...*underwater*. She was so oversensitive to some things I could scream, so compassionate in other ways I could weep. I guess it goes without saying, but I'll say it anyway: I love her so.

Then there were my pals, PK and Furbio (a.k.a. Pat Kerins and Paul Faerber), as good a set of friends as a fellow could ask for. We'd all been born in Newport Hospital a few months apart when Ike was still running the show, been constants in one another's lives for decades on end; stood up for one another at marriages; and been right there with an open ear and a shoulder to lean on when parents set forth to the great beyond. PK was Maggie's godfather; his daughter, Helene, and Furbio's youngest, Lauren, were both mine.

I had a long history with these lads, and for years and years we'd been talking about chartering a sailboat and taking a spin together through the B.V.I. And that's all it had been: talk. Then, somehow, all the planets in our different daily universes fell into alignment—the i's of school vacations were dotted, the t's of work commitments were crossed—and suddenly we were in Trellis Bay last spring with a freezer full of food, a chart spread out on the saloon table, and a week's worth of plans to be made. We were finally going sailing after all.

AT SEVEN, my Maggie was the youngest aboard. Helene, 10, and a terror on the lacrosse fields back home in Baltimore, was just enough older to think Maggie was at times goofy, and just enough more mature to be her good buddy anyway. Twelve-year-old Lauren was happiest listening to musicals on her portable DVD player, but she was a pacesetter when the activities turned aquatic. At 16, Furbio's eldest daughter, Molly, was the elder of the tribe in many ways: Her wry observations soared over the heads of the other girls about 99 percent of the time. And if Maggie grows up to be half the water-woman Molly is, I'll be very happy.

The first stop, naturally, was The Baths at Virgin Gorda. We ferried the girls in as far as the dinghy mooring on one of those days when the rollers were breaking on the beachfront and, when swimming ashore, you had to time your approach between the wave sets to avoid getting crunched at the last moment. I actually only learned this *after* Maggie's successful, if spluttering landing. She never would've tried it had the other girls not been over the side the moment we picked up the mooring—in other words, before I could say anything—and it set the tone for nearly all the adventures that would follow. The very last thing my daughter was going to be was left behind.

I've wandered The Baths a few times over the years, but it was all so very different with a bunch of kids who'd never been there before, whose joy and energy over all this new terrain was contagious, and this too would become a recurrent theme for the voyage. If you want to view something familiar through a fresh set of eyes, do not hesitate to bring a few fresh sets of eyes.

That night we anchored in Gorda Sound for another round of swimming and a barbecque, and next morning we hopped ashore for a tour of the Bitter End Yacht Club, a discovery for the girls that was on a par with Columbus's arrival to the New World. Luckily, since the next stop was the parched island of Anegada, I had a quick look at the water tanks before we shoved off, and promptly topped them off while I still had the chance. Do you have any idea how much fresh water four young ladies can consume in the space of 48 hours? Neither did I. For some reason, my lecture on the benefits of saltwater bathing was met with silence.

In Anegada, we ran into my old pal Bob Grieser, the marine photographer, who was there on assignment for another sailing magazine. Included in Bobby's wide repertoire of skills is his re-markable ability to imitate a barking hound, and thus the nick-name Photo Dog was bestowed upon him. If a voyage can have a mascot, he became ours, for the girls, especially Maggie, adored him. He joined us for the ride out to Loblolly Beach and an epic snorkel on the reefs—the new experiences just kept coming and coming—and when we returned to the harbor, he made chums of the local fishermen and did his best to get the girls to pose for a picture with a big, live Anegada lobster. Only brave Helene had the nerve, though they all made extremely short work of one after its brief detour to the open-fire grill.

Our little trip was flying by, but it was starting to get really good, and it would get better still.

ONE WISHES he could say the vacation was a success on absolutely all counts, that the girls took to sailing like the fish they resembled once they splashed the water, but that would be pushing it. For them, the sailing was a means to reach an island: Maggie generally hit the trampoline or the settee and zonked out for every passage; the other girls retreated to books and iPods or joined my daughter for a nap. But I made some serious inroads with the guys, neither of whom had sailed much before. By trip's end, Furbio was envisioning the day he retires as a firefighter to move aboard a catamaran, and PK, though not exactly bitten by the sailing bug, is now in the market for a nice cabin cruiser. Not bad, if I do say so myself.

But the longish sail from Anegada to Jost Van Dyke was one of my highlights, mainly because it gave me the chance to reflect on the trip so far. I was actually glad to see Maggie curled up and snoozing; her mother would've been scandalized by the hours she was keeping, and she clearly needed the rest. But her days (and nights) had been filled with swimming and laughter and camaraderie. She may have been the junior member of the sisterhood, and as such she spent equal amounts of energy learning from the others and seeking their approval. But in return she was granted generous helpings of time and patience and friendship. It was a wonderful thing to watch.

Yes, we could've taken the kids to Disneyland or on a ski trip, but what's better than a 24/7 sailboat excursion in the Caribbean, where the best lessons learned are the intangible ones—what it takes to be a good shipmate, to be considerate of others while living in a small space, to conserve water and energy and be immersed in nature and the outdoors? What other venue could give you what you get—what you *earn*—by being on a small boat for a real voyage?

As we dodged one squall after another on the sail to Jost, I realized our week together would ultimately become one seamless memory—all of us together, frozen in time, healthy and tan and very happy—like an image from a favorite old photograph. Who knows what the future will hold, what these little girls will eventually become, what grand adventures are waiting out there for them? At that moment, I couldn't have cared less. We were all together on a boat cleaving purposefully through the blue Caribbean. Whatever happens, I realized in a sappy moment for which I have no excuses or apologies, we'll always have these islands.

WELL, I'M sure you can guess what happened to the pink cap. By week's end, the sweat and brine had conspired to erase the reddish tint almost completely, and it looked just about brand-new. Like our little trip, now coming to an end, Maggie's pink present simply wasn't meant to last forever.

After Jost, we pulled into The Bight at Norman Island, where the piercing sound of a yelping mutt signaled a final drive-by dinghy visit from the beloved Photo Dog and where the girls had a quick and unfortunate glimpse of the antics atop the lewd and infamous Willie T's, which led to a round of questions that were simply impossible to answer and fingers crossed that the moms would never hear about this singular lapse of judgment.

Finally, we got up real early on our last full day and made our way over to The Indians—the B.V.I.'s signature outcropping of rock and sea life, one of the great snorkeling spots in the Carribean—where we scored the best mooring around and set up for a long morning and afternoon of water sports.

By 9 A.M., Maggie and I were in the water with masks and snorkels and making for the nearby reef. She insisted on leading and took right off, and I had to do some serious booking to keep up. I was a pretty proud papa, I must say, when something happened that will be with me for a long time.

I could see she was heading for simple trouble, a fringe of coral with no pass and small, breaking wavelets, where there was no option but to turn around. It was no big deal, really, but she had a moment of panic and started babbling away, her eyes very wide, though it was impossible to pinpoint the exact nature of her distress since she refused to take the snorkel out of her mouth. "Rrrrrrmmmmmmmmmrrrrr," she said. In any event, I waved for her to follow me in the opposite direction, and she dutifully collected herself and obeyed.

As we worked our way into deeper water, she sidled up alongside and grabbed my hand and she held on as we calmly resumed our way back to the boat, now enjoying the play of light on the reef and the schools of small, colorful fishes. It was much later, on the flight home actually, that it dawned on me that the entire little escapade encapsulated so many transitions one deals with as a parent: trust, discovery, discomfort, fear, support, recovery, more trust.

And the final little moment, just before we reached the boat, gave me a clear look at the coming attraction that all fathers of young daughters will someday inevitably face. As we approached the swim ladder to climb back aboard, she gave my fingers one last, tough, lovely squeeze. Then she let go and was gone.

# 12: A Merry, Moveable Feast

## SOUTH OF THE BORDER ON THE BAJA HA-HA

THEY CALL him the Grand Poobah, and there he was, in all his *Poobahness*. It was just before 1100 on a perfect October 31st (yes, Halloween) in the waters off San Diego, California, and the Poobah was about to perform the fall ritual he's practiced for each of the last dozen years. He was about to send hundreds of anxious sailors past the border to Mexico and due south on the annual 750-mile cruising rally and floating festival called the Baja Ha-Ha.

Some people know the Poobah as Richard Spindler, the publisher of the West Coast sailing magazine *Latitude 38*. Those people were not participating in the Ha-Ha. But to call him a mere Poobah is to ignore his many other talents and re-sponsibilities. In fact, His Grandness wears many Ha-Ha hats: radio man, cheerleader, race committee chairman (and we use the word "race" very loosely), party organizer, cruise direc-tor, force of nature. It is extremely difficult, if not impossible, to pinpoint precisely where the Poobah ends and the Ha-Ha begins.

As the ringleader of this oceanic circus, the Poobah over-sees the action from the deck of his 63-foot catamaran, *Profli-gate*, with a dozen or so pals, and chief sidekick Doña de Mal-lorca (who skippers the big cat in the Poobah's absence), lending assistance and enjoying the ride. As the rookie on the crew, I was taking it all in when Suzi Todd—a *Profligate* regular who just happens to be the chief of a California fire department when not chasing her sailing dreams—put everything into perspective. "Welcome to the insane asylum," she said.

Meanwhile, the Poobah was in VHF-radio contact with the skipper of the distinctive 97-foot schooner *Talofa*, a fellow with a first name as unusual as his boat: Cactus. The *Talofa* crew just happened to have a cannon at their disposal, and had volunteered to fire it at the start. With that, the 132 Ha-Ha boats would begin the first of three legs, the inaugural one en route to the remote fishing village of Bahía de Tortuga, or Turtle Bay.

"We'll give a countdown at 10 minutes, five minutes, and one minute," said the Poobah. "Then I'll count down the final 10 seconds. At zero, you fire the gun."

"Well, it's on a fuse," replied Captain Cactus. "We may not be right on the moment."

"Who cares?" exclaimed the Poobah. "This is the Ha-Ha! Twenty seconds late, thirty seconds, no worries!"

The forecast called for light winds but at the stroke of eleven, as if on cue, the flat sea darkened with fresh wind ripples from the northwest, and under bright sunshine and a cloudless sky, the moveable feast of merriment that would become Baja Ha-Ha XII was under way. Once the bulk of the fleet had cleared the starting line, we hoisted *Profligate*'s big asymmetric kite and began wending our way through the armada at an effortless ten knots. Many of the crew on the various boats donned Halloween costumes. All of them wore broad smiles.

In size, scope, and variety, this West Coast contingent of boats and sailors—some 525 of them—represented a true cross-section of the cruising world. There was a covey of Catalinas, a big bunch of Beneteaus, a slew of Swans, several Sabres, a hodge-podge of Hunters, tandem Tartans, and a parcel of Pearsons. There were big boats (the aforementioned *Talofa*) and small ones (the Elite 29 *Lonesome Dove*); cats and tris; schooners, ketches, cutters, sloops, and even a junk-rig or two; and hulls of wood, aluminum, and steel. (Heck, there was even a handful of *powerboats*.) There were kids, couples, families, and more than a few sailors well past their 70th birthday and going strong. There were several women skippers, a ton of first-time Ha-Ha participants (some of whom were also new to offshore sailing), and plenty of seasoned sailors who come back year after year. The one common denominator? The folks at *Latitude 38* put it very succinctly in their pre-rally preview: Everyone, to varying degrees, was "running from the rat race."

The Poobah and his posse were no different. Aboard *Profligate*, by early afternoon we'd launched out ahead of the pack, and when the wind began to falter just a tad, we swapped chutes and kept making tracks. A couple of fishing lines were deployed and everyone began settling into the shipboard routine. That is, until the breeze came on and—yikes!—the spinnaker exploded, torn from head to foot. The ensuing fire drill was brief, and it wasn't long at all before a back-up kite was up and drawing, and *Profligate* was creaming along at better than 17 knots.

It was almost all too much for the Poobah to assimilate, for as it turns out, *no one* appreciates a good, fast sail more than he. Grinning from ear to ear, he surveyed his domain and, clearly, he liked what he saw. "Is this great, or what?" he asked, of no one in particular. Oh, yes, it surely was.

IN THE November, 1995, *Latitude* preview of that year's Ha-Ha, a fellow by the name of James Yates discussed the open-ended, no-guarantees nature of the South Pacific cruising he and his wife hoped to accomplish: "A mentor of mine once told me, 'Leap and the net will appear.' For us, that's been the case."

It could certainly be said that for many sailors, the Baja Ha-Ha has been the very net into which they first leapt.

"The rally evolved out of a pre-existing annual migration south which had been going on for decades," said *Latitude* senior editor and Assistant Poobah Andy Turpin. "But nothing on the West Coast had ever been organized for cruisers, they just went off individually. Sure, there were Mexico races, but all were pretty serious and they didn't cater to cruising classes.

"But the most important thing about the Ha-Ha, really, is that it establishes a concrete deadline for casting off the dock lines and entering the, in many cases, long-anticipated cruising lifestyle. Hundreds of folks have told us that without the event, they'd probably still be stuck in a marina back home, procrastinating."

For a rally that over the years has attracted literally thousands of boats and sailors, the Baja Ha-Ha had an inauspicious beginning. The first one, in 1994, was held in conjunction with that year's San Diego to Cabo Race, run by San Diego's Southwestern Yacht Club. The race component was a no-nonsense affair for Grand Prix yachts, but the editors at *Latitude* convinced the yacht club to include a Cruiser's "Baja Ha-Ha" Division. That class, the magazine explained, was for "those of us who like to sail with women and children, three-bladed props, full water tanks, and that kind of stuff. Entrants will be permitted to use their engines if it gets too rough, too calm, or they just miss the throb of it." The fee was $100, there would be two stops—in Turtle Bay and Magdalena Bay (which has since been replaced by Bahía Santa Maria)—and everyone was invited.

Thirty-six cruising boats—Tayanas and Westsails, Cals and Bristols—and 125 "adventure-loving sailors" answered the call. By all accounts, it was a modest, but honest, success. "The racing, of course, was mostly casual," wrote the Poobah, in a subsequent story about the event. "The only people who really 'lost' were those of you who couldn't, or didn't make it. Like the T-shirts said, 'He who laughs first, laughs best.'"

As it turned out, however, there were plenty of folks quite happy to queue up for second, third, or even fourth laughs. The 1995 race drew 68 boats and 250 sailors; in 1996, the count was 78 boats and 350 participants; and the 1997 race cracked the century mark, with 112 boats and some 450 chuckling mariners crossing the finish line. Those numbers stayed fairly consistent over the next several years, until 2004, a record-breaking edition with 145 boats and 550 sailors.

Over the years, the rally has evolved slightly; citing liability issues, *Latitude* ceased running the event, the administrative duties of which now fall to an independent entity run by the Poobah's daughter, "Ha-Ha Honcho" Lauren Spindler. But the magazine remains a chief sponsor, and the Poobah remains its guiding light. He is also the event's historian, and each year takes pains to explain exactly what the Ha-Ha is...and isn't.

"We were distressed to learn that some folks feared the Ha-Ha is nothing more than a two-week bash during which men emboldened by strong liquor on ill-prepared boats harass women while pumping oil overboard—and all to the Grand Poobah's rigid schedule," he wrote in the 1998 rally round-up.

"On the contrary," he continued, "the Ha-Ha is a laid-back opportunity for responsible cruisers to have some fun meeting each other while sailing down the coast in a very loosely structured group. There's only one organized Ha-Ha party before the start, a daily roll call, two beach parties, and an awards party. And folks are welcome to customize their itineraries; this year several boats stopped at Islas San Benitos and Isla Cedros, and at Mag Bay. The few sailors who entered this year's Ha-Ha with trepidation—fearing either a tasteless frat-party atmosphere or a militaristic schedule—report being pleasantly surprised."

True enough. But of course, as I was about to learn, the parties are still pretty darned good.

IN THE couple of days it took for most of the Ha-Ha sailors to cover the 360 miles to Turtle Bay, they saw a bit of everything. Most of those who hugged the coast found themselves motorsailing for a fair stretch in dying winds, while those who chose the offshore alternative saw gusting breeze up to 30 knots, which caused a couple more blown-out spinnakers and other assorted minor dramas. Everyone got a good look at plenty of sea-life, from sunfish, dolphins, and porpoises, to orcas, sharks, and pilot whales.

"This is turning into a nature cruise," said the Poobah.

As the sailors came ashore in the rustic fishing village of Turtle Bay, most were drawn up the hill to the popular Vera Cruz restaurant, and on the first night in town an impromptu jam session—led by *Latitude*'s own "Banjo Andy" Turpin—took place on the porch and under the stars. It turned out that there were more than a few talented musicians sprinkled through the fleet, and they were packing their instruments. There would be many more evenings of fine tunes ahead.

But the following afternoon's beach party was the official Turtle Bay soiree, and the Ha-Ha fleet was there in force. Dozens of inflatables soon sprinkled the long, clean beach at the bay's east end, where a couple of beer and food vendors, and a pair of competing DJs, had all set up shop. There were plenty of villagers, too—the Ha-Ha arrival is perhaps the biggest local event of the year—all of whom were curious to see what this big gathering of *gringos* was up to.

As the Poobah said, the Ha-Ha is all about meeting and greeting like-minded individuals, and I had a great opportunity to do just that while sipping cold Mexican *cervezas* and scarfing down tasty tacos on the beach at Turtle Bay.

From the moment I met Christian Buhl, I was pretty sure I was in the presence of a fairly experienced sailor, and I was right. He'd first become entranced after moving to San Francisco and getting involved with the city's Maritime Museum. But his real claim to fame was being part of the *Mari-Cha IV* crew that set the West Marine Pacific Cup record of 5 days, 5 hours, in 2004. "The best part was approaching Hawaii and making 26 knots in fairly light winds," he said. Christian was doing the Ha-Ha on an Explorer 45 called *Morning Light* and was clearly having a wonderful time. So, too, was four-time Ha-Ha veteran Rennie Waxlax, a commercial airline pilot and skipper of the Swan 65, *Cassiopea*. Rennie's first boat was an Ericson 37, which he owned and loved for nine years. But he found the Swan perfect for the south-of-the-border cruising he now relishes. "I've rebuilt or replaced everything," he said.

"Plumbing, sails, electronics. It's a vintage Swan, built in 1975, and it's just a great boat: safe, comfortable, and sturdy." Like many in the Ha-Ha fleet, for Rennie, the rally was just the first act of what would become a pleasant sabbatical in Mexico. "I'll be in the Sea of Cortez for the spring, when the sea life and islands are just awesome," he said, with a faraway look in his eyes.

Under one of the beer tents I met a group of sailors who had plenty in common. Carl Mischka was the skipper of the Oyster 485, *Ti Amo*, while Dennis Knight held the same role on the Oyster 435, *Shilling of Hamble*. The only British entry in the Ha-Ha, Dennis and his wife, Janet, were outbound on a world cruise that had started six years ago. Carl had read about the Knights in an Oyster newsletter, and knew they were headed down the coast of California and past his Newport Beach home. "So I reached out to them, and they came and hung out for awhile," he said. "It's part of what cruising fellowship's all about." A smart man, Carl, for he hopes to follow the Knight's example and was using the Ha-Ha to launch an extended cruise.

Speaking of fellowship, there was a good bit of it on the Morgan Out Island 41, *Bronco*, as well. That's because skipper and retired pilot Nels Torbeson surrounds himself with sailors who enjoy the pure act of sailing as much as anyone. It turned out Nels was on his sixth Ha-Ha and was famous for completing nearly every race without ever turning over his engine. "We push the boat to its limits," he said, which is not something most Ha-Ha sailors would venture to say. "I've got guys who can push it, who can easily drop the spinnaker in 30 knots in the middle of the night. The boat sails great, much better than its reputation."

Finally, I couldn't help but say hello to the young lady with the wild red streaks in her hair. With her parents, Hugh and Karlene, 16-year-old Heidi Owens was off to explore the South Pacific aboard the family's Cal 48, *Koho*. Heidi was taking online courses from Brigham Young University, and having the time of her life on her first cruise ever. She couldn't wait to learn to surf and was looking forward to exploring New Zealand. The Owens' had left Jackson, Wyoming, and Heidi was happy to have the place in her rear-view mirror. "We're not going back!" she said.

I couldn't say the same, but I knew exactly what she meant.

MOVING forward is what the Ha-Ha's all about, and the next morning, the fleet gathered outside Turtle Bay for the second, 240-mile leg to Bahía Santa Maria. With light winds forecast, the Poobah authorized a "rolling start" in which skippers could motor for an hour without penalty. But it very quickly turned into another beautiful sailing day, with solid northwest breeze in the mid-teens. Aboard *Profligate* we had another wonderful sail, with an added highlight of catching not one but *two* yellowfin tuna, which resident Chef Sylvia transformed into a whopping, delicious platter of sashimi.

Some thirty-six hours later, the Ha-Ha fleet once again regrouped, this time in the other-worldly waters of Bahía Santa Maria. As far as I was concerned, we could've stopped right then and there; every year, several sailors come to the same conclusion, and forgo the final leg to Cabo until they're good and ready, which could easily take some time. For the attractions of the large, remote bay were plenty: vast sand dunes as far as the eye could see; board and body surfing along an inside bar or at the point break at the bay's entrance; eminently climbable, 1,200-foot peaks with jaw-dropping views of the Pacific Ocean and distant Magdalena Bay (not to mention the Ha-Ha boats at anchor); and an "inside passage" through winding mangroves and past simple fish camps, an ideal waterway to explore via dinghy or kayak.

And then, naturally, there were more parties. The first one was what the Poobah called "a dinghy-up affair" to *Profligate* for a tot of Pusser's Rum, free ball caps, and assorted games and mischief with big bottles of "Nelson's Blood" for the winners. Later, there was another good, old-fashioned beach party, this one catered mostly by the local *panga* fishermen, who somehow manage to throw a huge seafood feed of shrimp, lobster, and fish in the middle of absolutely nowhere for 500 hungry sailors—with live rock and roll to boot. It was another memorable occasion.

Then, way too soon, we were all under way again, this time for the third and final 160-mile jaunt to Cabo San Lucas, a.k.a.

Cabo & Gomorrah.  The Poobah had everyone under way at the ungodly hour of 0600, but it wasn't long before this memorable running of the Ha-Ha was blessed with yet more northerly winds, and the fleet was running down the rhumb line toward the finish.  "This is always the best and the worst day of the rally," said the Poobah, the former because the truly warm-weather conditions are fairly consistent for this last leg, and the latter because the end of the trip was drawing near.

*Profligate* arrived at Cabo shortly after dawn, and more of the fleet followed us in as the day progressed.  After a couple of weeks of anchoring out, most skippers chose to rent a slip for a few days at the swank Cabo Marina, where the cruising boats looked slightly out of place next to the rows and rows of tricked-out sportfishermen.

The rest of the Cabo stay was a whirlwind, from the first refreshing dip into the warm Pacific waters, to the final awards ceremony, where everyone—in the Poobah's secret, intricate scoring system for the 11 classes, no one finished worse than third—took home a prize.

But the craziest Cabo night was the last one, when 300 Ha-Ha sailors descended onto the raucous bar called Squid Roe to drink tequila, tell sea stories, and dance until the wee hours.  There were more than a few chuckles, but that was nothing new.  Sailing down the sunny coast of Mexico, nearly everyone in the Ha-Ha had been laughing all the way.

> Quite indirectly, my participation in the Baja Ha-Ha later led to one of my stranger career detours.  For two short and eventful months, I was the editor of the Bay Area sailing magazine, *Latitude 38*.  Two.  Whole.  Months.  True story.  You can look it up.

# 13: Across the Great Southern Ocean

## UNDER SAIL FROM AUSTRALIA TO ANTARCTICA

ALONGSIDE THE BAR at the Royal Cape Yacht Club in Cape Town, South Africa, where I'd found myself on a break from a magazine assignment, the chat had turned to the Southern Ocean. The crowd was a mix of doers and dreamers; the stories were loud and salty. Some rang less than true. Off to the side, quiet yet watchful, was a French sailor who was known to have vast experience in "the Roaring Forties" and beyond. Our eyes met.

"Ze waves and ze wind," he said. "Remarkable. 'Ave you been to *le sud*?" His tone was reverent, different from the others.

"No," I admitted, I hadn't been to "the south." But I wanted to go, to see with my own eyes what now flashed in his.

Time passed. Later that year, in the fall of 1995, out of nowhere I received a fax in my office from, of all places, Antarctica. An Australian friend of mine, ex-BOC solo around-the-world sailor Don McIntyre, and his wife Margie, were nearing the end of a year-long expedition where they had lived, on the ice, in an eight- by 12-foot hut. A spot had opened up on the sailboat bound from Tasmania to retrieve them. He wanted to know if I could make the trip down.

This was a once-in-a-lifetime opportunity, but there were problems. I'd just come back from a year's leave of absence at work, where I'd exhausted favors well into the next century. I was on the verge of getting engaged to a beautiful Australian gal who also had a few paybacks coming. There was no way in the world I could do this.  I faxed Donnie back: "I'll be there, no matter what."

Two months later, queasy from nerves, land legs, and a leftover easterly swell, I watched in silence as the stark hills of "Tassie' fell astern.  The island is a joke to the mainland Australian—"Tasmania?  Mate, I thought you said you were visiting Australia"—but I missed the place badly the instant it disappeared.  Next stop, Antarctica.  All we had to do was cross 1,500 nautical miles of the Great Southern Ocean.

> The Southern Ocean owes its richly deserved reputation as the world's roughest area to one simple accident of geography. It is the only stretch of water which completely circles the globe... Since there are no land barriers to check its progress, (the prevailing) westerly wind blows uninterrupted around the world...and in doing so builds up a very large westerly sea and swell. This is why the region between 40-50º south is called the Roaring Forties, and between 50-60º south the Screaming Fifties.
>
> —Robin Knox-Johnston
> *Beyond Jules Verne*

THE FURIOUS, dependable westerlies were what lured the Tall Ships laden with commercial goods in the Great Age of Sail, and they are what draw modern players such as Knox-Johnson who seek to harness their power to win races and set speed records.  But it was in the name of exploration that the visionary Portuguese navigators Dias and Magellan, respectively, first rounded the southern tips of Africa (1487) and South America (1520).  This posed the possibility of yet more land to the south— an idea planted by early Greek geographers who believed there must be a large landmass around the South Pole to "balance" the known land in the Northern Hemisphere.

But it was Captain James Cook who, in the course of three consecutive summer cruises between 1772 and 1775, circumnavigated the world in the high southern latitudes and crossed the Antarctic Circle (66° 20'S) for the first time. Though Cook did not set eyes on the continent, he did discover the Antarctic islands of South Georgia and the South Sandwich group and their wealth of marine life, particularly fur seals. It was the profit-minded sealers, in turn, who were the next to venture into the frigid Southern Ocean, and the first to set foot on the white continent of Antarctica.

By the mid-19th century, scientists and colonists had joined the southbound parade. Then, at the turn of the century, historic adventurers such as Scott and Shackleton from Great Britain risked all to become the first to reach the South Pole, a prize finally grasped by Norwegian Roald Amundsen in 1911. Later, Australia's greatest Antarctic pioneer, Douglas Mawson, left his own mark in the annals of southern exploring. It was to the site of Mawson's old base camp at Commonwealth Bay, where the McIntyres had erected their "hut" in commemoration to their countryman, that we were bound.

Slowly.

A huge high-pressure system stationed over southern Australia was frying the continent and providing our crew of eight aboard the ex-BOC round-the-world 60-footer *Spirit of Sydney* with unusual but favorable early conditions. Beating on port tack into moderate south-*easterlies*, we were fulfilling skipper Steve "Nig-Nog" Corrigan's (yes, every Aussie has a nickname) initial goal of working well to the west of the rhumb line and positioning ourselves for a favorable slant on our ultimate destination when the westerlies finally filled.

Four days into the journey, three days into 1996, five miles past the 49th parallel, progress stopped. The ocean was flat and gray. The sails hung flaccid and empty. It was foggy, like an early summer morning back home on Block Island Sound. We were on the bottom edge of the fearsome Roaring Forties. We hadn't seen a breath of westerly breeze. We were utterly becalmed.

Beyond 40° South there is no law. Beyond 50° South there is no God.

—Old sailor's adage

DAYS PASSED. We slipped beyond 60° South. Never mind "no law" or even "no God." Aboard *Spirit of Sydney*, there was no bloody heater. The wetness and cold were numbing. A makeshift clothesline strung over the propane oven was home to a suite of dripping off-watch mitts. Another pile baked on the engine block. Steamy breath was visible above and below deck. The cabin sole was soaked in condensation, a puddle of problems for those foolish enough to exit berths sans boots. I slept in doubled-up sleeping bags, wearing a jacket, pile pants, and long johns, and awoke shivering. I pulled on a watch cap and went back to bed.

The aluminum-hulled *Spirit of Sydney*, in addition to her outstanding and natural powers of refrigeration, was in excellent condition after a recent, extensive refit. Originally built for Australian Ian Kiernan to a Ben Lexcen-design for the 1986-87 solo BOC race, the interior plan had been converted to fit the needs of a full crew. Water-ballast tanks had been replaced by a series of pipe berths and snug, bunk-bed-style settees. The overall effect, especially when going forward, was reminiscent of certain below deck scenes in the German U-boat movie *Das Boot*.

At the foot of the companionway, someone had erected a tacky Christmas tree music box in honor of the season.

For all this luxury, our passage down the fifties had been a chilling descent. A 15-knot west-southwest wind, accompanied by thick cloud on the horizon but clear skies above, greeted us at 51°S. The sailing was crisp and fast. By 54°S, the sun was gone. The lower boundary on our favorite daily weather fax map abruptly stopped at 55°S.

As we tracked our progress for that waypoint, there was a sensation of sailing toward The Edge. We should have been so lucky. The plummeting seawater-temperature thermometer, registered in degrees Celsius, could have been a misery meter. Around 56°S it dropped several degrees in 24 hours, to a new low of 3°C (37°F). We had apparently entered the Antarctic Convergence Zone, where the cold, dense Antarctic waters meet the warmer subtropical seas. It would eventually bottom out just this side of freezing. On deck, be-gloved and be-goggled, no one needed reminders to clip on his harness. Falling overboard would be a death sentence.

> And now there came both mist and snow,
>    and it grew wondrous cold:
> And ice, mast high, came floating by,
>    as green as emerald...
> At length did cross an Albatross,
>    thorough the fog it came;
> As if it had been a Christian soul,
>    we hailed it in God's name.
>
> —Samuel Taylor Coleridge
> *The Rime of the Ancient Mariner*

THE MIGHTY albatross ("sea gulls on steroids," said one onboard comic) were by now old friends; the cold, misty fog a familiar nemesis. But where was the ice? On *Spirit*'s voyage a year earlier to drop off the McIntyres, the northernmost iceberg was spotted at 53°S, a waypoint we'd put hundreds of miles astern, with nary a 'berg in sight. "You're going to go wild when you see the first ice," said Nig-Nog. "And you're going to be amazed how close it was before you saw it."

Visibility was poor, but there was consolation. The daylight hours lengthened; at 62°S it was dark less than four hours each night. And we'd caught another break. The high that had stymied us early on drifted south too and, as a farewell gift, it blasted us with three days of 30-knot northwesterlies. We scurried over the 60th parallel running hard wing and wing with a deeply reefed main and poled-out staysail, notching a string of 200-mile days.

The 0300-0600 watch on the eighth day was outstanding. Some 120 miles west of the rhumb line we jibed onto starboard to gain the favored tack, unfurled the headsail and staysail, and shook the reefs out of the main. A dusting of snow settled on deck, and half a dozen snowy petrels flittered in the sail exhaust. With spray flying and *Spirit* creaming along at 12 knots on a wicked beam reach, it was a Southern Ocean scene.

To punctuate it, five hours later came the cry, "Iceberg!" Well to weather, long and angular, it was a twin-peaked tower of blue. We slalomed through its downwind brash—the cubes ranged in size from microwaves to minivans—and wondered how many 'bergs lay ahead. Reassuringly, it had popped up on radar like a pimple on prom night. At 63°S, we were 600 miles south of the first sighting a year before.

The next night, at the tail end of a wearing watch, my watchmate Mary Ann Stresau said, "What we need are Show

Tunes!" With freezing rain plinking off the hood of my jacket for accompaniment, she broke into a painful medley from *Oklahoma*. Mary Ann, an American, is a longtime friend of the McIntyres, who had cruised to Australia with her husband. She is a good sailor. She is a bad singer.

I recorded the moment in my journal, a capsule account of the kinds of things that can drive offshore sailors crazy in the confines of a small boat at sea: "She asked me what I thought. I told her she sounded awful. She asked me if I was a music critic and I told her I knew what I liked. She told me she'd stop if I was really serious. I said, 'Please! Stop!' There was almost the sound of a splash. It wouldn't have been me."

Finally, just before reaching the Antarctic Circle and a hundred miles from Commonwealth Bay, we copped our first true gale. The anemometer recorded a steady 35 knots, but it felt like much more. Nig-Nog attributed it to the sheer pressure of the moisture-laden air. "It's like 40 in the Atlantic or 50 in the tropics," he said. "More force is needed to move this air." I wrestled with the science but the evidence was unimpeachable. The low, white continent hove into view hours later. After a 10-day passage from Hobart, we were there.

"Good to see ya. Where are the sausages?"
—Don McIntyre's welcome speech to *Spirit*'s crew
Commonwealth Bay, Antarctica
January 9, 1996

WE FORGAVE Don his cravings. It'd been a long time since he'd fired up "the barbie." A cruising man at heart, he'd roamed the Pacific in his beloved 30-footer, *Skye*, until his ambition for more adventure overwhelmed his wallet and he sought highly creative methods to finance his dreams. His wife, Margie, dropped her nursing career and, with $5,000 to their names and a small marine-supply business to fall back on, Don put in motion his plan to race the 1990-91 BOC Challenge.

He scraped and borrowed, and built a 50-footer that he named with his banker in mind: *Sponsor Wanted*. At the midway point of the race he landed support from an Australian baked goods company and the boat became *Buttercup*. He sailed to a terrific second-place finish in his class, and afterwards his backers sponsored a voyage to Antarctica. While there, bitten by the adventure bug, he envisioned a grander scheme—a completely self-supporting, yearlong husband-and-wife expedition to the ice. Expedition Icebound was under way. The McIntyres sought and received permission from the Australian Antarctic Foundation to camp near Mawson's Hut; set up an education program with Australian and New Zealand schools; found partial sponsorship from communications giant COMSAT; secured film and book contracts; and headed south.

The McIntyres are imbued with the same entrepreneurial spirit that enabled Magellan and Cook and others to find funding for their explorations. In fact, they'd chartered half-a-dozen berths aboard *Spirit* for our voyage, and have begun a commercial adventure-travel concern with the boat for future trips. The Southern Ocean remains open for business. On our last day in Antarctica, after a long week on the ice communing with the penguins and closing up the Hut, a QANTAS jet day-tripping from Sydney flew low over the McIntyre's camp on a regularly scheduled tourist flight. During our layover at Commonwealth Bay, a Soviet research vessel-turned-New Zealand tour boat visited us in the midst of an extended luxury cruise. In the southern summer, Antarctica is still lonely, but you're not necessarily alone.

That had not been the case months earlier. The McIntyres endured the hellish conditions of the long, dark winter when their 8- by 12-foot prefab hut was completely inaccessible. They were tested by and survived windstorms that neared 200 knots, and they were rewarded with a year of indescribable experiences.

While preparing for the return voyage, over a four-day stretch of 50-knot winds, we received a taste of the wild weather they faced. When it finally eased, we were out of there. I felt privileged to have witnessed the wildlife, the raw country, the amazing vistas...and I was damned glad to be headed home.

> He sent the others below to get some warmth and sleep
> in the reindeer-skin bags while he kept a sharp lookout
> for ice . I steered; [Shackleton] sat beside
> me... By midnight the sea was rising, and every other
> wave that hit her came over, wetting us through and
> through. Cold and clear, with the Southern Cross high
> overhead, we held her north by the stars..."
>
> —F.A. Worsley
> *Shackleton's Boat Journey*

THE MOST remarkable Southern Ocean voyage ever recorded occurred in 1916. Sir Ernest Shackleton and a crew of 28 were en route to the Antarctic when their square-rigger *Endurance* was beset by ice and crushed. The sailors spent five months drifting on an ice floe before it too broke up beneath them and they were forced to take to three lifeboats, reaching remote Elephant Island. From there, Shackleton, his trusted captain Frank Worsley, and a crew of four set out on a creaky 22-footer bound for a whaling station on South Georgia Island. It was 800 miles away.

A copy of Worsley's account of the nightmare journey, a passage from which is excerpted above, was with us onboard

*Spirit.* When anyone dared complain, Nig-Nog recited specific incidents of terror and triumph as if they were biblical lore. Furthermore, he'd conclude, "Shacks didn't have GPS."

In fact, we had our own "Shacks" onboard in the personage of David Nelson, an accomplished Alpinist, new to offshore sailing but quickly proving himself a natural. So too was his watchmate, Cameron Aird, a commercial diver from New Zealand with scant previous experience who'd taken the moniker "Mawse" after Douglas Mawson. Used to hard work in rugged wilderness, "Shacks" and "Mawse," our A-Team, greeted each watch with high fives and a hunger to take on any task.

Mawse was also proving to be a fine sea cook, and he perfected a thick pumpkin soup he called "hoosh," the name of a staple mush aboard Shackleton's ships and a delicacy that prompted Worsley to wax lyrically: "In cooking, the aroma of this ambrosia rose as incense to the gods."

Our own hoosh had much the same effect, even though I had burned my mouth crispy weeks earlier gulping down a giant mug of the stuff. But my true vice was an insipid Australian cocoa called Milo, which tasted like a single Hershey Kiss boiled in hot water. I was addicted to the heat of the stuff, and couldn't get enough of it its scalding ride from tongue to gullet. In essence, food and drink had become more important for their warmth than their flavor.

With a batch of hoosh on the stove and a building southeasterly gale, we had a fast start to our northbound leg, registering 176 miles in the first 18 hours of sailing. It appeared that the unusual string of northerlies in the latter part of the first leg had blown the 'bergs and pack ice fortuitously out of our path. But the first night's clear, chilled sunset saw us weaving through a massive ice field whose grand monoliths were Stonehengian in shape and assemblage. Backdropped by a fiery horizon and capped by a pastel orange-blue ceiling, it was worth every minute it had taken to get there.

> At midnight, the wind was north-northeast, Force 7. Down to topsails now, her upper and lower yards naked, gleaming yellow like great bones in the moonlight, she was a terrible wild stranger to us. At the wheel a Swede and a Dane were fighting to hold her as she ran at 13 and 14 knots in the gusts. I knew then that I would never see sailing like this again. When such ships as this went it would be the finish. The wind belts of the world would be deserted and the great West Wind and the Trades would never blow on steel rigging and flax canvas again.
>
> —Eric Newby
> *The Last Grain Race*

IN 1938, 18-YEAR-OLD Eric Newby signed on as apprentice aboard the four-master *Moshulu* for a voyage from Europe to Australia and back by way of the Southern Ocean—outward by way of the Cape of Good Hope in ballast and homeward around Cape Horn with a cargo of grain. A dozen or so ships were still active in the trade, and they raced annually to make the shortest passage home. Newby was right about one thing: It was the swan song for the Tall Ships.

But it was not the end of outrageous southern sailing. In 1994, co-skippers Robin Knox-Johnston and Peter Blake drove their 92-foot catamaran *Enza New Zealand* to a new world record for the fastest circumnavigation of the planet with a time of 74 days, 22 hours. Deep in the Southern Ocean, daily runs of 450 miles were not uncommon. Their *average* speed was almost 15 knots.

Following the same route that Newby had sailed 56 years earlier, *ENZA* reached the halfway point of the trip in 32.5 days (*Moshulu*, with the second fastest time that year, took 82); and covered the second half in 12.5 days (the fastest time for a Tall Ship along that course was *Cutty Sark*'s voyage of 71 days in 1888).

(In subsequent years, the round-the-world record was slashed with startling regularity. In 2010, the maxi-trimaran *Groupama 3* established a new benchmark of 48 days, 7 hours, 44 minutes.)

We'd had an easy passage south, but now it was our turn to realize what had lured generations of sailors before us. With the barometer at 975 millibars and plunging, and fueled by a 35- to 45-knot gale, we crossed 60°S in three fast days while again putting a heap of westing in the bank. For a North American sailor like me, it seemed odd to sail *north* for the sun and warmth, and the clockwise-spinning low-pressure systems added to the novelty. Between the weatherfax and a radio schedule with Australia's Casey Australian research station, we were receiving dependable forecasts. The lows were stacking up to our west like jets over O'Hare. With apprehension and anticipation, we pressed forth toward an inevitable rendezvous.

The westerlies, when they came—and they were precisely what we came for—did not disappoint. In the course of three full gales on the homeward board, we faced winds that topped out near 60 knots and seas down which one could ski. We were on the right side of two of the three lows, which brought winds abaft the beam and long, wicked surfs up to 20 knots. *Spirit* reveled in the rough weather she'd been built for.

Snapshots in the mind's eye are the souvenirs of any long voyage. From those miles I have these memories: steering on a dark night, hitting an unseen wave just so, the shudder of the boat and the dreadful silence before the deluge of cold spray; driving through an ocean of phosphorescence, disoriented by the celestial seaway juxtaposed against a black, starless sky; the eerie light of an aurora; a brilliant double rainbow; weird dreams.

A week into the trip, two days out from Tasmania, smack-dab in the Roaring Forties, we had a fire drill. A building breeze, an uncontrolled jibe, and suddenly a bunch of us were on deck striking the main in a wild seaway and hanging on for dear life. The job done, my sweat freezing, I gathered my breath and looked around at what had to be one of the most inhospitable scenes on the planet. It was good to be there.

**In the windswept waters of Antarctica's Commonwealth Bay, the 60-foot cutter *Spirit of Sydney* is paid a visit by the local welcoming committee.**

In 1994-95 I took a yearlong sabbatical from my job on the editorial staff of *Cruising World* to serve as the media manager for the BOC Challenge, a job that took me literally around the world.  I hadn't been back in the office long when Don McIntyre contacted me about sailing to Antarctica.

After covering the round-the-world race, it's safe to say I was obsessed with the Southern Ocean; I had to see it for myself.  If I hadn't received permission to go do this story, I might've resigned.  But it never came to that.  My boss at the time, Bernadette Bernon, rolled her eyes mightily, but gave me the green light. I'm forever grateful.  And after a couple of subsequent trips to the high southern latitudes, I've finally got those tempestuous waters out of my system.

# 14: "Good Morning, Georgetown!"

## THE EPIC BAHAMIAN CRUISER'S RENDEZVOUS

ROCKIN' RON is ready. The tools for his job are close at hand. It's 0745 on a blustery March morning in the otherworldly harbor of Georgetown, the glorious centerpiece around which life revolves on the striking Bahamian island of Great Exuma. Assembled near Ron in the comfy center-cockpit of his Morgan 45, *Sea Dancer*, are the following, crucial items: a large cup of coffee; a pen and legal pad; a boom box; and finally, the device that will play the central role in the upcoming enterprise, a VHF-radio, switched to "high." Down below, the Rockin' one's better half, Karen, mans a second VHF.

At the stroke of eight, Ron switches over to Channel 72, hits the boom box on-switch, and presses the transmit button on his cockpit-mounted VHF. As music cascades across the vast anchorage via the dozens and dozens of boats tuned into the broadcast, Rockin' Ron, with the polished delivery of a seasoned radio DJ, lets her rip:

"Good morning Georgetown AND CRUISERS! And what a NIGHT it was! This is ROCKIN' Ron and COOL Karen aboard *Sea Dancer*, broadcasting to you LIVE on WGTWN-VHF 72. Welcome to the 29th ANNUAL Georgetown Cruising Regatta.

"Today it's TENNIS at February Point, and later this afternoon it's the Bridge Tournament at St. Francis Resort. Let's see how our day's going to be weather-wise by switching to our weather guru, ELECTRIFYING Ernie, anchored somewhere north of Hamburger Beach. Ernie, come on and tell us what the weather's going to do!"

And thus, another hectic day begins.

For the next half hour, Rockin' Ron will choreograph a seamless, wide-ranging show packed with oodles of useful information and broken down into several dedicated segments: Business, Regatta, Community, and Boater's General. At sea and on land, listeners will be updated on topics ranging from today's special at Eddie's Edgewater (meatloaf) to tomorrow's big awards ceremony (and the Rockin' Ron Dance Party) at the beach bar (and unofficial regatta headquarters) called the Chat 'n' Chill. We'll learn that John on *Buddy* needs crew for his trip to Puerto Rico, that Doug on *Bad Boy* is flying to the mainland and is happy to take any "flat, stamped mail," and that Bob on *Kavali House* is offering "safe, secure, non-live-aboard boat storage" for the summer over in the anchorage known as Hole 3.

But my favorite bit comes from a fellow named Dan on *Borrowed Horse*. "Good morning, I'm your self-appointed spokesperson for ARG," he growls. "The Alcohol Research Group. We're announcing an impromptu get-together today at five at Hamburger Beach. We'd like you to bring a dish to share, some research material, possibly a musical instrument, and your well-behaved pets and children. We'll look forward to seeing you there."

When all is said and done, Rockin' Ron wraps it up quickly: "I'm going to sign off here, switch to 6-8, and go back to low power. Have a great Exuma day. The net is clear."

Like everyone else in this (and almost every other) cruising community, in these parts Ron and Karen Sobon aren't known by their last names, but simply as "Ron and Karen on *Sea Dancer*." Having retired from their respective careers in New Jersey—he at Verizon, she in commercial real estate—they've been making an annual pilgrimage to Georgetown for ten years now. "That seems to be a good average for how long people last," said Ron. "We're there. We're the oldies now."

Though working the Georgetown Cruiser's Net is supposed to be a week-long duty before getting passed on to another cruiser (it's an ongoing, year-round affair), because he's so good at it, Rockin' Ron has been asked to take over for the duration of the Cruising Regatta. He's happy to do so, as it fits in naturally with the prevailing vibe, which has brought him back year after year.

"It's the camaraderie," he said. "Everybody helps everybody. If someone's dragging anchor or has some other issue, people are running over to help you out. There's just such a good attitude. What we always say is that Georgetown is the way the whole world should be."

Rockin' Ron is a cool cat and I have lots of other questions, but he has to run. The other day he was on the four-person team that made it to the finals of the ridiculously competitive Regulation Volleyball Tournament (there's also "Fun Volleyball" for mellower players) and today he's off to compete in the Tennis Tournament.

The following bears mention, because along with the general Georgetown attitude, another recurring theme among the cruisers is afoot. Like many of the folks I'll meet at the event, Rockin' Ron is trim and fit, vital and energetic, and could easily be mistaken for a fifty-year-old. In reality, he's 67.

It can't be a coincidence. Somewhere in Georgetown, along with such popular local waypoints as the towering Monument on Stocking Island and Mimm's Market, downtown, there's got to be a Fountain of Youth.

ONCE UPON a time—before the variety shows, athletic competitions, ham-radio seminars, arts and crafts, sand sculpture contests, pet parades, scavenger hunts, bridge and trivial pursuit tournaments, poker nights, and so forth—the Georgetown Cruising Regatta was, well, a sailboat race. Given what transpires today, it's almost impossible to fathom.

Mickey Walsh was there at the beginning. These days, he lives aboard in Georgetown Harbor with his wife, Joyce, aboard their Hardin 45, *High Hopes.* But for many, many years, he'd set out from New York each fall with his three daughters aboard the family's 29-foot Garden-designed double-ender, *Valkyrie,* and wander through the Bahamas until it was time to sail home and get back to his seasonal occupation grooming the beach at the Fire Island National Seashore.

Walsh says it was a wild group of Texas cruisers that used to sail in company who launched the inaugural edition of the event during the winter of 1979-80. "We used to call them the Texas Navy," he said. "They'd cruise down from the Abacos like a bunch of locusts. They were all kooks but they were active and did a lot of things. They said, 'Let's have a race,' and that's basically what the first year was. Later on, a lot of other people got interested in it and said, 'Oh, let's do this and that.'

"I personally never got too involved," he added, voicing a sentiment that many other visiting sailors have subscribed to over the years. "I kind of resented it a little bit. They organized *everything*! I came down here to get away from all that."

An ex-pat American dentist known as Dr. Joel took the baton from the rambunctious Texans, and as Walsh recalled, "started making an enterprise out of it." It was the entrepreneurial doctor who came up with the tradition, which holds to this day, of selling distinctive regatta t-shirts each year, the proceeds from which largely cover the costs of the event. Anything left over, then and now, is donated to the National Family Island

Regatta—the colorful races conducted in local Bahamian sloops and dinghies each April—as well as other local causes and charities. Over the years, literally tens of thousands of dollars have been funneled into the local economy.

The one thing, Walsh said, that Georgetown always had going for it was the incredible natural harbor: "I call it a 'Captain's Resort.' Think about it. It's got the most beautiful anchorage you could ever imagine. If you cruise the Bahamas at all, you know you have to anchor in the wind and current (on a Bahamian moor), which is a pain in the ass. You don't have that here. Any place in this harbor you've got a beautiful anchorage and great holding. We've made a lot of friends here over the years. It's like home. I see a lot of boats come through here on the way to Puerto Rico or the Caribbean, and they get in here and just say, 'Why? Why leave?'"

Ultimately, Dr. Joel and the event parted ways in what's been described as "difficult" financial circumstances. Today the management of the regatta is in the hands of the cruisers themselves, with oversight provided by a local Georgetown merchant, Mike Mimms, the proprietor of the busy local market. A dedicated regatta chairman is responsible for the overall organization, while individual chairs oversee the respective seminars, contests, and shows. On average, each costs a mere $2 to enter.

In both 2008 and 2009, retired Canadian swim coaches, Stuart and Marilyn on *Union Jack*, a Nauticat 33, shared the chief duties. "Two years ago, to our great surprise, the previous chairmen, from Tennessee, came by one day and asked if we'd like to take over for them," said Stuart. "I said, 'No.' Marilyn said, 'Yes.'"

"So," he laughed. "We took over for them. Okay."

The couple first ventured to Georgetown in 1988, and Stuart, an avid bridge player, volunteered to teach the game for the simplest of reasons:  He wanted partners so he could play on the beach.  After retirement, in 2000, their visits became annual. Marilyn said that at the high point, a few years ago, as many as 500 boats visited the harbor for the regatta.  In 2009, with the downturn in the economy, she fretted that they wouldn't be able to recoup their investment, in both time and money—the event takes a full year to organize, with an annual budget of around $20,000—for the 800 T-shirts and hats they'd pre-ordered.

"But we still had 350 boats at the max this year," said Marilyn, "and every single item was sold."

Stuart said their management philosophy, as regatta chairmen, was very straightforward.  "Our goal was to make it as much fun as possible, to be nice to everybody, and to be as inclusive as we could to the people that live here:  Non-controversial. Non-exclusive.  We just wanted everyone to participate."

In Georgetown, as I'd soon discover, participation was not a problem.

WITH PHOTOGRAPHER Bob Grieser, I arrived in Georgetown some nine days into the two-week regatta, so among the many early events I missed was the opening variety show, which everyone agreed had been a doozy.  But I was just in time for the finals of the Regulation Beach Volleyball Tournament, which turned out to be an ideal place to jump in.

The tourney chairmen were Wayne and Isabel on *Cassiopeia*, a good old 1966 Pearson Vanguard from Marquette, Michigan.  Sweaty Wayne was not only helping organize the event, he was also on a team wending its way through the round robin, but he stopped for a breather between games.  Recently retired from the art department at Northern Michigan University, he'd taken the plunge as both a sculptor and a sailor.

"I'm going to try and be a real artist instead of an educator," he said. "Sailing will be a big part of it: the inspiration, the people you meet, it just gives you a different perspective. We're on one of the smaller boats out here but it's the boat we had, and the boat we like. Plus, I've got a good woman. It's tough to find a good woman to stick with you, especially on a small boat."

Over at the scoring table, the good woman in question, Isabel, was busy filling in the brackets and keeping the action moving. "It's our second season coming down here," she said. "We just loved it, so we volunteered to chair an event. Get involved. Do your part. That's the way it is here in Georgetown."

The top teams were playing a skilled and spirited brand of volleyball, but after a while, it got a little tiring just *watching* them battle under the blazing sun. Over by the regatta bulletin board, under some shady casuarinas, I ran into Mark and Gwyn on *Ala*, a Leopard 40 hailing from Chesapeake Bay, as they scanned the scratch sheet for the next day's race around Stocking Island. It would be their first sailboat race ever.

"We didn't plan on being plopped in this place for so long," said Gwyn, echoing yet another familiar and oft-repeated refrain. "We were warned if we got to Georgetown and put the anchor down it might be a while before we picked it up again."

Over on a picnic bench, George and Toby on *Puff*, a neat little houseboat tucked up in the shallows, said they felt no desire to pull up stakes. Then again, *Puff* has no engine and is permanently moored. Like many other cruisers, the couple made a permanent move to Georgetown after many years of regular visits aboard their Tartan 37, and later, their Morgan 44.

"When we first started sailing to the Bahamas, all we heard about were the great crowds in Georgetown, how there was no room and all that stuff," said George. "So we ventured on down and found out none of it was true. There's always room to anchor. It's a big, huge, immense harbor. And it's a lot warmer here than the Abacos."

George and Toby insisted we meet some friends of theirs, French-Canadians Michel and Louise on *Marie-Antoine*, a 42-foot trawler. The Canadian presence is strong in Georgetown; in fact, it seems like every other boat in the anchorage sports the familiar red-and-white Maple Leaf flag snapping off the transom.

Like many of their countrymen, Michel and Louise commute back and forth to Canada every six months in order to meet the residency requirements to retain their health insurance. But Michel, a former executive at Xerox who left the company in 2000, reckons that the time he spends in the islands play the largest role in his wellbeing.

"Those last five years of work, from 1995-2000, I took quite a beating. I aged quite a bit," he said, in a pleasing French accent. "I was looking at my body decreasing. It wasn't good. Since then, I don't feel like I've aged too much at all."

If you stick around Georgetown long enough, you begin to hear the same things over and over from different people. Louise's parting comment was one more increasing recognizable proclamation.

"This place," she said, "is a summer camp for adults."

YES, IF you're patient, there actually is a "regatta" at the Georgetown Cruising Regatta. Actually, there's a pair of races, the first a point-to-point contest of about 20 miles, starting and finishing in the main harbor after a circuit out in the ocean and around Stocking Island, and the second a round-the-buoys in-harbor match. The former drew a couple of dozen monohulls and nine multihulls, the latter about half those numbers.

For the distance race, I'd scored a spot aboard the St. Francis 50 catamaran, *Artemis*. The boat's owners, George and Jillian Godfrey, and their son, Greg, had originally sailed to the islands from their home in South Africa. After a career in banking, George started building the St. Francis line of cats and has since erected a multi-purpose resort/sales office/bar and restaurant on an arresting parcel of land on Stocking Island, the scene of several regatta parties and gatherings.

Our crew for the race included Pam and Ollie on *Let it Go*, a Beneteau 41 (Ollie, I'd soon learn, has a serious problem keeping his pants around his waist, particularly when sailing close abeam another boat); Eric and Susan on *Elysia*, a Formosa 46; and Willis from *Whistling Winds*, a Contact 35. The actual racing, however, was but a sidelight to the overall proceedings. Other prizes, of equal merit, would be awarded for the Best Photograph, the Best Baking, and the Longest Edible Fish Caught, all of which had to be addressed under way.

Soon after the start, four fishing lines were streaming astern. "If we run into a school of Mahi, we're in trouble," said Eric. Moments later, Pam disappeared into the galley to whip up an incredible chocolate pecan pie (which turned out to be the winner). "This isn't the Jenny Craig Race," she said.

Meanwhile, as event chairman Stuart, in his soothing English tones, narrated the action on VHF Channel 78, the rest of the crew put *Artemis* through her paces. Skipper George was obviously a very solid and accomplished sailor, and he orchestrated a smart game plan from start to finish. In a fading breeze, *Artemis* glided past the finish line and the huge, raucous raft of inflatables partying off the race-committee boat, the first cat home.

Pam's pie was an incredible success, but the two smallish barracuda in the fish hold were far less promising. "Maybe we could sew them together," sighed Eric.

Two days later, for the in-harbor race, I joined Charlie and Terry on *Voyager*, their immaculate Jeanneau 43. It was, as they say, blowing the dogs off the chains, and things were definitely more chaotic than they'd been on *Artemis*. But Charlie had done his fair share of PHRF racing back in the day, and he managed to (mostly) keep his cool as we negotiated the two laps around the cans. Even though it was 10:30 in the morning, the icy cold beer was a welcome treat when all was said and done.

THE DILEMMA when trying to write a story about the Georgetown Cruising Regatta is perplexing: Where do you begin? Where do you end? After all, all the sailors who've managed to extricate themselves from the so-called "real world" and make it all the way to the Bahamas have a great tale to tell. Nowhere was this more evident than at the post-racing regatta awards ceremony at the Chat 'n' Chill.

For instance, take Charlie and Lizz on *Kaya*, a Catana 401, who cleaned up in the multihull division. The "Charlie" that everyone on the beach knew was a laid-back dude who was clearly having the time of his life. But Charlie Ogletree was also probably the best mariner in the harbor, a four-time Olympic cat sailor who'd earned a silver medal at the Athens Games.

Then there was Marc and Angie on the Manta 42, *Side by Side*, cruising with their children, Parker and Sabrina. The Johnson family was conspicuous in an unexpected way, for the one thing that seemed to be missing from the regatta was a big posse of cruising youngsters. Marc acknowledged it was true. "There were a whole lot of families who rolled back home after their savings tanked," he said. "We're on year three of a five-year plan, and we can't see a reason to stop now."

Then, at the epicenter of the gathering, was Kenneth Bowe, better known as K.B., the Bahamian-born proprietor of the Chat 'n' Chill and the owner of the nine acres of pristine beach on which many of the regatta activities take place. "I figured out what the people wanted and what they needed," he said. "I separated the wants from the needs and started with the needs. From there, the business has gone straight up."

"Without K.B., there'd be no Georgetown," said Rockin' Ron, who was hosting the awards presentation.

"And without us," whispered one cruiser, "he wouldn't be a multi-millionaire."

The Saturday night awards ceremony segued into the Rockin' Ron Dance Party, and before long a big group of cruisers were rollicking on the beach. But I decided to head for town to take in the Bahamian Music and Heritage Festival in "downtown" Georgetown at Regatta Park.

A group of cruisers in a band called Folks on Boats (previously known as "White Folks on Boats," but since shortened for perhaps obvious political reasons) were playing, led by none other than the volleyball chairmen, Wayne and Isabel from *Cassiopeia*. They even sang an original tune called "Down and Out in Georgetown":

> *We packed it up and sailed away,*
> *We'll go to work another day,*
> *I don't want to LOOK at my 401-K!*
> *Just want to drink some rum,*
> *get some sun, have some fun,*
> *down in Georgetown.*
> *Yeah, down in Georgetown.*

After their set, I was having a beer with the couple when the noisy, boisterous, local Junkanoo band came rolling through the crowd.  Suddenly a guy with a big green conch shell was beside us, blowing away.  He handed it to Wayne, a natural musician, who gave it a hard look, blew a tentative note, realized he had it, and joined in step with the band, Isabel close behind.

The last I saw them, they were dancing away, jiving and swinging, two more fully grown cruising kids, off to yet another Georgetown sandbox.

*Herb McCormick*

**The incredible natural harbor of Georgetown
on the Bahamian island of Great Exuma
is renowned for its many anchorages
and fine holding ground.**

*"Good Morning, Georgetown!"*

The thing I took away from this story, which I didn't fully address in the article that appeared in *Cruising World*, was the lack of kids and families at this popular event, which used to be crawling with them. The bulk of the fleet hailed from Canada, and most were retired couples.

It's one of the sadder truths about the economic meltdown. As never before, younger sailors are averse to leaving a good job for a family adventure, not knowing if it'll be there when they return. Sailing is becoming an ever-grayer pastime.

# 15: Enthralled in the Land of Smiles

## ALLURING THAILAND, AFTER THE TSUNAMI

ON MY FIRST afternoon in Thailand I did something that, in retrospect, was both incredibly stupid and totally inspiring. On a bustling street a block behind crazy Patong Beach on Thailand's signature island of Phuket, I handed a fellow 250 *baht*—about six bucks—and in return received the key to a deceptively peppy, Honda 125-cc motor scooter. Donning a helmet a couple of sizes too small, I wheeled into traffic and headed south, down the coast.

That, surely, was the dumb bit.

Driving alongside the locals was fine; scooters are a primary form of transportation and the Thais know what they're doing on them. More troublesome was negotiating the steady stream of maniacal tourists, most of which were a) clearly operating a two-wheeled motorized vehicle for the very first time and b) drunk. I was nearly done in by an inebriated pack of whooping, sunburned *farangs*—white people—of undetermined nationality who believed they were in a motocross event and liked to pass on the inside. This was all idiotic for the obvious reason: the odds on developing a severe case of road rash were exceedingly high.

But once down the coast a ways, things got better fast. The winding road passed through a series of resort towns with gleaming beaches, then ascended rapidly through lush, green forest that opened up to one amazing ocean vista after another. I stopped at a small roadhouse nestled into the trees with a breathtaking western view of the sun setting into the Andaman Sea. It was some sort of Thai-Rasta bar—photos of Bob Marley were plastered all over and they had one CD, Marley's *Legend*, which they played over and over—and the attendant mood was, well, let's just say that "mellow" would be an overstatement. I ordered a big platter of shrimp and crab with a spicy salad that left me panting. I had little choice but to down a second cold Singha beer (the local favorite) before resuming my journey south.

And that's when my little ride became inspirational.

For sailing in Thailand had long been a dream of mine; over the years I'd heard the stories and seen the pictures from countless cruisers who ranked the country as one of their all-time favorites. This thought was very much on my mind as I rounded a cliff-side bend near the southwestern tip of Phuket and, quite unexpectedly, came upon the expansive, remarkable anchorage off Nai Harn Beach. There below me were a couple of dozen cruising boats—sloops and ketches, monohulls and catamarans—and looking farther south were a smattering of the islands accessible to these seaworthy craft.

The scene jolted me. I took a big gulp of air. That's when it really hit me: I was in Asia, and I wasn't dreaming. And the best part of all? Tomorrow I'd be on a cruising boat, too, just like those other sailors, and all those islands would be mine to explore.

LET'S GET one thing clear right at the outset: Thailand is hot. I don't mean uncomfortably warm; I'm talking searing, sizzling, nuclear heat. The only way to survive the middle hours of the day, when the sun is high, is through repeated immersion in the clear waters and total shade when you're not in the drink.

Luckily, *Constanza*, the Beneteau Oceanis 461 we'd chartered from Sunsail, was equipped with a nice dodger and a big cockpit bimini, so shade was plentiful.  And as the voyage progressed, on especially toasty afternoons we'd drape towels off the bimini with clothespins for even greater protection, or scurry beneath the shadows of the sails like old dogs in an alley, always lurking toward the dark spots.

We were a crew of four aboard the 46-foot bareboat—photographer and longtime traveling companion Billy Black, delivery skipper Jon Eisberg, sailing buddy Jeff Roy, and me—and Thailand was a first-time destination for all of us.  After stowing gear and taking on provisions on a still morning last February, we were both sweaty and more than ready to get away from the close quarters at Sunsail's docks within the fine marina facilities of Phuket's ultra-modern Boat Lagoon.

The two-mile journey from slip to open water began inauspiciously.  We had no trouble wending our way through the mangrove river just beyond the marina, but we then came to an abrupt halt on a sandbar at the entrance to the narrow, curving main channel.  We were pushing the tail end of an outgoing tide and for a second there it looked like we might be stuck for a while.  We were finally able to rock free and clear out on the very last bit of the ebb with the keel just kissing the bottom.  We could've cut our departure a little closer, though not by much.

Still, the collective onboard stress of having furrowed our way seaward disappeared instantly the moment we set the sails.  Isn't it funny how that always works?

Earlier, Sunsail base manager Ian Hewett—a cheerful Welshman who'd said farewell to the British isles, married a Thai woman, and was settling in for the duration—had laid out a chart and given us a pretty good idea where he'd go with ten days to fritter away on a sailboat. He suggested a fairly ambitious, clockwise tour of the immediate islands, starting with a left-hand turn out of the Boat Lagoon and on to a northerly heading toward the Ao Phang-Nga National Park.

"What's up that way?" I'd wondered.

Ian began to describe the attractions but then seemed to think better of it. "You'll see for yourselves," he'd said, smiling. So northbound it was, close-hauled on a light, warm, but thoroughly refreshing northeast breeze. In Thailand, even a little wind brings a lot of comfort.

We decided that our first night's anchorage would be somewhere off the skinny island of Ko Phanak, a distance of about 16 miles. We later all agreed that the short afternoon sail would be one of the most memorable of our lives. But truth be told, it was the scenery that made it, not the sailing, for the fluky northerly soon disappeared and we were reduced to motorsailing. But the farther along we went, the more incredible our surroundings became. There was no longer any doubt whatsoever: We were in Thailand.

Words barely do justice to the visual spectacle that is Ao Phang-Nga. Jeff's travel book, the *Rough Guide to Thailand's Beaches and Islands*, gives it a pretty good shot: "Covering some four hundred square kilometers of coast between Phuket and Krabi, the mangrove-lined bay is littered with limestone karst formations up to 300-meters in height, jungle-clad and craggily profiled. The bay is thought to have been formed about twelve thousand years ago when a dramatic rise in sea level flooded the summits of mountain ranges, which over millions of years had been eroded by an acidic mixture of atmospheric carbon dioxide and rainwater."

Approaching this wondrous otherworld by sailboat was perfect, as it gave us the chance to slowly drink it all in. Appearing slowly out of the haze, the sharp, dramatic mountain peaks seemed like something out of Jurassic Park. Even more remarkable were the bizarre islands that rose dramatically from the sea like giant exclamation points. Frankly, it was almost all too much to take in.

We dropped anchor in a notch off the northern flank of Ko Phanak and tried to grasp the scale of our surroundings, which was impossible. I dove in and swam for the island, guessing it was three or four boatlengths away; it turned out to be several hundred yards. Once alongside—it was steep, you couldn't get ashore—I kicked in under its weird limestone overhangs, which reminded me of the wet sand a kid might dribble off a sandcastle. Then I started up a dark cave, which seemed to go for a while, until I scared myself witless and beat a hasty retreat.

At dusk, a passing fisherman in a longtail came alongside and sold us a heaping pile of fat shrimp, which were tasty indeed after a quick singe on the grill. When night fell I couldn't resist one more plunge into the soupy green sea, which was rich in bright, sparkling phosphorescence. Come dawn, the waters were shrouded in low mist, a vision that was surreal, spiritual, and spooky, all at the same time.

If we made one mistake in our week-and-a-half aboard, it was not spending more time kicking around the countless isles of Ao Phang-Nga. It would be a wonderful place to linger for many days, or even weeks, of quiet exploration and reflection. As it was, we weighed anchor and motored up between the fissure of deep water separating the stunning islands of Ko Yai and Ko Hong; we dropped the hook again off the latter and split up in pairs to have a look around in the dinghy and two-person kayak.

In Thai, the rough translation of *hong* is "room"; the word is used to label the caverns and open-to-the-sky enclosures that are a feature of many of the islands. Not surprisingly, Ko Hong had a dandy one that was accessible via a dark cave that opened up into a large, circular grotto with high, slab-sided walls to which clung all manner of tough scrub, trees, and brush. It was, quite simply, majestic.

THERE WERE many miles ahead of us, though, so before long we were under way again, perhaps a tad too anxious to check out the clearer waters to the south. Jeff Roy, however, would never have forgiven us had we not made at least a quick stop at, ahem, Ko Roi. It proved to be a worthy detour, with yet another impressive *hong*, this one several hundred feet high and partially surrounded at its base by thick mangrove. One thing about Thailand—you never have to wait long for the next visual delight.

If Ko Hong and Ko Roi had been peaceful and serene, however, with just a handful of cruising boats and longtails roaming about, our next layover, off Railay Beach on the Krabi peninsula, was a veritable beehive of activity. Railay was certainly a scene, with plenty of guesthouses, backpackers, restaurants (several of which were Muslim-owned and did not serve alcohol, though you were permitted to bring your own), massage parlors, and a row of longtails at the water's edge ready to be pressed into service as water taxis.

The next day, Billy and I hailed one for the 45-minute trip into the bustling city of Krabi for ice, beer, and groceries. For 1200 *baht*, or about $30, we basically hired the boat and driver for the afternoon, and it was worth every penny. With their high prows and narrow hulls, the ubiquitous longtails are fast, dry, and extremely seaworthy. What's more, they're generally powered by standard car engines that spin an open prop on a long shaft which the helmsmen—Billy respectfully referred to them as "water Indians," and they truly appeared at one with the sea— wield with remarkable deftness. We had an up-close view of a string of climbers working their way up a sheer face before entering the pretty, mangrove-lined estuary leading to Krabi town.

The highlight of the journey was lunch, and it was so good we had it twice. The first was on a street corner where the cook whipped up a fine plate of rice, shrimp, and vegetables, which she adorned with fresh herbs and a hard-boiled egg as we ate. The bill, for two, was 40 *baht*, or fifty cents apiece. The second was in a busy lunch spot run by a Chinese family, who served us large, steaming bowls of noodles, chicken, and fresh kale. This was much more up-market, as reflected by the tariff: a whopping seventy-five cents each. We didn't have a bad meal in Thailand, but this simple fare was as delicious as anything we tasted.

While on the subject of pleasurable experiences, let's digress a moment to discuss the rejuvenating benefits of Thai massage, a topic about which I gained considerable knowledge during the course of my visit. In fact, there was hardly an afternoon that passed when I didn't lighten my wallet of 300 *baht* (about $7) for what always proved to be the best hour of the day. There are few creatures on this planet less flexible than I, which made the entire exercise all the more beneficial. Thai masseuses give it their all, working every part of *your* body with nearly every part of *theirs*: hands, knees, elbows, and fingers. Every masseuse has her own variation on the theme, but the final result is always the same: After the stretching and kneading and caressing, you emerge with a complete and total body buzz that lasts for hours. Don't even get me started on the foot massages.

The anchorage off Railay was so lovely, and the treats ashore so wonderful, that we spent a couple of days there before shoving off for popular Ton Sai Bay at Ko Phi Phi Don. On the way, we made a short tour of the uninhabited islands of Ko Dam Hok and Ko Dam Khwan, the latter of which sports a strange, distinctive rock called Chicken Head. We stopped long enough to pick up a mooring at one of the adjacent islets for a long, fun snorkel along its sheer rock wall.

Any discussion of sailing in this part of the world would be remiss without addressing the devastating tsunami that wreaked such widespread havoc in Thailand, Indonesia, India, and Sri Lanka following a powerful Indian Ocean earthquake on December 26, 2004. The most visible reminders, particularly in populated areas, are the warning towers with loudspeakers that are dotted along the beaches, and the Tsunami Evacuation Route signs on every coastal road. An amazing fact about the tsunami is the surprising lack of evidence, just a little over a year later, that it ever happened. Clearly, it didn't take the resourceful survivors of the catastrophe long to rebuild so many stricken areas and resume their lives.

One exception, however, is the low-lying spit of land at the head of Ton Sai Bay, where several hundred people were killed and a slew of ruined buildings stand testament to the ravages of that awful day. The main beachfront strip at Ko Phi Phi Don was open for business and over the top, with a complete collection of dive shops, restaurants, bars, resorts, hotels, Internet cafes, jewelry stores, and on and on. But for some reason it didn't feel so merry, and we were back on board after a rather quick look around. Besides, we were planning an early start the next day.

We hadn't had an abundance of breeze thus far, but of course that changed during our stay at Ton Sai, when a big southeasterly kicked in and made for a rocking, roiling evening on a lee shore. I slept fitfully in the cockpit and was up and down all night making sure we stayed put. Dawn and low tide arrived at just about the same time, and in the fresh light we could see we were closer than 100 yards from a nasty, exposed reef. There was no reason to stick around, and we didn't.

We were headed southeast, to a series of outlying islands where we hoped to escape the hue and cry of the madding crowd. But we'd been advised that a tour of Maya Cove on the nearby island of Ko Phi Phi Leh was worth a visit; furthermore, we knew to get there early, before the small fleet of tour boats made their advance.

Maya Cove is home to the sea swift, a tiny bird whose cliffside nests are the primary ingredient for bird's nest soup, a prized delicacy in the Far East that is widely touted as an energizing aphrodisiac. It's also a tourist attraction for several reasons, not the least of which is the starring role it played in an otherwise forgettable Leonardo DiCaprio movie called *The Beach*.

Motoring down the west side of the tall, dramatic island was cool, but it paled in comparison to entering the wide, circular lagoon itself, which was extraordinary. We picked up a mooring and settled back to watch the sun rise over a stark limestone cliff. As the sun crept higher, the cove's coral reef became most alluring, and we all had a good, long snorkel and swim before wandering ashore for a stroll on the fantastic white-sand beach. As movies go, *The Beach* may have been a critical disaster, but the filmmakers got one thing right: If you wanted a place that evoked the elusive notion of paradise, Maya Cove was an outstanding choice.

FOR GOOD reason, Thailand is nicknamed the Land of Smiles, and nowhere was this more evident than on the remote islands of Ko Muk and Ko Kraden, our next destinations. It's impossible not to truly like the Thai people, who are industrious, proud, handsome, friendly, and possessed of a quiet humility that's rare and admirable in this day and age. They love and honor their country and their monarch, King Bhumibol Adulyadej, who has reigned for the last six decades. They are deeply religious Buddhists, and the robed monks one encounters everywhere are reverential figures. On top of everything, they seem to be genuinely happy folk, and you never happen upon a group of Thais who aren't laughing and joking and basically choosing to embrace the sunny side of life. And there is no more civilized gesture in any society than the *wai*, the gentle bow with clasped hands that is exchanged regularly as a token of greeting and respect.

The anchorages off Ko Mok and Ko Kraden were calm and lovely, much like the villagers ashore. But we had an eventful time getting there. We'd been lulled into complacency in Maya Cove but that changed in a hurry soon after rounding the southern tip of Ko Phi Phi Leh. Out of the lee, the southeast breeze was still pumping and an opposing current was churning up standing waves just off the headland. One of those waves buried the bow and swept *Constanza* from stem to stern, which is when we discovered we'd forgotten to dog the boat's series of opening portlights. To say things got a bit damp down below would be putting it very mildly.

With a reefed main and full genoa we ultimately got our act together and managed to sail roughly half of the 35 miles to Ko Muk before the wind died and we again engaged the engine. We arrived off Ko Muk late that afternoon at the same time as a cool, brief squall, the first rain we'd seen all week. Deploying the dinghy with the last of the shower, we made our way up and into long, dark Emerald Cave, an excursion I found to be exceedingly creepy. But it was worth it, as the cave opened up to a large, towering *hong* with a sandy floor that was breathtaking. On the way out, I slipped over the side and swam out of the cave and directly into the setting sun. It was my favorite souvenir of the trip.

We lingered for a couple of days off these terrific islands, picking up a mooring off Ko Kraden the second night. There, we went ashore for dinner at an interesting spot called Paradise Lost, run by an ex-Hawaiian chap named Wally who sailed here some 11 years ago and built his restaurant and guest house from scratch. It was a bit hard to hang with Wally without thinking of the Marlon Brando character in *Apocalypse Now*, but we had a fine time at his establishment, even though the latter part of the evening remains hazy thanks to a generous serving of the lethal, local brew called Chang. "Every batch is different," Ian had warned us during our charter briefing. "Chang definitely has some quality-control issues."

Next morning, with ringing heads, we were under way at 0530 for the 60-mile, open-water passage to a set of islets called Ko Racha Noi and Ko Racha Yai. We anchored off the latter's picture-perfect harbor that fronted a swank resort that wanted absolutely no part of a motley crew like ours. Happily, a fine, inexpensive hillside restaurant was more than happy to take our business.

Our time in Thailand was coming to an end and the boat was due back in Phuket, but we had one more stop. Ao Chalong, at the southern end of the island, is a bustling port and we had our best sail of the voyage to get there, making a solid 7 knots in 12 knots of perfect northeast breeze. We stopped for a beer at the Ao Chalong Yacht Club and then strolled over to a joint called Jimmy's Lighthouse. I'd loved every Thai meal I'd eaten over the last 10 days, but at Jimmy's I couldn't resist a big cheeseburger slathered in mushrooms with a side of onion rings. It was perfect.

From the deck at Jimmy's we could look out over the harbor at a fleet of truly international cruising boats. From big Hallberg Rassys to funky little Wharram cats, every size and style was on display, and it reminded me of the scene at Nai Harn I'd witnessed from my motor scooter on what now seemed a quite distant time and place. For at that stage, all I wanted to be was an honest-to-goodness sailor in Thailand. Now, lo and behold, I was one.

*Billy Black*

**The scenery and anchorages along the remarkable coast of Thailand and the islands of the Andaman Sea seem to be from another planet.**

If you've never been to Thailand, one word: Go. After this story appeared in *Cruising World*, my experiences there were later summarized in a chapter of Chris Santella's book, *Fifty Places to Sail Before You Die.*

*Bobby Grieser*

**On the remote island of Vieques, pristine, white-sand beaches like this one at Ensenada Sun Bay—with nary a soul in sight—are pretty and plentiful.**

Part of my crew for our trip to the Spanish Virgins was my longtime friend and sailing pal, Ian Scott, with whom I co-owned my first boat, a J/24 called *Crack 'O Noon*. You can blame Ian's dad, the late Bud Scott, for this entire book—Bud literally taught me the ropes, racing out of the Newport Yacht Club on both of his Pearsons, each of which was called *Swanya Vah*.

# 16: Secrets Revealed

## THE SPANISH VIRGIN ISLANDS, STILL PRISTINE

ARMED WITH Off!, we spun the inflatable away from our chartered Bahía 46 catamaran, *Ricky Dee*, and pointed it towards the dark, narrow cut leading into Puerto Mosquito. The name alone made me itch.

It was late evening on a Tuesday in March, and my three buddies and I—escapees from a long stateside winter—were on a bona-fide tropical adventure that was getting more interesting by the day. Ours was the only boat in the reef-fringed anchorage on the south coast of the outlying Puerto Rican island of Vieques; the eco-tourists on their kayaks who'd also been drawn to this unique inlet earlier in the night had long since departed. Like the anchorage just outside, we now had the inner bay all to ourselves.

We approached at a snail's pace, a big moon above casting a warm glow to the proceedings. Despite its name, we had no use for insecticide in Puerto Mosquito; the air was silky and bug free. It practically invited us to eschew the outboard and paddle in, and we happily obliged.

But the real reason one visits the shallow, plankton-rich cove in the dead of night isn't to idle, but to swim in its warm, soupy, bioluminescent waters. And when my friend Ian took leave of the dinghy and knifed into the sea in a flat, perfect dive—leaving a glowing wake like a launched torpedo in a U-Boat movie—we instantly understood the attraction. Seconds later we were all in, plunging, kicking, and choreographing our own personal underwater light shows.

A few months earlier, I'd barely even heard of the Caribbean island of Vieques, or its nearby neighbor, Culebra.  But as
I scrambled back into the tender, cracked a cold beer, and took
in the quiet, stunning night, I was already wondering how and
when I might return.

FIRST OFF, a confession:  I broke a promise.

For when John Jacobs of CYOA Yacht Charters in St. Thomas agreed to let my pals and me take the slick, quick *Ricky Dee*
for a week's sojourn to the nearby Spanish Virgins, he did so on
one condition.  John wanted us at some point to fetch up on the
main island of Puerto Rico to visit the El Conquistador marina,
spa, and casino complex at Fajardo.  As a veteran of the charter
business, his reasoning was straightforward.  John knows that
the fairer sex sometimes gets short shrift on charter vacations—
after all, it's often the women who end up toiling in the galley
and succumbing to the Island Boy fantasies of the skipper and
his fellow cronies—and he wanted us to sample and report on
the sumptuous facilities and creature comforts of what is from
all accounts a remarkable resort.

So here's where I come clean.  We never got there.  Not even
close.

Perhaps if we'd had our wives and girlfriends along it
would've been a different story.  Certainly, we were soon to
learn that in Vieques, and later, in neighboring Culebra, the
shoreside bars and restaurants that one comes to reliably
expect in countless anchorages in the USVIs and BVIs are few
and far between.  Ditto for moorings, aids to navigation, and
all the general support services that are part and parcel of many
Caribbean cruising grounds.  To cruise the Spanish Virgins, you
must assume and embrace a level of self-sufficiency that's sim-

ply not required in the immediate waters around St. Thomas and Tortola.

In other words, if you go chartering to eat out every night, you'll probably want to give Culebra and Vieques a miss.

However, if you do as we did, and stock the larders, freezer, and fridge with food and drink from the excellent, one-stop-for-everything Pueblo supermarket in St. Thomas, then augment that with a pile of fresh fish from the open-air Frenchtown markets just down from the CYOA docks, you definitely won't go hungry. If you've got a couple of frustrated chefs aboard (photographer Bobby Grieser and me), and another pair of willing guinea pigs (friends Ian Scott and Charlie Zechel), all the better.

Still, it wasn't like we set out planning to dodge the nightlife on the main island. Quite the opposite. But after just a few days in the out islands, we quickly realized it would take much more time than we had available to really get to know them. And we didn't want to waste a single minute.

THERE IS, of course, a very good reason Vieques was off the radar screen of most sailor's island itineraries for so long: the bombing range. The possibility of getting strafed is a strong deterrent to fun in the sun.

In fact, for much of the last fifty years, the eastern half of Vieques was a "live fire" training facility for the U.S. Navy, and off limits to the public. By the late 1990s, however, protests against the bombings mounted and the Navy faced considerable pressure to cease the practice. On May 1, 2003, they did so, handing over nearly 80 percent of the island to the United States Fish and Wildlife Service. With the swoop of a pen, Vieques was transformed from what was largely a military installation to the Caribbean's biggest wildlife refuge. And tourism suddenly became an important sector of the economy.

On the day we flew into St. Thomas, coincidentally enough, that very point was underscored by a story in *The New York Times* travel section entitled, "Vieques, Far From the Lounge-Chair Crowd."

"Modern-day Vieques feels more like a border town than an emerging tourist destination," wrote Pableaux Johnson. "For years it managed to keep a low-key image, known mostly to veteran Caribbean travelers and others willing to keep a secret. But the last two years, glossy travel magazines have lavished attention on Vieques... [It's] still best known for the natural attractions that inspired the island's newfound fame—secluded beaches, crystal-clear snorkeling waters, and stunning forest vistas. They are open to any traveler willing to work a bit for the experience and adapt to the island's relaxed pace."

As we beam-reached toward Punta Este, the island's eastern point, in a delightful 10-knot southeasterly, we could relate to the part about relaxation though we'd hardly begun to expend much energy on the experience. Indeed, clipping along at an effortless six knots on a brilliant afternoon, the snowy days of winter seemed far away. The distance between the CYOA base and Punta Este is roughly 22 miles, and as we ticked them off it wasn't long before the hustle and bustle of St. Thomas felt equally remote.

"If you are looking for the Caribbean as it was three decades ago, head west for Culebra and Vieques!" exults Don Street in his excellent guidebook on the region. But Street didn't make it easy to pick our first anchorage; both Bahía Icacos, on the north coast, and Bahía Salina del Sur, to the south, make his top-ten list of best anchorages in the Eastern Caribbean.

We flipped a coin and opted for the former, which turned out to be a wide, beautiful bay surrounded by reef with the exception of a pair of passes to the north. We chose the more westerly of the two and Charlie and Ian hopped into the dinghy to scout the reef before entering. Once inside, just as Street said, we discovered a sensational anchorage that we shared with three distant powerboats. As would often be the case as the trip unfolded, we were the lone sailboat there. And Street was right: the stark, bare landscape, without a house or soul in sight (though we did spot a couple of wrecked tanks while sailing in), looked and felt like a scene from a bygone era.

If we made one mistake on the trip, it wasn't spending more time in Bahía Icacos. For a few weeks later I received an email from cruising sailor Stacey Collins, who was anchored in the bay with her family at the time. "I think we could stay a week," she wrote. "Neil's having the best spear-fishing since the Bahamas, and we have the beaches all to ourselves (except for the sea turtles, manta and eagle rays, birds, and the occasional pickup truck from the observation post)."

We saw a few folks from the powerboats who must enjoy living dangerously—hey, what's a little undetonated ordnance?— wandering inland from the beach a ways, though by the letter of the law it remains a restricted area. But as we had a quick errand to run, we never even went ashore, preferring instead to set out early the next day.

WE'D TRIED from Bahía Icacos to clear customs by phone—a requirement for all vessels, even those transiting from the U.S.V.I.—but were informed that since our vessel had not been issued a user-fee decal by the U.S. Customs Service, we'd need to pay a visit to their airport office (we later learned this can be done in advance online). So we hoisted sail and set a course for Esperanza.

The 15-mile run around Punta Este and down the south coast in a light northerly breeze was simply exquisite. The shore-line was mostly empty, save for mile after mile of white, sandy beach. We saw exactly two boats, a Mako runabout and one other catamaran. The water was crystal clear, the bottom easily visible 70 feet below. At one point, as a school of flying fish took flight, a huge, gleaming dolphin broke free of the water in a long, wet arc, then locked on to one of the flyers. Back in its element, it zigged and zagged like a tracer missile and was right there— Chomp!—the instant its prey hit the drink. That's the problem with flying fish: At some point, you have to land.

Once in Esperanza, the south coast's only real village, Bobby and I rented a Jeep and drove out to the airport, where we quickly cleared customs. On the way back we decided to stop at the tony new Wyndham Hill resort on Martineau Bay, the sole facility of its kind on the island, for a rum punch. At the pool-side bar, Bobby struck up a conversation with a lithe, clueless young woman from Philadelphia with a penchant for laughing, annoyingly, at her own jokes.

"I told my travel agent to get me Puerto Rico without the Puerto Ricans," she said, clearly oblivious to the fact that half a dozen Puerto Ricans were four feet away and waiting on her hand and foot. We backed down the rum, made a dash for the gates, and never looked back.

Back in town we soon discovered that Vieques owed much of its charm to the very people Miss Philly was trying so desper-ately hard to avoid. In an open-air bar along the main street's lovely promenade, the salsa music was blaring and local couples of all ages—and I do mean all ages—were sipping Coors Lights and dancing Sunday afternoon away. We couldn't help but join them.

For most of the next day we put the Jeep to hard use and tried our best to see all the places *The New York Times* advised intrepid tourists to see, and then some. From the bustling town of Isabel Segunda on the north shore to the inviting waters of Ensenada Sun Bay on the south, we took it all in. We honked down the old Naval airstrip, already being reclaimed by nature, and four-wheeled it up a wild dead-end road to an ancient water tower.

Moving on, we swam at three more of the island's best beaches—that's a subjective statement, there are dozens and they're all terrific—which are still known widely by the names the gringo sailors gave them: Red Beach (Bahía Corcho), Blue Beach (Bahía de la Chiva), and Green Beach (Punta Arenas). All are accessed by rough dirt roads, though the drive to Green Beach, on the western flank of Vieques, also takes you up and through a lush rainforest before descending into open pasture that serves some of the island's countless wild horses. The beach itself provides a nice view of mainland Puerto Rico, the east coast of which is only 6 or 7 miles away.

Having done the tourist bit, we retired to the boat early and the next day made our way towards the solitude and pleasures of bioluminescent Puerto Mosquito. From there, we had new islands to explore.

IN RETROSPECT, I made a tactical error on our long beat, in steady 14- to 18-knot northeasterly tradewinds, from the east end of Vieques to neighboring Culebra. Much too late in the exercise, I decided to bear away to the isle of Cayo de Luis Peña— an uninhabited wildlife refuge to the immediate west—rather than making for Culebra's main harbor, Ensenada Honda. It cost us a livelier, cracked-off reach and added a few more upwind miles.

Still, it was a great day of sailing, highlighted by the unforgettable sight of a pair of breeching humpback whales. And at trip's end, we found yet another solitary anchorage in 18 feet of crystal clear water, where we torched the grill and took in a fine sunset behind the distant, majestic Puerto Rican peaks of the El Yunque rain forest.

It turned out there was a fair bit of current around Cayo de Luis Peña, which at one point had our bow spun due southwest though the breeze remained steady out of the northeast. The next morning we motored around to the island's northern end and anchored in a clear, sandy thoroughfare between two lanes of coral. There was good snorkeling right off the boat, though we found even better in the rocky outcroppings known as Las Hermanas, a short dinghy ride away. There, I dropped into the water and came face to snoot with a medium-sized barracuda lurking ominously off the transom. The fish shot me a quick look of disdain and frittered off at the pace of an extremely bored teenager.

We sailed to Ensenada Honda later that day and picked up a mooring in the anchorage behind the reef off Punta Colorada just beyond the entrance to the large inner harbor. Calm and lovely, Street declares it "certainly one of the better anchorages in the Caribbean." Ho hum. Like, what else was new?

Like Vieques, Culebra's history also holds a closed chapter on a U.S. military presence, and the main town of Dewey—to which we soon dinghied—is named after a Navy admiral from a distant past. We stopped at a liquor store for some rum and directions and ran smack into yet another one of those pesky

Puerto Ricans. "There's a saying here," said the shopkeeper, and her smile was sincere. "Stay for a weekend on Culebra and we'll be friends. Stay for a week and we'll be family."

A fine anchorage in its own right, in 1989 Ensenada Harbor, and the scores of cruising boats that had sought shelter in its protected enclosure, were pasted by Hurricane Hugo, and upwards of 300 boats were washed ashore. Today, especially compared to almost anywhere in Vieques, the harbor and Dewey seem like veritable beehives of activity. Over the next couple of days we treated ourselves to lunch at the Dinghy Dock—a sailor's haven where big tarpon linger right off the pier—and to dinner at Mamacitas—on the small canal that links the main harbor with a little inlet called Bahía de Sardinas—where the fresh dorado was killer.

As we stepped ashore one morning we ran into a shaggy fellow gringo pedaling out of town with a surfboard under his arm. "Where're the waves, mate?" I called. "North shore today," he yelled back. "It's going off!"

We hired a Jeep and aimed it north towards one of Culebra's more famous beaches, Playo Flamenco, where there was indeed a huge, frothy break off the bay's eastern point but some very rideable three- to five-foot bodysurfing waves right off the beach. After a good session in the surf we drove around to the island's eastern edge and kicked back on the much more placid but no less beautiful Playa Zoni. On the mile-long beach, there may have been a dozen other bathers.

Our time was growing short and the boat was due back in St. Thomas the next day, but we had one final stop to make on the return trip. The little refuge island of Culebrita, just three miles off Culebra's east coast, boasts a couple of fine anchorages. We made a quick attempt to motor into the more protected option to the north but chose discretion over valor at the first dip and roll from an impressive northerly ground swell. Instead, we backtracked to the west and dropped the hook in ten feet of water.

We scrambled ashore and made the short but sweaty climb up to the Culebrita Lighthouse, built by the Spanish in the mid-1880s to confirm their sovereignty over the Brits and Danes also sailing these waters. Because of weather and neglect, these days the lighthouse itself is in rough shape, but the view from its tower remains breathtaking.

From there, we could practically retrace the high points of our cruise: the open-water passages, the remote anchorages, the coral passes, the sensational beaches. It had been a straight-forward trip but there had been some challenging moments, and we all agreed it would be a fantastic destination not only for experienced charterers and southbound cruising sailors, but also to anyone on the verge of an extended voyage who wanted to sharpen their skills before setting out.

If you want to go, don't tarry, for the secret's getting out on the Spanish Virgins. And from what I understand, there's a pretty good casino nearby, too.

# 17: In the Wake of 9/11

## MANHATTAN, AFTER THE TOWERS FELL

IN A PERFECT world, the educator and adventurer Rich Wilson would be hoisting sail today (September 11, 2001) aboard his 53-foot trimaran, *Great American II*, and setting a course past the Statue of Liberty to begin his longstanding plan of chasing a 150-year-old voyaging record from New York to Australia.

But as the events of last week have proved, the world is not a perfect place. So Wilson, his co-skipper, the veteran offshore sailor Bill Biewenga, and *Great American II* are securely tied to a dock this Sunday morning at Manhattan's Chelsea Piers. Their sails are furled. Today, they are going nowhere.

Last Monday evening, however, *Great American II* had no forebodings of evil. They had made landfall in New York after an overnight passage from Marblehead, Mass., and as many sailors who have approached the city by sea can attest, Wilson and Biewenga were transfixed by the sight of downtown Manhattan. It was, Wilson said, "a really moving experience."

Neither heavy rains nor sporadic lightning altered the vision of the skyline's grandeur. "Even from a far distance offshore, you could see the World Trade Center and the Empire State Building sort of lined up with the Throgs Neck Bridge," Wilson said.

The thrust behind *Great American*'s record attempt—to better the 70-day mark to Melbourne set by the clipper ship *Mandarin* in 1856, during the Australian gold rush—is to provide school material for the website that Wilson founded, www.sitesalive.com.

For that reason, Wilson was especially aware of the historical significance of the waters through which he sailed on his approach to New York. "We passed Ellis Island on the same route that immigrants came in on," he said. "The great strength of this country comes from the diversity of those people."

Like countless sailors before them, as they made their way into the Hudson River, the crew of *Great American* snapped pictures of the twin towers. They might have been the last to do so from the deck of a sailboat. Some 12 hours later, the towers were no longer standing.

Wilson and Biewenga have known both adversity and triumph. Biewenga is a Marine Corps veteran who saw duty in Vietnam. In 1991, Wilson was rescued in appalling conditions off Cape Horn after his previous trimaran capsized in 50-foot seas. And in 1993, they had set the sailing record from San Francisco to Boston via the Horn.

But none of their previous experiences prepared them for the events of last Tuesday, September 11th. And in the immediate aftermath, both men struggled with the notion of whether or not to continue with their plan. "We discussed the entire range of possibilities and options," Wilson said.

Wilson said he was compelled to continue by the students who would participate in the program, and by the gist of a message put forth by Mayor Rudolph W. Giuliani.

"We need to delay going in respect for the tragedy and the deceased," Wilson said of the decision to postpone the start of their voyage until Sept. 19th at noon. "But we also have to get back to doing the things that we do. We can't let terrorists stop our way of life or stop our individual endeavors. That's what America is all about. You get a chance to do the things you want to do."

And he was also persuaded by an email message from a man he had never met, but who watched him leave Massachusetts under sail last weekend from the vantage point of the Marblehead Lighthouse. The man had struck up a conversation with Wilson's relatives, who were on shore to bid farewell to *Great American II.*

"In spite of the tragedy unfolding around you, we hope you'll begin your great journey without mishap," wrote the correspondent, Peter Lake. "Ernest Shackleton was about to set off for the Antarctic in August, 1914, when the Great War broke out."

He continued, "Shackleton offered to volunteer his ship for the war, but Churchill sent him on his way with the single word: 'Proceed.' He did, and endured his great adventure to become a legend.

"Shackleton and Churchill and all the great heroes of the past would want you to proceed now with great success. Show our flag proudly to the world."

Wilson said: "When someone sends us off like that, we have to go. And in the context of all that's happened, the name of our boat, *Great American II*, was never more fitting."

So at midday on Wednesday, Wilson will point the bows of his trimaran past New York City's forever altered silhouette and into the Atlantic Ocean, swapping the unfathomable shoreside storms for the less complicated ones of the open seas.

*Courtesy of Rich Wilson*

**On September 19, 2001, the 53-foot trimaran *Great American II* left New York on an attempt to break a 150-year-old voyaging record to Australia, a goal which crewmen Rich Wilson and Bill Biewenga ultimately achieved.**

On September 16, 2001, the "SportsSunday" section of *The New York Times* was abbreviated, and this story, originally titled "Great American II to Stay Course and Set Sail From City's Altered Silhouette," was one of three that appeared on the front page. The photograph of the inscription on the Yankee Stadium message board that accompanied one of the other stories ("Can American Sports Ever Get Back to Normal?") said it all: "God Bless America."

# 18: *Stranger in a Strange Land*

### IN PATAGONIA, BOUND FOR CAPE HORN

"SO YOU are the *gringo*," she said.

Yup, I was the *gringo* all right, the only *norteamericano* in sight. Disoriented by the overnight flight from New York to Chile—and my third pisco sour, a close resemblance to its whiskey cousin—the preposterousness of that fact was just dawning on me.

I was standing by the sunny gardens of Santiago business-man Mauricio Ojeda's lovely suburban home, and the handsome woman addressing me was the wife of Mauricio's 71-year-old pal, German. The conversation, inevitably, shifted to Cape Horn: That's where the three of us lads were supposedly bound.

I'd only met Mauricio face to face an hour before, though we'd swapped emails about sailing in Chile for quite some time. In one he shared his dream of rounding the Horn with his friends under sail. He even asked me along. I said great (as if it would really happen). Then, last spring, Mauricio rang and said pack your seabag.

My bluff had been called.

A man of action, if not reason—I actually knew little about Mauricio and nothing about his friends—I immediately booked a ticket south. But now I faced the consequences.

At 61, Mauricio was trim, fit, and clearly up to the task of a harsh trip in high latitudes. But frankly, German didn't instill a lot of confidence. Broad of beam and barking a rheumy hack, he appeared a long shot to make it around the block, never mind Cape Horn.

Still, in such fine surroundings, the talk was as light and refreshing as the cocktails and hors d'oeuvres. However, my butt had already been kicked in the Southern Ocean once, so when German's wife whispered in my ear to look after her dear one, reality's wake-up call stung like the cold hail of a Screaming Fifties gale.

And I was visited by that old, familiar question: What in the hell was I doing there?

IT HAD been five years since The Dream (the exact span since I'd last sailed south of the fiftieth parallel), but it was as vivid as ever. Standing on a street corner conducting a normal conversation, I inexplicably rocket skyward like a character out of *Crouching Tiger, Hidden Dragon*. Over and over. The annoying ascents negate the excellent points I'm on the verge of making, which pisses me off no end.

I awoke to find I indeed was being launched—from an upper bunk of a Nauticat 52 crashing into a fierce seaway in the general vicinity north of Tierra del Fuego. Fumbling to rig the lee cloth in the dark, it seemed like a poor place to be.

Hours earlier, with Mauricio and German, I'd flown into the distant Chilean outpost of Punta Arenas. On the lam from various escapades involving cash and trains, Butch Cassidy and his trusty sidekick, Sundance, had preceded us by 96 years. So I wasn't the first *gringo* to arrive there with a cloudy past and an uncertain future.

Shortly after landing, while clambering around the obstacle course of a Chilean naval vessel's busy deck, I realized this would be no ordinary cruise. And as I hauled myself aboard the 52-footer rafted outboard and met the other sailors with whom I'd cast my lot—who'd sailed the rugged thousand miles from the boat's homeport of Puerto Montt—I also understood this was no ordinary crew.

It would be awhile before I deciphered the onboard dynamics, but the basics were simple. Ronald Phillips, *Chucao*'s jovial owner and a man of clear intelligence, had in a lapse of good sense been coerced by Mauricio into lending his Finnish-built, Chilean-flagged motorsailer for a reunion of several retired navy buddies, all of them now successful in other fields. Their navy connection had sealed the prime parking place.

To the core group Ronald invited his cousin, German, and another pal. Age-wise, all were north of 60. Another three guys in their 40s, myself included, were along to pull strings and address other shipboard matters. There were lots of nicknames: Cucho, Chuma, Beta. To see Cape Horn from *Chucao*'s deck was our common wish.

*Chucao*'s command had been more or less handed over to a man called Lolo, who'd segued from a distinguished naval career to a long run as a ship's pilot through the southern canals and the Straits of Magellan. The soundness of this decision would be exhibited time and again in the days ahead.

After first setting out from Punta Arenas, the downwind sailing was sweet and the view arresting. Running south along the final miles of the continental mainland, the flickering lights of the shoreline *estancias* were straight out of Bruce Chatwin's *In Patagonia*. High above, moonbeams glanced off craggy snow-fields. Passing Cape Froward, mainland South America's final landmark, was a milestone.

But as the evening wore on the clouds thickened and matters deteriorated. Below, the barometer's arm pointed hard to port in a fine imitation of the nine o'clock hour. The translation: 980 mb., and falling. The midnight squall arrived in sync with

Mauricio's and my going off watch and our departure from the open waters of the Magellan Strait and into the maze of islands and waterways south of the continent. We helped shorten the mainsail from a full hoist to the second reef, then retired below, where I'd soon experience The Dream and its immediate after-math, which also was a nightmare.

By daybreak, it was worse.

A stated option had been to roll down Canal Cockburn, into the open Pacific, and then on to the Horn. But with 45 knots funneling down the channel, Lolo had moved to Plan B: hang a left at the canal's mouth, turn tail, and scamper downwind through Canal Breaknock to a taut anchorage north of Isla Londonderry. (Note: A retired pilot who's logged hun-dreds of thousands of incident-free miles is very handy in these waters.)

The miserable ride might've been smoother had we em-ployed a steadying sail, but the main had blown during a pegged, pre-dawn 50-knot-plus blast. As waves swept *Chucao* while we pounded upwind under power, with the voice of experience Cucho said, "This is like submarine duty."

Exactly 24 hours after leaving Punta Arenas, we eased into the cove at Londonderry and, on second try, set the anchor in 20 feet of flat water while a half-dozen fat skuas looked on. Soon after, Chuma laid out a sensational meal (he'd soon join my list of all-time favorite sea cooks), after which I noticed my bunk was still and inviting. I got right into it.

NOT THAT it was very restful. Unsettled on one hand, yet also awed by the vigor and resonance, I was open-eyed as the chorus of snores—from the v-berth to the aft cabin and every-where in between—rattled *Chucao*'s world. I inserted those traveller's friends—foam earplugs—but they were powerless. Sleep was a train I'd be missing.

And there were more interesting surprises.

In the Defense Mapping Agency's *Sailing Directions* for this part of the world in the month of January, under the category of precipitation, it says: "Snow rarely falls except at elevated stations and in the extreme south."

The trouble there was that through the wide windows of *Chucao*'s raised saloon, glistening with condensation, it was definitely snowing—quite hard, in fact. The surrounding hills, last seen laced with tough, green shrub, were now whitewashed. Aloft, it was solid, gray, and nasty. Before this scenario Cucho sleepily sat down, rifled through the CDs, and without irony chose an Ella Fitzgerald collection. Her perfect voice soon filled the cabin: "The sky IS blue...and high UH-bove..."

As we powered down Canal O'Brien with an unrolled staysail for a touch of balance, Lolo may have given a nanosecond's thought to careening off for Bahía Cook and into open water, but he sanely pointed us down the protected waterway. It was bloody nippy but at least the steady 30-knot westerly—gusts to 50 were forecast—was dead astern.

Swaddled in fleece and foul-weather gear, I was dazzled by the piercing salt air, the heavy flurries, and the corridor of frosted mountains through which we sailed. As we passed the first of five glaciers indented along Tierra del Fuego's south coast, Mauricio—who as a young navy officer had patrolled these waters forty years earlier—was also transfixed. "I love this place," he said. "I love the brutality of it."

We spent the night 60-odd miles down the track in a dramatic anchorage called Caletta Olla, with the pick set in 23 feet of water beside a slab-sided rock that rose, literally, into the clouds. A stern line was run ashore. It snowed hard again.

The next morning Beto and Juan, the younger Chileans and skilled sailors who ran boats for a living, rose early, bagged the torn main, and swapped it for the mizzen. A comparative scrap of sail, it was better than nothing. On deck, their seaboots left tracks in the snow.

By now, my concerns about German were few. He admittedly could take or leave the boat trip, and he didn't roam far from the saloon settee, from which he held court for hours on end. But there were no straight faces during his constant rants on the general state of affairs, which he found (wink, wink) utterly deplorable.

In fact, I was completely cured of my Santiago doubts. Hanging out with these old friends, some of whom hadn't seen each other in decades (but acted as if it were last week), was an honor. That they were all terrific seamen made it even better.

BEFORE getting under way I picked up my copy of Hal Roth's fine 1978 book *Two Against Cape Horn*, about his eventful Chilean cruise. At one stage therein, Roth seeks advice from a wise navy captain, Luis Mesias. The name was oddly familiar. I thumbed to my notebook's back page, where Mauricio had spelled out everyone's proper name for later reference, then looked up at our skipper, poring over charts. Lolo. Luis Mesias. One and the same.

The *gringo* named Roth stirred his memory. "Ah, yes," he said. "*Whisper*. Black hull. Pretty boat. Yes, I remember."

The day's plan was to follow Roth's previous wake along the Beagle Channel, then wind through the narrow Canal Murray, and emerge into the open waters of Bahía Nassau. Though Roth passed freely through the canal, more recently it's been closed by order of the Chilean navy; a small outpost stationed along its banks monitors traffic. It had just re-opened to Chilean-flagged vessels.

Lolo and Ronald had been in constant radio contact with naval officials, who keep a close eye on vessels transiting the region, since leaving Punta Arenas. Now we were instructed to bypass the canal entrance and call at the navy base in Puerto Williams, a 60-mile detour, for official clearance. To this decree the two men exchanged "Yeah, right" glances. Strings were quickly pulled and permission to enter the canal was granted.

Before doing so, we motorsailed past the Chile/Argentina border to the north, an invisible line of demarcation which no doubt was linked with the low-level paranoia. In 1928, the two nations averted war over the three islands that stand before the Beagle's eastern approach (Picton, Lennox, and Nueva) only after the pope intervened and ruled in favor of Chile. Today the countries are friendly, if wary, neighbors.

Just weeks earlier Mauricio sent me a note saying, "Not much wind this time of year, but wet." I reminded him of it as the ever-present westerly built to 30 knots, with heavy puffs into the 40s, as we reached down Bahía Nassau. But, like O.J. in the face of overwhelming evidence otherwise, he remained steadfast in his stance. "There is not," he insisted, as my ball cap nearly blew away. "I am convinced of it."

Our anchorage that evening in Bahía Allen Gardiner, on Isla Hoste's Peninsula Hardy, wasn't perfect, but with the barometer at 975 mb. and another gale forecast, we were safely parked before it really started hooting.

And blow it would, with sustained 50-knot winds after midnight.

In retrospect, our biggest mistake the next day was moving. We should've sat tight. But the breeze had moderated by morning so we set a course for Puerto Maxwell on the northeast side of Isla Hermites, a good staging area before the final run for the Horn.

We didn't get far. Once out of the bay, though still in the peninsula's lee, we watched the westerly again begin to fill, and fill. At the same time the anemometer settled at a steady 40 knots, the tackle for the self-tacking staysail exploded, and the sail began to flog mercilessly. Fire-drill time.

I ran up to overhaul the furling line while Juan tailed aft at the winch. We quickly had the instantly shredded sail furled, but with the sheet blown free it wasn't necessarily going to stay that way. Grabbing a short length of line, I again scampered forward to lash it tight.

With my back to the bow, I saw the whole foredeck start to slowly levitate. Unharnessed, I applied a bear hug to the furled sail and thought: *This isn't good*. Then, as if an elevator cable had parted, down we plunged. After an abrupt stop at the bottom of the trough, I got that cool, surfer-movie view of the big breaking curl. It was right over my head. Welcome to the green room, dude.

Someone's suggestion of bailing back towards the peninsula, with its selection of wide bays, seemed like an excellent idea. But we could only make good a violent three knots bucking directly into the brunt of the blow. When we anchored in Bahía Orange after a short eternity, as the crow flies we'd gained about ten miles.

Though onboard morale wasn't necessarily terrible, to some of the crew the enterprise was losing its luster. It was understandable; I'd been onboard less than a week, and most everyone else had been pushing hard for over a month.

Then again, we were only 60 miles from Cape Horn.

LOLO CAME up with a plan. We'd rise at 0200, radio the Chilean outpost at the Horn for a current-condition update, and if the coast was clear push ahead for a mid-morning rounding. At the appointed hour, after learning that the narrowest of weather windows had opened in our favor, we again set a course south.

Mauricio and I drew the first watch and it wasn't long before we were picking our way via radar through the most godforsaken string of spooky islands I'd ever seen. I half expected a giant winged reptile to swoop in and nab Mauricio. But as the day's first light softened the edges, in the distance we got our first glimpse of what had brought us here: Islas Hornos. Cape Horn.

At sunrise, with a blessed 15-knot northerly rippling the waters, we snapped portraits against the backdrop of the island's western flank. Shortly later, we were due south of the famous rock. We'd damn near run out of sails, but under our funky "mizzen main," we rounded the Horn. One can count on two hands the number of sailboats that have passed Cape Horn flying a Chilean flag. With champagne toasts, the proud *Chucao* crew saluted their addition to the list.

The rest happened fast: a dinghy ride ashore. Mutts yapping at my heels (Horn dogs?). A wobbly climb to the observation post. A three-year-old planted before a TV set. Cartoons on Cape Horn. Her young parents: a fresh-faced sailor in a sweater and tie and his pretty wife. A prayer in the tiny chapel. The striking steel monument of an albatross in flight. The lighthouse. A long look towards Antarctica that couldn't be beat. And, amazingly, another sailboat rounding Cape Horn.

Northbound again, Mauricio picked up my copy of Roth's book, and added up the collective years of our not-so-virgin crew. "Two against Cape Horn?" he asked. "We are 522 against Cape Horn!"

Under bright sunshine, we anchored in a perfect nook of a cove on the eastern side of Isla Wollaston. Before we tied up in Puerto Williams days later we still had one more pasting to endure, but at that moment life was as grand as could be. A wonderful bottle of Chilean red appeared, then another, then another still. Tending to a stupendous slab of beef on the aft grill, Cucho tilted his mustachioed snout towards the sky, a leathery old seal basking in the afternoon sun. "Who would believe this weather?" he asked no one in particular. "Here in the ass of the world."

A good friend of mine, Alvah Simon, an accomplished offshore sailor himself, once wrote that to truly be called a Cape Horner—to wear the golden earring symbolic of that passage— one must fight the good fight for weeks on end, and negotiate the milestone after a testing Southern Ocean voyage.

It's a view I largely subscribe to. Though I did round Cape Horn, my contributions to the effort were pretty meager. As far as the Horn is concerned, I have unfinished business. Still, I am considering the purchase of a golden stud in the shape of an asterisk.

But what about my shipmates? What about these fine men who realized their collective dream, who planned and schemed and left their comfortable homes and stations in life in quest of a good old-fashioned adventure under the flag of a country they love so dearly? Who's to say these fellows aren't genuine Cape Horners? Who's going to tell them their accomplishments are any less grand than Simon's or Knox-Johnston's or Moitessier's or any of the others?

Not this *gringo*.

*Herb McCormick*

**The striking statue of the silhouette of an albatross in flight greets the visitor who anchors off Cape Horn and ambles ashore.**

When you round Cape Horn, as legend has it, you earn the right to wear a golden earring in the lobe facing the famous rock (i.e., if you sail past from west to east, as we did on this voyage and as most modern sailors do, you can pierce the left ear). In 2010, as part of the Around the Americas expedition, we tackled the Horn from east to west. Theoretically, I can now wear earrings in both ears. Too bad I don't wear earrings.

*Gone to the Sea: Places*

*Part 3*

*Races*

Finishing a Sydney-Hobart Race was a major check-mark off my personal Bucket List. I've been fortunate to sail in a few Newport-Bermuda Races, but have never done a Fastnet, the third event in what I consider the Triple Crown of offshore ocean races. Anybody out there know of a ride?

# 19: Third Time Charmed

## THE ONE AND ONLY SYDNEY-HOBART

CRIKEY.

The simple expression, of course, was the all-purpose catchphrase employed by the "Crocodile Hunter" himself, the late Australian naturalist/huckster Steve Irwin, whose astonished, wide-eyed days on this Earthly sphere came to an abrupt conclusion in September of 2006 when the barb of one spooked stingray, incredibly, pierced his fragile heart. The truth is, most Aussies found Irwin to be a bore and a yahoo until his untimely demise, after which he became universally (and correctly) hailed as a goofy-but-loving husband and father, and a fierce champion of the great outdoors and all its creatures.

But that's not the "Crikey" I'm talking about.

What I was after was the sweet chocolate candy bar of the same name (an item I'm sure has Irwin spinning in his grave). I'd never actually tasted a Crikey bar but for the previous two hours, while driving the 35-foot sloop, *Morna*, southbound along the windswept Aussie isle of Tasmania before a 25-knot northwester, I'd obsessed over the confection's mouth-watering possibilities. Once relieved of the helm, I dove into the galley in search of a Crikey. I knew they were down there somewhere.

We were just over two-thirds down the 635-nautical mile track in the 63rd running of the famous Rolex Sydney-Hobart Yacht Race, and things, quite frankly, were going swimmingly. Our crew of six, including *Morna*'s skipper and owner, Greg Zyner, had enjoyed extremely favorable sailing conditions and, with the exception of one notable glitch, was sailing fast and well. Our unflappable navigator and tactician, Jim Nixon, a 13-time veteran of the Hobart Race who'd seen it all and then some, was calling a flawless race and consistently putting us in the most favorable breeze and current.

Nothing could go wrong, right?

Well, yes. We'd weathered one southerly blow earlier in the race, but it was relatively quick and, by Hobart Race standards, a piddling zephyr. Another was forecast later in the day but suddenly, in an instant, the wind shifted forward and we broached hard, sails flapping everywhere. A moment later, we broached again. Harder.

A yelp came from above and before I could strike caramel pay dirt I was on deck scrambling to help get the chute down, a jib up, and a reef in the main. It had all gone to blazes as I hunted for my snack.

Yeah. What the Crocodile Man said: "Crikey."


LET'S PUT it this way. I had a bit of history in the Tasman Sea, particularly when it came to sailing from Sydney to Hobart. I'd tried twice before, and failed miserably on each occasion. My grade, as it were, was incomplete.

The first time had been in 1986, en route to Fremantle to cover the America's Cup. I had a week to kill and made a bee-line to the Cruising Yacht Club of Australia (CYCA) on Sydney's Rushcutter's Bay in an attempt to land a ride for the annual Sydney-Hobart Race, which starts on Boxing Day—December 26th—each year. I was much too late to find a spot on a racing boat, but ended up aboard a big American ketch owned by a trust-fund heir on a world cruise who planned on accompanying the fleet to Hobart for the post-race party.

It was a voyage from hell.

Twelve hours into it, in the black of night, we were slammed by a so-called Southerly Buster, a fierce, cold gale that caught us largely by surprise and rendered many of the guests—airline and cruise-ship hostesses whose primary attributes involved bikinis and tanning oil—supine and miserable. The owner retreated to his cabin and his copious supply of weed, which would ultimately lead to costly, difficult engagements with Australian law-enforcement agencies. We limped into the fishing village of Eden on the southeast coast with a broken rudder, and the proverbial rats bolted the sinking ship, me first among them.

It was almost ten years later that I again fetched up in Eden, this time aboard a 60-foot converted ocean racer headed for Antarctica on a long-range expedition. After pounding into another awful December southerly for several days outbound from Sydney, I was put ashore to fly on to Hobart and secure fuel and provisions before everything shut down for the Christmas holidays. It took another week for my shipmates to catch up with me, and they were a mess when they did, having endured a severe spanking on the voyage across the Bass Strait to Tasmania. The voyage on to Antarctica across the wild Southern Ocean, they all later agreed, was a day in the park compared to the shocking trip from Sydney to Hobart.

My persistent failures, however, had quite the opposite effect than one might've expected, particularly after planning to spend a couple of months in Australia for the winter. They made me more determined than ever to see the voyage through successfully, and led me back to where I'd ultimately started: Scouring for a crew berth on the famous race to Hobart.

When I first laid eyes on the Australian-built Cavalier 35, *Morna*, on the CYCA docks, of one thing I was certain. There was no bloody way in the world I'd be getting aboard the rather squat, somewhat under-rigged cruiser/racer to sail to Hobart, or anywhere else for that matter. (The Cav 35 actually comes in a racing version with a taller rig and completely different deck and interior layout, but *Morna* was the conservative cruising model.) I was desperate, yes—at my urging, the Hobart Race press officer had sent my name out to the fleet and I'd had a couple of interesting offers, both contingent on some pre-race practice sails that I couldn't attend—but not quite that desperate.

But skipper Greg Zyner proved to be a passionate and persuasive sailor. I accepted his invitation for a day race on Sydney Harbor and met some of *Morna*'s Hobart crew, who were fine, veteran sailors. Then, on a funky afternoon with the promise of an advancing cold front, we sailed out past Sydney Heads and into the teeth of the freshening blow. And it quickly became apparent that *Morna* was a tough cookie equipped with a complete inventory of good sails, a boat that would handle whatever was tossed at her at least as well as I would, and probably better.

Besides, if it all hit the fan, I certainly knew how to get into Eden, a small snippet of information I chose not to share with my new shipmates.

OVERHEAD, a half-dozen helicopters whirled about. All around us, a spectator fleet numbering hundreds and hundreds of boats churned the blue waters. Ashore, on balconies, in parks, and atop the headlands, tens of thousands of picnicking "Sydneysiders" soaked in the glorious harbor view. The start of the Sydney-Hobart Race is a fabulous, breathtaking scene televised live across all of Australia, and the 2007 edition was launched on a sensational summer day with light breezes of 6-8 knots and barely a cloud in the sky.

Pudgy little *Morna* was smack-dab in the middle of it.

Along with skipper Zyner, navigator Nixon, and me, our six-man crew was rounded out by bowmen Alex Seja and Geoff Hickey, and trimmer and helmsman Dan McHolm. There were actually two separate starting lines cordoned off from the spectator craft, one for the Grand Prix race boats like the big 100-foot maxis *Wild Oats XI* and *ICAP Leopard* in quest of first-to-finish line honors and record-setting passages—a mark held by *Wild Oats* after a voyage of 1 day, 18 hours, 40 minutes—and the other for less ambitious steeds in the 35- to 50-foot range, like *Morna*. Overall, there were 84 boats on the respective lines, all intent on getting to Hobart as quickly and safely as possible.

They've been racing sailboats from Sydney to Hobart since 1945, when the 35-foot *Rani* topped a fleet of nine boats to win the inaugural race in a time of 6 days, 14 hours, 22 minutes. In 1994, on the event's 50th anniversary, a fleet of 371 vessels showed up for the contest, the largest ever. Many sailors find it to be an addictive experience and come back year after year; the 2007 race was Tasmanian legend Lou Abrahams' 45th Hobart. But it also has a storied reputation for angry, harsh conditions, a point underscored in the 1998 race when a "weather bomb" went off in the Bass Strait, sinking five boats and killing six competitors.

Our forecast, however, could hardly have been more favorable. After a light-air start, the wind was predicted to build steadily from the north to provide a nice spinnaker run for the opening stages. A southerly change was due about a day later and then the pattern would repeat itself: more northerlies, a second southerly, and finally north again near the finish. Most everyone agreed conditions weren't likely to produce a record run for the big boys, but it all sounded pretty civilized for the smaller boats like *Morna*.

It seemed too good to be true.  But, as predicted, the initial northerly filled in as advertised and after a hectic but solid start, *Morna* tacked out through the mighty Heads and into the open Tasman.  It wasn't long before we hoisted our .9 oz. asymmetric spinnaker and ran up the No. 4 jib, as well.

"It's all horsepower, mate, it's all working," said Nixon, a raffish, True Blue Aussie who looked like a cross between the actor Tom Selleck and Australian tennis legend John Newcombe.  "You get an extra tenth of a knot for a hundred hours, it all adds up."

We were trucking along making a good 8-10 knots through the water, aided by the southerly flowing coastal current that added another knot-and-a-half of speed over the ground.  The lovely day gave way to a beautiful night, with *Morna* sliding down the shoreline of New South Wales under a nearly full moon and the iconic Southern Cross.  It was blowing a good 25 knots and steering was a bit of a challenge, but *Morna* was hauling the mail and knocking off the miles, hitting speeds as high as 14.5 knots.

Back ashore in the early evening of the 26th, our wives and girlfriends were checking the event website to track the positions of the various boats, and when they scrolled down to see where *Morna* stood in the fleet on corrected time they were in for a surprise, one that we on the boat wouldn't hear about until later on, which was probably just as well.

That's because we were winning.

WE'LL NEVER know what our fate would ultimately have been if our .9 oz. workhorse of a chute hadn't burst into pieces later that first evening, but Nixon was probably prophetic when, after we cleaned up the debris and hoisted an older, tired re-placement, he said, "We'll rue losing that kite later on."

And by 0300 on the morning of the 27th, it was all academic anyway. For that's when the breeze swung into the south at a staunch 25 knots. We briefly ran up the No. 1 genoa, soon changed down to the No. 2 jib, and finally tucked a reef into the main. It was a brutal slog with the breeze stacking up short, steep waves against the opposing current, but we were at least making tracks at a good eight knots.

"This is where you make some ground, right here, in this horrible seaway," said Nixon. "If you keep your foot on the pedal."

At 0800 we learned at the first official position report that order had been restored to the universe (we were no longer the overall leader), but that we still held a second in our 12-boat division, in close proximity to several of the other smallest boats in the race: a pair of S&S designs, the 34-foot *Huckleberry* and the 36-foot *Stormy Petrel*; the 33-foot Farr 1020, *Zephyr*; and the 33-foot Doug Peterson-designed *Impeccable*, owned and skippered by the race's oldest competitor ever, 85-year-old Johnny Walker.

Walker was a long-time sailing mate of our navigator, Nixon, who'd decided to enter the 2007 race at the last minute, which is why Nixon had signed on with *Morna*. Originally from Eastern Europe, Walker was a concentration camp survivor who later immigrated to Australia and changed his name in honor of his favorite beverage. I sensed that Nixon didn't care that much where we finished, with one exception.

"As long as we beat *Impeccable*," he said, over and over again.

The Hobart Race can basically be broken down into three separate sections: the first third, from Sydney to the Bass Strait, a.k.a. "the Paddock"; the middle section, across the Strait itself;

and the final stretch, down the coast of Tasmania, and then up the Derwent River to the finish line off Hobart. *Morna* knocked off the first bit in just over 24 hours.

Ever since that tragic 1998 race, before setting out across the Paddock, each skipper must hail the race committee via SSB and make a formal declaration that he's carrying forth. Zyner's call was a highlight of my sailing career. I'd finally made it past Eden, and into the Bass Strait.

Not that it had been all that easy, particularly the last part, when we had to tack around Cape Howe at the southeast flank of the continent, shortly after which the breeze shut down completely. We were more or less becalmed for a good six hours before the northerly reappeared and we once again got a spinnaker up in the very early hours of the 28th.

There were dolphins in the bow wave, albatross wheeling overhead. The sun was shining brightly, and we were sailing in shorts and T-shirts. "Now this," said Nixon, "is the way to cross the Bass Strait." He'd later say that of his 13 Hobart Race crossings, the 2007 run was by far the easiest.

But we still had to pay the piper one more time.

THE "CRIKEY" moment came as we hammered our way down the coast of Tasmania on the final third of the voyage. The breeze actually swung aft again, briefly, before well and truly settling into the south for our last full night at sea. It was a wretched one.

We were in the Roaring Forties, the wind was a brisk 25 knots with higher gusts, the seas were gray and lumpy. It was a black night, zero stars, an invisible horizon. With no frame of reference, driving was a nightmare. Worse, I had six layers of clothes on—T-shirt, long-sleeve T-shirt, crew polo, vest, fleece jacket and pants, foul-weather gear—and remained frigid. At one point, sitting on the rail, I was struck by a distinct, foul odor. I looked down and saw a big flying fish sloshing in a puddle by my butt. Once off-watch, I didn't sleep a wink; I was too damn cold.

"Welcome to the real Hobart Race," said Nixon. "It's hard to believe some guys do three or four. Or forty."

Amen, brother.

But the fresh dawn was clear and bright, and before long, it was still as well. And when the new breeze did arrive, in mid-morning, it was a final, blessed northerly. Back up went the kite and good old *Morna* was again a going concern.

It turned out to be a magical day of sailing, one of the best of my life. Boats were converging on Hobart from Sydney and from a race that started in Melbourne, too. Colorful spinnakers dotted the horizon. The dramatic backdrop of bold Tasman Island was mesmerizing, as were the stark rock formations known as the Lanterns and the Organ Pipes, which have greeted thousands of Hobart racers over the years.

We carried the chute into Storm Bay and nearly right up to the small island called the Iron Pot at the mouth of the Derwent River. The last eleven miles passed quickly as we held a tight, fast, close reach to the finish line off the modest city of Hobart, which we crossed just before sundown in the last gasp of the dying breeze after a passage of 4 days, 7 hours, good enough for second in Class E, behind the well-sailed Farr design, *Zephyr*. Skipper Zyner, also finishing his first Hobart Race, was a happy man, and rightly so. *Morna* didn't surf, as we'd constantly reminded ourselves, but she was impeccably prepared and gave us everything we'd asked of her.

The end of the Hobart Race was as cool as the beginning. The big boats like *Wild Oats*, which was first to finish after a

one-day, twenty-one-hour trip, and the overall winner on corrected time, the lone U.S. entry in the event, Roger Sturgeon's
spanking new 65-footer, *Rosebud*, had obviously been there
awhile. Their decks were clear and orderly, and there wasn't a
sailor in sight.

But the scene was quite different in the protected basin of
Constitution Dock, which we entered through a swing bridge
to a round of applause from the tourists lining the wharf who'd
turned up for the party. A bunch of other small boats like ours
were in the process of arriving and as we tied up someone tossed
a case of cold beer aboard and it wasn't long before we were enmeshed in the festivities.

We did indeed beat Nixon's good pals on *Impeccable*, which
finished shortly after us, and many hours, and beers, later, I
found myself down below in the cramped quarters of Johnny
Walker's boat reliving the events of the past few days.

Walker's personal story was a great one. He'd never sailed
until well into middle age, but once he started, he stacked up
several lifetimes of voyaging, including 23 Hobart races, mostly
aboard his beloved little 33-footer. The flash yachts like *Wild
Oats* and *Rosebud* got all the headlines, and deservedly so, but
at the back of the fleet we'd enjoyed a race within the race with
our own little pack of modest boats, and I wouldn't have wanted
it any other way. The competition was fun, but it was the camaraderie that made it such a fantastic experience, a point that
Walker drove home when he briefly mentioned his three years of
captivity in World War II.

"It's funny, but what I remember the most is the laughter," he
said. "You wouldn't think that, but it's true. It's the same with this
race. Sometimes it's horrible. But that's not what you remember.
You remember the good parts. You remember the good people."

I stumbled back to *Morna* not long after, in the middle of the night after a trip I'll never, ever forget. I had one more brief, unrequited search for that elusive Crikey bar, but the still, warm berth was more alluring. Like the race itself, the sleep that followed was deep and wonderful.

DanielForster.com

**The 35-foot sloop *Morna*—one of the smallest yachts in the fleet—rolls south under spinnaker at the outset of the 2007 Sydney-Hobart Race.**

Bobby Grieser

Mark Schrader's Cal 40, *Dancing Bear*, in the
early stages of the 100th running of the Transpac from Los Angeles to Honolulu.

It doesn't get much better than racing with old friends
Mark Schrader and Dave Logan, my shipmates on this
edition of the Transpac as well as our 27,000-mile circumnavigation of North and South America in 2009-
10. (www.aroundtheamericas.org)

# 20: Loaded for Bear

## THE 100TH TRANSPAC, ABOARD A CAL 40

REGAINING CONSCIOUSNESS, even if you've only lost it for a second or two, is a strange experience. You need to sort things out slowly, one step at a time, maybe try to work the whole sequence backwards to get a real grasp on the matter.

Let's give it a shot.

First off, that was my old friend Mark Schrader with his hand on my shoulder, asking if I was okay. Yup, a little hazy but just fine.

The scratches on my cheek and nose were a sure sign I'd done a face plant on the foredeck—where I was now slowly regaining my bearings—an observation reinforced by the salty taste on my lips from lapping up the nonskid. That lump on my head? No doubt about it, that's where the spinnaker pole had met my noggin. And just why had I been standing under the pole? Oh yeah, the massive spinnaker wrap around the headstay told that story. I was futilely trying to undo it when the rope clutch bearing the line that controlled the pole's topping lift was suddenly, fully, mistakenly released.

Crack. Ouch. Good golly: Look at all the pretty stars.

The episode had unfolded on Mark's Cal 40, *Dancing Bear*, the vessel I'd stepped aboard nine days earlier to begin the 100th edition of the venerable Transpac ocean race from California to Hawaii. So there we were, two-thirds of the way to Honolulu on a beautiful, windy morning with *Dancing Bear*, having finally found a groove, suddenly wallowing in a following sea with her twisted spinnaker wound tighter than ever. It was all coming back, all right, and it wasn't pretty.

But I'm getting way ahead of the story.

IN CELEBRATION of the class's 40th anniversary of Transpac participation, 14 Cal 40s set out on July 11, 2005, to begin the 2,225-mile passage to the islands. Many in the fleet reckoned they were racing for second. That's because the clear favorite was a two-time Rolex Yachtswoman of the Year, Sally Lindsay Honey, and her all-woman crew on *Illusion*. With her husband, Stan—one of the best offshore racing navigators of this or any other era—Sally had helped guide *Illusion* to the Cal 40 winner's circle in the 2003 Transpac. For this running, Stan had returned to his familiar spot at the nav station on *Pyewacket*—an 86-foot rocketship owned by movie mogul Roy Disney, sailing his final Transpac—but *Illusion* was a fast, proven entity, and few, if any, had any doubt that Sally and her talented crew would skillfully negotiate the Pacific High and tap the boat for every last iota of speed.

Sprinkled through the rest of the Cal 40 class were several other veteran boats and crews from the 2003 field, including *California Girl*, *Ralphie*, *Seafire*, and *Willow Wind*. Then there was a whole other group of boats that had been refit or overhauled specifically for the 2005 event. Among those was a very unusual Cal 40—complete with its own stuffed teddy-bear mascot—called *Dancing Bear*.

Fresh from a refit on a horse farm north of Seattle, *DB* had been brought back to racing trim by veteran solo sailor Mark Schrader and his cousin, Quinn Olson. Unlike all the other Cal 40s lining the pre-race docks at Long Beach's Rainbow Harbor, *DB* sported nary a splinter of teak on her deck and coamings, and that was just the very beginning of how she differed from her sister ships. To say she garnered a fair bit of attention from the competing crews would be putting it mildly.

Truth be told, *DB*'s crew could be characterized as "different" as well. Only Mark—a two-time solo circumnavigator, the second during the 1986-87 BOC Challenge—and Quinn had any real offshore Cal 40 experience, and theirs had come in the rushed delivery from Seattle to Long Beach for the start. Dave Logan, a craftsman who'd fashioned wholesale sections of *DB*'s new interior layout, was an excellent, experienced racing sailor, but he was a Cal 40 rookie. The same could be said for the remainder of the crew, multihull veteran Peter Hogg—who holds the singlehanded Transpacific record from Japan to San Francisco—and me.

On a related note, was I concerned how Mark and Peter, two renowned, hardscrabble solo sailors, would handle the dynamics of a fully crewed effort? Well, um, yes.

But I was pleasantly surprised and even encouraged by our start, which took place off the Palos Verdes Peninsula in a light, six- to eight-knot southwesterly. Technically, it wasn't perfect, but thanks largely to Dave's expert touch on the helm, we absolutely rolled by the Hawaii-based *Seafire* and, for the first few hours, at least, held our own with the fearsome *Illusion*.

We were going just fine, it seemed, given the light air we had to work with. But six short hours into it, we fell into an absolutely windless hole, and the boatspeed instruments soon registered every racing sailor's most dreaded trifecta: 0.00.

The first night was ugly. There wasn't much breeze, but at least it was cold, damp, and foggy. At times I'd look up from the tiller to see the masthead fly spinning around endlessly like some maniacal Wheel of Fortune. The only real consolation was the sea life we'd seen—pods of leaping dolphins, seals, sea lions—which was abundant. And in the dead of night we were treated to the remarkable vision of schools of fish, thousands upon thousands of them, clearly visible in the phosphorescence of our wake: rush hour in the blue Pacific.

At the 0800 morning report we received the brutal news that we'd made some 33 miles in the 21 hours since our start. Furthermore, the forecast told us the murky "marine layer" under which we labored (on the I-405 Freeway, this might also be called "smog") wouldn't be going anywhere for the conceivable future.

On we pushed, relatively speaking. In a four- to six-knot headwind, with our speed topping off at some 4.5 knots, we crawled past the Channel Islands of Santa Catalina and Santa Barbara. The latter was close enough to swim ashore, and the thought briefly crossed my mind. By the time we reached San Nicolas that evening, the sky had merged with the sea and visibility was nonexistent. We couldn't see St. Nick, but we definitely could smell it and hear it; alive with honking seals, it was noisy, rank, and redolent. The next island we'd encounter, of course, would be much more fragrant and inviting. But that would be Hawaiian, and it was a long way away.

WHEN ONE signs on to do a Transpac race, the operative vision is fluffy white cumulous clouds, blue following seas flecked with pleasing whitecaps, and billowing spinnakers harnessing reliable trade winds for mile after downwind mile. This vision, I was learning the hard way, is pure fiction.

Instead of crossing the ridge of high pressure, easing sheets, and hoisting chutes, 48 hours into the race, with the breeze filled in cold and hard from the north, we found ourselves pounding to weather with a reef in the main and a blade jib. Yes, we were moving, at times up to eight knots, but in the confused seaway, the motion was plain awful and I'd been reduced to munching on ginger snaps chased by occasional swigs of water. Down below, the saloon looked like a train wreck with all the detritus of modern ocean racing—sails, boots, harnesses, jackets—scattered hither and yon. Throw in the occasional prone crewman, and the picture was complete.

It'd take a good 10 minutes to struggle into foul-weather gear, and at one point, while changing watch, Dave looked up at me as he tried his best to pull his pants on and said, "Three thousand years of civilization, and it's come to this."

To which I could only reply, "Some would say we really haven't made much progress."

But we were moving, knocking off 183 nautical miles on our third full day at sea and holding seventh position among the Cal 40s, with a handful of boats within nine miles on the distance-to-finish column of the race standings (though *Illusion* and *Ralphie*, to the south, seemed to be pulling ahead, perhaps with more favorable breeze). It was still a close race, and we were right in the hunt.

That was the good news. The bad came from the forecasters, who gloomily predicted that "the 100 percent marine cloud cover" would persist for, probably, the next *thousand miles* or so. Except for one or two extremely brief snatches, we'd yet to see the sun or the moon, never mind the stars, and it sounded like a good long while before we would. And never mind the trades; it was impossible to guess when they'd arrive.

Navigator Peter, a born-and-bred New Zealander, stated the obvious in his best Kiwi twang: "It seems we've not yet completed our entry procedures to the trade winds portion of our voyage."

**THE 100TH TRANSPAC, ABOARD A CAL-40**

Mark was less poetic, but more pragmatic:  "I'm wondering if I can get a refund on these spinnakers?"

Just around midnight on our fourth night at sea we almost literally ran into a bit of trouble in the form of a gigantic, stationary fish-processing ship that was lit up like Fenway Park on a Friday summer's eve.  After our repeated VHF hails went unanswered, we decided to reach off and cross its bow, which is just about the time some joker decided to ease the beast forward.  Realizing it had some way on, I came back up on the breeze and sailed down its considerable length before skirting past its transom unscathed.  There's nothing like a little adrenaline rush to spice up the routine.

By late afternoon the next day, July 15, we had a tactical decision to make.  We'd eked our way up to a tie for fifth on the distance-to-finish column, but the downloaded weather files showed an anomaly—what appeared to be a strange, isolated low-pressure cell—smack-dab in the southern rim of the Pacific High (which was already stationed a bit farther south than usual).  From the morning fleet update on the SSB, we knew *Illusion*, holding second, was dipping farther south and that class-leader *Ralphie* was already down there.

Our options:  Follow *Illusion* south.  But she'd be difficult, if not impossible, to pass using that strategy.  Or we could hold course with the majority of the fleet on a more northerly heading closer to the rhumb line.  It was the shortest distance to the finish.  If the info was correct, we ran the risk of encountering squirrelly winds or no wind.  But if it was wrong, we could be golden.  Finally, we could split the difference.  Dive south a bit to skirt the disturbance—but not as far as *Illusion*—and try to execute an end run around her.

We chose Door Number Three.

UNBELIEVEABLY, we'd yet to hoist a spinnaker. That miserable fact was finally corrected at 0300 on the morning of the 16th when the breeze veered sufficiently aft and built to around 20 knots, and we set the 1.5-oz. yellow-and-black kite Mark called the "bumblebee." At last, we got to see what the fuss over designer Bill Lapworth's 40-year-old creation was all about. No doubt about it, chugging along at up to 10 or 11 knots, *DB* was an absolute joy to steer. If and when the gusts came, or the helmsman steered a bit too high, there was no drama whatsoever. A quick twitch of the tiller was all it took for the big, deep, forgiving rudder to take command and carve the boat back on its proper heading. And she was a dry boat, too, even when the fur started to fly. Generations of sailors had experienced the same thrill we were now happily enjoying. Clearly, the Cal 40 had stood the test of time.

But the good times weren't meant to roll.

At the 0800 position report, we were chagrined to learn we'd dropped back to eighth, but not particularly surprised, given our course change the day before. Peter allowed that we might've "gone over the ridge" of high pressure the evening before, but I wasn't quite sure. We'd yet to shirk the murk, and the celestial bodies we so longed to see were still invisible markers from some other time and place. By late in the day the wind had eased well off, and by evening it threatened to disappear altogether. All through the night we chased and chased it, trying our best to keep the spinnaker full and the boat beneath it. It was maddening work.

Such was the drill for the next several days.

More than once, I was reminded of the strange Bill Murray movie *Groundhog Day*, in which the protagonist, a Pennsylvania weatherman, is doomed to live the same day over and over again. Life on *DB* became an endless succession of driving and sleeping in up-and-down breeze, always under a leaden sky, with two daily milestones to break up the routine: suppertime, which was always a treat—as Mark concocted one fantastic meal after another—and the 0800 position report, which was nowhere near as rewarding.

Morning after morning, we'd await the news that our mighty efforts had propelled us forth in the standings, and morning after morning we'd learn we were snatching defeat from the jaws of victory. At one point, we'd dropped all the way to 11th, then in small steps we worked our way back to ninth. The one consolation was that *Illusion*, too, was slipping, bottoming out at eighth.

*DB*'s mascot is a fluffy little teddy bear, which lived on deck in good weather and bad, and which Mark took to rearranging from the mast to the cockpit to the stern pulpit, perhaps in hopes of changing our overall luck. The bear, however, wore a perpetual scowl on its stuffed little mug, and at 0800 every morning during this *Groundhog Day* stretch of the race, Mark's dark countenance very much resembled the teddy's. But you know what they say about people and their pets.

Were our tactics paying off? It didn't seem so. But Peter remained optimistic. Stuck in the back half of the class on another *Groundhog Day*, he put forth this analysis: "We've chosen a strategy that may yet provide us with an opportunity of success. Whether that opportunity arises within the time frame afforded us on the race course remains to be seen."

That's also how you say "bullshit" in Kiwi.

IT TOOK us the better part of nine days to finally get a taste of the reliable northeast trades we'd lusted after for so long. The first inkling came around dusk on the 18ᵗʰ, when the fitful breeze we'd be wrestling with all day started to build into the mid-teens. As darkness fell, we changed spinnakers from the light, half-ounce kite we'd been flying for a couple of days to our newest, fastest 1.5-oz. chute, which held its shape better in stronger breeze and sloppy seas.

Then, a miraculous thing happened. The glorious orb of a nearly full moon made its first real appearance of the voyage. It cast a glow on the waters like a giant spotlight, and the seas began to sparkle.

A brief squall left us truly spinning in circles, but even this hiccup was welcome, for localized squalls are yet further proof of the trades. Once this passed, the skies began to break; thank the heavens, the stars were still up there. By 0400 on the 19ᵗʰ, about the time we broke the thousand-mile-to-go barrier, Mark was steering *DB* straight down a wet, silvery avenue cast by the reflection of that bountiful moon making its way around to the west: the Highway to Hawaii. His watch ended, but he wasn't going anywhere—not on this night. He just wanted to steer and steer.

Dawn broke, and with it came the very first sunrise of the voyage. Things briefly got murky, but by early afternoon, the sky was a deep blue and so was the sea. In the receding distance, the brutal "marine layer" lurked ominously in the rear-view mirror. But that was the past, not the future. Overhead there wasn't a cloud in the sky, and Mark took the opportunity to take a sextant shot of the sun, a requirement of all Transpac crews. It was the very first chance he'd had since we'd started.

For the next couple of days the sailing was fantastic, and while we didn't make much ground on the fleet, with a few hundred miles to go we were still within striking distance of a handful of boats. *Ralphie*, the southernmost boat in the fleet, seemed destined to record a wire-to-wire victory. *Illusion*, after a mid-race slump, was back on pace and charging toward second. But on the distance-to-finish scale, we were within 30 miles or so of no fewer than five boats; with a bit of luck, it was conceivable that we could make the leap from ninth to fourth, or better, before all was said and done.

That's when it all went haywire.

Just before noon on the 21$^{st}$, we suffered a massive wrap of our best 1.5 oz. kite and, in the comedy of errors that followed while attempting to sort it out, I was laid low by the spinnaker pole in the incident described at the outset of this story. (Note to self: When working on the foredeck with a spinnaker flying, make sure your skull is on the opposite side of the headstay from the pole.) Once I took a deep breath or two, I was fine. The same couldn't be said of the kite, which we tore badly while finally wrestling it down. Our workhorse sail for the crucial last stretch was out of commission.

Then, not an hour later, with the second-string bumblebee kite up and flying, we managed a second mighty wrap—one that wasn't sorted out until we hoisted Mark aloft to release the halyard. But by the time we'd completed that task, from the start of the snafu to its conclusion, when we rehoisted the kite—we'd somehow avoided shredding this one—we'd lost nearly three hours, which translated into maybe 30 miles.

And that, as they say, was that.

THE LINE honors winner of the 2005 Transpac was the 86-foot *Morning Glory*, which set a new elapsed-time race record of 6 days, 16 hours. On the other hand, the winning Cal 40, *Ralphie*, having sailed the southernmost course in the class, finished after a passage of roughly 13½ days. It was a solid victory; *Illusion*, in second, was another 11 hours in arrears.

However, the difference between second and ninth, where we wound up, was only about seven hours, so the racing was incredibly close. In hindsight, could I see where we might've saved a few? Well, our spinnaker problems alone cost us a handful. We should've cracked off farther south, where *Ralphie* and *Illusion* demonstrated there was more breeze; there's another couple. And we could've been more aggressive jibing on the many 10- or 15-degree shifts. So the answer is: Absolutely.

A couple of weeks after the finish, I was swapping emails with an old friend, veteran Southern California racer Tom Leweck, complaining about the lame conditions we encountered and the wimpy trades. Tom laughed and replied, "It's always like that!"

A few days later, I received a membership card from Tom for a group he's jokingly formed called Transpac Anonymous. A 24-hour hotline number was on the bottom of the card, which stated: "A nonprofit organization designed to protect yachtsmen from unscrupulous boat owners who make promises about sunny July sailboat rides to Hawaii. Call the HOTLINE before making any commitments so we can talk it through."

I get it. My only problem is, I can't stop thinking about the race's last few hours.

The final stretch down the Molokai Channel was quite simply the best afternoon of sailing I'd ever experienced. We jibed for the finish line off Diamond Head about 20 miles out in 30 knots of breeze and held on for dear life. The sun was searing, the wind was howling, and the deep blue Pacific was all the more glorious against the amazing backdrop of the green volcanic isles. After all the days of zephyrs and gloom, it was practically sensory overload.

I was nearly thrown off the tiller once, twice, three times, as I tried to pinch up a bit to lay the finish line and a big puff coursed down the channel and threatened to lay us over. But *DB* was game for anything, and always managed to shake it off and stay on her feet. God, I love a boat that's better than I am.

Every third or fourth following roller was ripe for surfing, and once the boat was aligned with the wave, the helm would go real light and we'd just start flying, touching 12 knots, 13, 14. It was wild, wild, wild. I didn't want it to end. But of course it would.

After two hours of this, drenched in sweat, I handed the tiller over to Mark, and he drove us past the finish buoy in lovely late-afternoon light.

So now I maybe know why Tom's hotline number is so infrequently called. Mark's already made some noises about taking another swing at the Transpac aboard *Dancing Bear*. If he's there, so am I.

# 21: Slidin' to the Island

## RIDING THE ELUSIVE PACIFIC CUP TRADEWINDS

THE FIRST day was the wildest, the weirdest, the most un-expected. Well, of course, not counting the last one, but we'll get to that later. Point is, when I signed on with the crew of the 65-foot, Bob Perry-designed sloop *Icon* to sail the 2004 West Marine Pacific Cup from San Francisco to Hawaii, I wasn't sure what I was getting into. Sure, I harbored the usual Sailor Boy Island Fantasies, of deep bluewater and billowing spinnakers, of flowered leis and tall mai tais. And all those visions did, in fact, come true. So it's safe to say that my dreams were well founded. It was, as usual, reality that threw me.

Take, for instance, that cool, fresh, 25-knot southwesterly pumping across the starting line just off the St. Francis Yacht Club on that July 2nd morning. It felt much more real than the forecast (but AWOL) 6-9 knot breeze that was overruled with gusty authority. "So, is this what 6 to 9 feels like on the East Coast?" asked my Canadian watchmate Kevin McMeel, one of the regulars on *Icon*'s mostly Seattle-based crew. "The air's a bit denser out here, eh?"

Perhaps the air was dense, but I wasn't, and the weather had nabbed my full attention. But so too had our competition. The Pacific Cup employs a staggered start over five days, with the smaller boats and cruisers setting out early and the bigger vessels, including *Icon*, bringing up the rear. That way, in theory, everyone fetches up at the finish off Oahu's Kaneohe Yacht Club at roughly the same time. Our four-boat Division F—the last to begin, with the rest of the 49-boat fleet already under way—was the fleet's smallest in number but included another Seattle entry, *Braveheart*, a flat-out Transpac 52 racer, and a brand-new 80-foot maxi from Long Beach, *Magnitude 80*. They looked formidable indeed.

That is, until compared with the remaining vessel in our foursome, the otherworldly, 140-foot *Mari-Cha IV*, owned by Duty Free magnate Robert Miller, whose sole interest in our little boat race was stomping the bejesus out of the 6-day, 14-hour course record for the 2,070-mile passage. Bent to their coffee-grinders with arms flailing, *M-C IV*'s small army of paid maritime mercenaries from France and New Zealand hoisted the main and mizzen in unison just minutes before the start, then buzzed our transom on a screaming reach at a good 20-knot clip. Aboard *Icon*, eyebrows skied and jaws dropped.

But not for long, for we had our own voyage to get on with. Skipper Jim Roser nailed the start and three tacks later the Golden Gate Bridge was overhead and the vast Pacific Ocean all before us. Not much later the tall rigs of *Magnitude 80* and *M-C IV* were little more than angled slits on the horizon, and then one was gone, followed by the other. We'd wondered all week how long we'd have *Mari-Cha* in our sights. It'd been a great two hours.

Our own little match race with *Braveheart* came to a close when we changed headsails from our number three jib to a blast reacher and footed off to the south, leaving our closest competition to their own devices on a more northerly heading. We were yet to realize the error of our way.

At dusk, we cruised out from under the blue skies above and into a dense, gray murk. There were gusts to 28 knots. We tucked the first reef in the main. For some, dinner was a two-part affair: Down, then back up. Chris Roberts, our wiry bow-man, took the helm and recorded a top speed of 18.3 knots, but mostly we averaged between 12 and 15. From the windward of her twin wheels, *Icon* was a blast to drive. We all took our turns. The full moon made only intermittent appearances, but cast a hazy, welcome glow to the proceedings. That said, the first night at sea was eerie, tiring, damp, and long. Tradewinds? Spinnakers? Not so fast, pal.

Morning broke. We saw a whale. And 24 hours into it, navigator Bruce Hedrick—my old buddy from a crazy race we'd contested in Alaska many years before, my link to the *Icon* team—came up on deck with the seemingly good news that we'd already knocked off 303 miles.

But he wasn't smiling.

NO, WE WEREN'T having many yucks yet. So for owner Dick Robbins, the voyage thus far was fatally flawed. Having a good time sailing had always been a clear priority for Dick, first aboard his old Maple Leaf 48, *Sea Bear*, and certainly with his next boat, the S&S-designed, 57-foot *Charisma*. Of course he wanted to win, but he also wanted everyone aboard to thoroughly enjoy the experience. It was the reason he'd decided on a light, fast, striking sled like *Icon* in the first place.

A mechanical engineer by trade, for some four decades Dick had been the driving force behind The Robbins Company, a pioneering firm in tunnel-boring technology whose latest major achievement was the boring of the English Channel "chunnel." He inhabited a high-tech world and was also an adventurous sailor, bush pilot, and survivor, having walked away from a commercial airline crash in Africa that took scores of lives. Little wonder that when he ultimately commissioned his own custom racer/cruiser, it had to be bold, lively, and cutting edge.

In Jim Roser, the professional skipper and competitive racing sailor who'd overseen a major refit with *Charisma* and then helped Dick cruise and campaign the boat throughout the Pacific Northwest and on offshore races like the Vic-Maui (from Victoria, British Columbia, to Hawaii), he had a very willing co-conspirator. But the central member of the design team, naval architect Bob Perry, at first glance might not have been as obvious a choice for the project. Bob had certainly made his mark with such seminal modern cruising designs as the Valiant 40, but he was equally renowned for heavier, full-displacement, Taiwan-built boats like the Baba 30 and many others. And *Icon*, most assuredly, was not your daddy's Baba 30.

But Dick, like Bob, resides in Washington State, and he was a long-time admirer of the Seattle-based designer's work. A collaborative effort to bring the notion of *Icon* to ocean-sailing fruition was soon under way. The boat they envisioned had to be nimble and quick, but strong—"bulletproof" was the operative word—and easily cruised by two couples. It took a full year of weekly visits to Bob's office before the design team had what it was searching for.

For reasons of cost and quality, *Icon* was built in New Zealand at Marten Marine of high-modulus, pre-preg carbon fiber. And *everything* was carbon: the hull, deck, interior, and Southern Spar rig. A retractable keel was specified to provide upwind grunt on the race course and shallow draft when cruising. Wholesale portions of the accommodation plan and other hardware—some 4,000 pounds worth—were fitted so they could be readily removed to transfer the boat from cruising to racing mode. And in every nook and cranny, the attention paid to style and detail was impressive.

Jim Roser once said the seed that became *Icon* had been planted during a Vic-Maui Race aboard *Charisma*: "We buried the bow quite successfully a couple of times, and Dick learned what it's like to not surf. We came to the conclusion that it'd be real cool to have a surfing boat, one that could go destination racing and then cruise wherever you wound up."

It proved to be a doable plan, and since her launch in 2001 *Icon* had already finished a Sydney-Hobart Race, a Transpac, and a Vic-Maui, and cruised the coastlines of New Zealand, Australia, and Alaska. Now, pounding to weather off the coast of California in the Pacific Cup, we all wanted a taste of what had been the boat's genesis and inspiration. We were ready for a little surfin', too. But it was going to take a little patience.

OUR INITIAL mistake had been diving south too early, for it soon became apparent that, weather-wise, the 2004 edition wasn't going to be a "typical" Pacific Cup. But we'd dealt ourselves this hand of cards, and now it was time to play them.

The one thing we had going for us was a versatile, talented, and motivated nine-person crew, which skipper Roser divided into two watches designated as the Sharks and the Jets. The latter was comprised of the captain himself; his wife, Robin (not only an excellent driver, but one of the great sea cooks of our time); owner Robbins; navigator Hedrick, who'd been this way many times before; and bosun Joe Greiser, whose constant attention to the serious, never-ending matter of chafed spinnaker halyards and other potential breakdowns was unsung and unwavering.

We Sharks were led by watch captain McMeel, with an endless supply of raucous sea stories from his 80,000 miles of offshore voyaging that kept us entertained through many a long evening's trick; bowman Roberts, a transplanted Bostonian whose love of sailing was pure and infectious; and young sail-maker Karl Funk, a late addition to the team who brought an inshore racer's unrelenting focus to the long-haul enterprise. As the resident cruiser in this mix of vastly experienced racing sailors, my main goal was to avoid mucking things up. At times, I enjoyed mild success. But not always.

For I was soon to learn that driving a rocket like *Icon* at double-digit speeds on a black night in shifty breeze under a big kite can be a mighty challenge. And I was in for yet another surprise. Especially in the wee hours, the Pacific trades were anything but a flick-the-switch phenomenon of steady, pumping, reliable pressure. They were fluky, fluctuating, and maddeningly elusive, with instant, radical shifts of 20 through 50 degrees, and more. At least when I was at the bloody helm.

When the wind clocked to the north just before dusk on our second day under way, we'd hoisted a reaching spinnaker, hung a slight right, and had begun making tracks directly towards the islands. With that, the official rivalry between the Sharks and the Jets was on. Bruce filed the following Fourth of July dispatch to *Icon*'s shoreside followers the next day: "The slow watch (the Sharks) set a new record for round-ups early on until skipper Jimmy Jet went on deck to teach them how to sail."

It was a bit more than I could take, and when Bruce was sleeping at the next watch change, I issued my own email rebuttal: "Let's just say there are two ways of steering to Hawaii FAST under spinnaker. One is 'low and slow' (Jets style), one is high and quick. Yes, at times, when chances are being taken, when miles are being made, the occasional spin-out does occur. When you're trying to make up for the off-watch, there's no other option. So now, while the Jets are cooled, it's time once again for the Sharks to get *Icon* up to speed. Fins up! *Icon* clear." That was my story and I was sticking by it. I could've signed it, "Easily Amused." But in fact, *Icon* was a very happy ship, and the sailing was getting better by the day.

We peeled spinnakers from the reaching kite to the big A2 masthead asymmetric, a sail we'd carry for several days and well over a thousand miles without ever considering a change. Though the boats to the north of us were pulling steadily away, we continued to knock off daily runs in the 250-mile range. There were small changes from the daily routine: one afternoon we backed down the boat to clear a fishing net from the keel, another we were hailed via VHF by a lonely solo sailor who'd lost her SSB and wanted her friends to know she was okay. But mostly we worked together to sail *Icon* as fast as we could, for she was the center of our shared universe.

And by coincidence, Chris, Joe, and I celebrated birthdays within a day of one another, and Robin's great meals made them very special occasions. Chris took to the keyboard to post this birthday greeting: "Magical moments aren't hard to come by on this amazing body of water. Karl saw his first flying fish and then his second, which soared a solid 75 feet before plunging into a wave. The ocean makes a sweet, harmonious hum as it whizzes past the hull. The clouds—black, gray, white, purple—all billow and swirl with sunbursts and blue skies busting through. And speaking of blue, the color of the ocean is amazing. It's everything you can imagine in the word 'aqua' and then some.

"We all collaborate and work hard at finessing the sails to the wind, which in turns caresses us, teases us, and punishes us, but always keeps us guessing, optimistic, and busy. Meanwhile, *Icon* delivers us safely through this magical nature."

It was pretty hard to think of a better present.

"DRIVE IT like it's stolen!" were Jim's parting words of advice as he disappeared down the companionway at the change of yet another watch. And we did as instructed, tweaking and trimming for all we were worth. As we closed to within a couple hundred miles of the islands, our fate was sealed: *Mari Cha IV* had already finished in foregone conclusion, posting a new Pacific Cup record of 5 days, 5 hours, and it was clear we'd bring up the rear in our class. But we were still sailing hard, jibing up to six times a day to optimize our course heading or try to sniff out better breeze.

Even so, the Transpacific veterans in the crew remained chagrined by the relatively light conditions we'd experienced. "Even the squalls on this trip have been a little disappointing," said Kevin. "El Pacifico has lived up to her name." But for me, a rookie in these waters, ignorance was bliss. You will never, ever hear me complain about steady boat speeds of 12 to 14 knots, or better, hour after hour after hour. It'd been a funky beginning, sure, but the foulies and headsails were distant memories of a trip that'd gotten warmer, clearer, and more fun with each passing day.

So I guess it was only poetic justice that on our last night racing we'd have to pay the piper one final time (make that two) before that first, fruity libation ashore.

We Sharks had drawn the 2200–0200 watch and, as predicted, the compressed trades were staunch and building as we closed in on the peaks of the island chain. The anemometer hadn't risen above twenty knots for over a week but it was there now, and was that more breeze under the dark cloud closing fast on our hip? At precisely that moment, the big A2 exploded,

Chris hollered, "All hands on deck, the chute's gone!" and *Icon* descended into a scene of controlled chaos. As I ran forward and began a mad grope at the untamed masses of sailcloth, all I could think of was that famous if apocryphal ocean racer's lament: "We put 'em up, God takes 'em down."

Twenty minutes later, we had a rugged A3 spinnaker up and drawing. Dick was philosophical about the destroyed A2, saying, "I guess we got our money's worth out of that sail." But after changing watches, we learned the night wasn't through with us yet. Only now it was the Jets' turn.

Jim took the wheel and wouldn't let go as the wind gusted to 30 in a fresh squall, and *Icon* plowed through the waves at 20 knots. All well and good, except for one thing: There was a large island directly in front of us. At 0430, the call came below, "Everybody up. Time to jibe."

The lights of Maui were *right there*; yup, it was definitely time to swing the wheel. We'd already pulled off countless jibes, day and night, without a hitch, but not this time. Something happened to the tack line, or maybe the spin sheet; it was under the bow! "Sheet on," someone yelled. "Well, um..." said I. The sail took a big, flapping wrap around the headstay, and then another twist, just for good measure.

At least it was dark. We could sort out the mess without anyone seeing.

HOURS LATER, with those leis around our necks and another round of cold cocktails by the yacht club pool, there was little mention of the two hours it took to clear the decks and hoist one last chute one last time. It was much better to recall that crisp, early light over Oahu, and how we all got a final turn at the helm, and what a joy it was to notch 17 knots on the speedo as *Icon* rose, plunged, and surfed before the big following swells. Spinnaker wrap? What spinnaker wrap?

As expected, our time of 8 days, 22 hours earned us fourth place in a fleet of four, in both elapsed and corrected time. Did last place, I wonder, always feel this good? Truthfully, it didn't matter to me one way or the other. All I really wanted to do was go back to California and try it all over again.

**The powerful 65-footer *Icon* reels off the miles in fresh tradewinds en route to Hawaii in the 2004 edition of the Pacific Cup.**

Two of the best days of my sailing life were finishing races to Hawaii, the aforementioned Transpac and this Pacific Cup. Creaming towards the Big Island under spinnaker in the accelerated tradewinds in the final hours of the race is something every sailor should experience.

# 22: A Robust Spot of Yachting

## THE SURPRISINGLY FRISKY WORLD
## OF CLASSIC YACHT RACING

EDGAR CATO got bitten by the bug. Sure, he had his share of not-so-subtle persuasion, but ultimately, when the daydream required massive infusions of cash, it was Cato entranced by a compelling spell from the distant past. It was the tail end of 2005, just after the annual Fort Lauderdale to Palm Beach Race, and on the delivery home, Cato and his crew aboard his Farr 60, *Hissar*—conspicuous among them the three-time J/24 world champion Brad Read, a long-time ally of Cato's and an aficionado of antique, classic yawls—started shooting the breeze about boats.

By chance, while recently surfing the web, Read had happened upon a brokerage listing for the famous 52-footer *Dorade*, the winner of the epic 1931 Transatlantic Race, a breakthrough offshore design built by Minneford Yacht Yard in City Island, N.Y., that helped launch the career of one Olin Stephens, who'd sailed the boat to victory with his brother, Rod, and returned triumphantly to a tickertape parade through the streets of Manhattan.

"The prettiest boat ever drawn," said Read of the vessel that's been dubbed "the mother of modern ocean racing."

Not so coincidentally, Read had cell-phone coverage, an Internet connection, and a captive owner with a deep love of sailing. He wondered if, you know, since they had some time on their hands, Cato might like to see the listing? The boat was lying in Italy, having recently undergone an extensive refit. Yes, said Cato, that would be fine.

Now Cato speaks in a languorous Southern cadence, a throwback to his boyhood in South Carolina, and after he looked and chatted for a while, he made what turned out to be a prophetic observation: "I think it would be *wonderful* to have *Dorade* back on a mooring outside the New York Yacht Club." And it wasn't long at all before that split-rigged vision was actually bobbing at her bit off Harbor Court, the club's "station" in Newport, Rhode Island.

Cato, however, is but one in a growing collection of Grand Prix sailors with strong mainstream roots who've been smitten by the notion of owning, and sailing, a slice of yachting legend. Multiple America's Cup winner Dennis Conner has thrown himself wholeheartedly into the classic era, first with the vintage 1925 Q-class sloop *Cotton Blossom II*, which he lovingly restored and then shipped to the Mediterranean, where he cleaned up on the European classic circuit; and more recently with the S&S-designed 51-foot *Brushfire*, which he's campaigning vigorously in West Coast events.

Another Cup veteran, naval architect Doug Peterson, has owned, sailed, or restored a veritable fleet of classics, including the 1898 cutter, *Bona Fide*; the 1933 Marconi sloop, *Tamara IX*; and currently, the Concordia yawl, *Skye*. Fellow yacht designer Greg Stewart, of Nelson/Marek—a regular on *Dorade*—has owned his classic 6-Meter, *Sprig*, for over a decade, and even drove her cross-country one year for the class's World Championships.

More recent classic converts include NYYC stalwarts Joe Dockery and former commodore George Isdale, Jr., who co-own the 1935 S&S-designed 53-footer, *Sonny*; Richard Breeden, whose latest *Bright Star*, a TP 52, has been displaced by the 68-foot S&S designed *Black Watch*, built in 1938; and veteran Caribbean-based racer Tom Hill, who switched over from the latest in his long string of boats called *Titan*, a 75-foot Reichel/Pugh sled, to the more refined pleasures of a 1935 Q-class sloop called *Falcon*.

"These guys are the (new) rock stars of classics," said Terry Nathan, the president of the Newport-based International Yacht Restoration School (IYRS). "They've brought some very important boats into the fold. They understand the importance of restoration and that it's not being done universally. It's not something we can take for granted anymore. These guys get it."

According to the sailors who've ridden the rise of the classic tide, there are many aspects to their appeal.

"You're right down in the water, it's like sailing a Soling," said Hill. "And the ride is so great. Six, seven, or eight knots on *Falcon* is like fifteen or sixteen on a big boat. And it's a fraction of the cost. Let's face it, the cost is getting out of sight for a lot of people."

"You go to a regatta and start looking around and you see all these really cool, one-of-a-kind boats," said Stuart. "You can go back and read about them and research them and figure out what other people did, what worked and what didn't."

"If there's one thing in common among all these guys who are sailing classic boats," said Read, who now serves as *Dorade*'s tactician, "it's their appreciation for the history of the sport. And the events are a blast. There's just a totally different vibe to them. Between the boats and the regattas, racing a classic is just completely different than any other kind of sailing you do."

An important aspect of this classic renaissance has been the long-term commitment promised by the Italian watchmaker, Panerai, which now sponsors an annual series of events in the

Antigua, Europe and New England. Panerai began producing dive watches for the Italian Navy in the mid-1930s and, says Alexandra Zoller, the president of the company's North American division, the alliance between the manufacturer and classic yacht racing is a "perfect" fit.

"You have all these elements in common: history, tradition, craftsmanship, passion," she said. "So it makes sense that we're working together. It's the DNA of the brand."

Panerai has become so enmeshed in the culture and framework of classic yachting that it took the extraordinary step of acquiring a forgotten 73-foot William Fife-designed ketch called *Eilean*, which it's restoring to its full, original glory.

"I like the fact that they just don't talk it, they're trying to live it," said Nathan. "Panerai has provided some critical financial support but in each of the regattas they're associated with they're trying to create a spirit and momentum that's larger than any one single event. I think that's so important."

Cato's *Dorade*, of course, has become a regular fixture on that classic circuit. "It's an icon, kind of a national treasure," he said. "Right now, I'm just the new custodian. I'll fix her up and pass her on to the next custodian. A boat like *Dorade*, you just want to treat it like a piece of antique furniture for as long as possible. It should go for another fifty years now."

Cato should know. After his first season with the boat, in 2006—the highlight of which was the guest appearance of none other that Olin Stephens, who took the tiller during that summer's Classic Yacht Regatta in Newport and regaled the crew with sea stories from his eventful career—Cato and his team discovered that *Dorade* was suffering from serious structural issues in the form of countless cracks in her white oak frames.

His first reaction, according to a fine article by Joshua F. Moore in *WoodenBoat* magazine, was to donate the boat to a museum or school. Instead, Cato reversed course and underwrote a massive restoration project spearheaded by Peter Cassidy of Buzzards Bay Yacht Services. By August of 2007, *Dorade* was once again a going concern. Furthermore, she was no longer burdened by an engine and other modern conveniences, having been transformed to the same precise level of fit and detail as when she conquered the Atlantic some seventy-six summers before.

Since then, *Dorade* has been collecting silverware, with numerous first-place finishes in events from Maine to Newport. But the real reward of campaigning *Dorade*, it would seem, is in the pure, sensual joy of sailing a boat with such a rich offshore pedigree. "It has an easy motion because of the displacement hull," said Cato. "It's not like a modern boat that's like a feather on top of the water. Out at sea, in big seas, *Dorade* is really comfortable."

"It sounds very Sixties, but you become one with the boat," said Read. "Do you go with the Yankee or the big jib? You can't roll 'em out on a furler, you're hanking and unhanking. The boat really screams at you when you're not in the sweet spot with the sail plan. And nothing happens quickly. Four seconds in a fin-keel, spade-rudder boat is like thirty seconds in a classic fleet. My advice to everyone who comes on board is, it's going to take you four times longer to do anything than you think it is."

The simple time/space equation may be at the root of probably the one controversial element in classic sailing: As the sailors who participate get better, the racing becomes tighter, and close calls become more frequent. Even a small dust-up can lead to a nightmare repair job for an antique woody, and never mind the emotional currency expended as well.

There's a rule in place that obliges classics to remain a boat-length apart, no matter the tack. But it's impossible to enforce, and when things go terribly wrong, the consequences can be disastrous. That point was underscored in an event off Newport in 2007 when the New York 30, *Amorita*, sank after a violent encounter with a 94-foot Fife ketch called *Sumurun*. The story had a happy ending, as no one was injured and *Amorita* was subsequently raised and recovered, and has even returned to competition, but the incident left everyone involved shaken.

As it turned out, however, even hearty old *Dorade* isn't immune from trouble, as I discovered firsthand while crewing aboard her during last August's Classic Yacht Regatta. It happened moments after the start, with *Dorade* on port and Hill's *Falcon* on starboard in the race's very first crossing situation. When *Falcon*'s bow cleaved into *Dorade*'s aft quarter and the splinters flew and *Dorade*'s mizzen folded over, it was a surreal scene of the highest order. The burden was on *Dorade*, which immediately retired, while Hill actually managed to continue and finish the race. Afterwards, he was a gracious sportsman.

"I've been racing all my life," he said. "Those things happen. Not only in racing, but in life. Things come up that you never expected. But you deal with them and move on."

Happily, Edgar Cato took the same tack. Though it was *Dorade*'s last regatta of the year, he vowed to have the mizzen replaced over the winter and was looking forward to racing her again in 2009. "In all my years of racing, that was my first collision," he said. "I was a virgin."

So maybe that's the final lesson to take from the episode. Only in the classics can an 83-year-old sailor say it was his very first time.

**Edgar Cato's famous Olin Stephens-designed *Dorade*
loses her mizzenmast after colliding with *Falcon* in
the Classic Yacht Regatta off Newport, R.I.**

I first met Dave Reed, the editor of *Sailing World*, who
commissioned this story and many others over the
years, when he showed up to do foredeck on our J/24
when he was all of 17 years old. I helped him land his
first internship and have sailed many a mile with him
in the intervening decades. Now I work for him. God,
I'm getting old.

**THE SURPRISINGLY FRISKY WORLD**

247

**Frank Savage went from rank beginner to a force to be reckoned with in international yachting circles, and named all his boats after his wife: Lolita.**

*Herb McCormick*

Months earlier, when *Sailing World* assigned me this story, I had no way of knowing that I'd show up to race aboard *Lolita* the day after she was creamed in a collision at Antigua Sailing Week, thus setting the stage for this rather dramatic and inspirational piece.

Again, sometimes it's better to be lucky than good.

# 23: The Lolita Way

## FRANK SAVAGE'S UNLIKELY JOURNEY TO ANTIGUA RACE WEEK

FRANK SAVAGE glanced at his watch—a little before 0900—then gathered his crew around him. By any measure, it had been a long, difficult, and emotional twenty-four hours. It was hard to believe that precisely a day earlier, to the very minute, all had been so right in his world. Of course, that was before the collision; before his beloved Swan 56, *Lolita*, had been fiercely strafed by the 115-foot behemoth; before his hopes and ambitions for this comeback regatta, this grand opportunity to reunite the faces and forces that had given him such joy and satisfaction, had been punctured like a birthday piñata.

He'd brought his boat and his team back down to Antigua in April of 2008—a return to the scene of perhaps their most memorable of the many, many victories, the overall winner of Sailing Week in 2003—for the simplest of reasons: He missed them. For the previous couple of years, competitive racing had been placed on the back burner while he concentrated on another of his passions, the career in international finance whose vast successes have made the sailing career possible.

"The boat had been in Europe," he said. "I'd cruised through Croatia and figured I'd leave it over there. Then last November, something just hit me. I realized I wanted to come back to the Caribbean and do Antigua Sailing Week. I told myself: I want to do that."

The wheels were set in motion, the calls went out to the *Lolita* legion, the worldwide network of committed sailors that have been at Savage's side since he launched the brand-new yacht back in 2000.  Some of the old guard, guys like Geoff Ewenson and Jon Ziskind, were busy with other projects and commitments.  But Savage has always had a loyal pool of regulars on which to call, and folks like Phil Garland, his long-time co-helmsman, were right back in the saddle.

"I just missed being together with my crew," said Savage, who leans heavily on those words he wants you to fully comprehend.  "They've become part of my *family*. They are a part of my *life*."

It had all started out according to plan.  Savage liked what he saw during the first practices, could see that the handful of new crewmembers were meshing well with the veterans.  For Savage contends that being a part of the *Lolita* squad has always been about much more than wins and losses, that the price of admission means subscribing to a code of behavior that, for lack of a better term, might be called "the *Lolita* way."

"It starts with respect for people," said Savage.  "Everyone who comes aboard is an individual in their own right.  But we share a common psyche, a common philosophy.  We are team players.  There is no screaming.  I don't care how good you are if you can't fit into that *Lolita* culture."

*Lolita* was just a hair off pace on the first of the five-day series in Antigua, but still registered a solid second on Day 1's opening distance race, a good beginning.  But the second race, on Day 2, a 26-mile point-to-point contest down the island's western flank, was barely under way when it all went horribly astray.

Things happened fast.  *Lolita* had just negotiated the short beat and the quick reach to an offset mark before a jibe set to begin the long run along the coastline. Suddenly, the overtaking Farr 115, *Sojana*, barreling along at some 15 knots, attempted to squeeze past to weather, a maneuver that proved to be impossible. It was *Sojana*'s responsibility to keep clear. They didn't (a fact later substantiated in the protest room). *Sojana*'s carbon mizzen boom raked *Lolita*'s rig, notching a 20-degree bend in the port upper shroud and busting the spinnaker pole.

"They're fast," said Savage. "It was a violent collision. Luckily, the Swan is a strong boat. I thought the mast was coming down. It was a dangerous situation. We retired. And we were devastated. Depressed. People were in a state of shock."

But slowly, collectively, the *Lolita* crew regained their focus. And they got lucky. The local rigger, Antigua Rigging, had the precise length and diameter of rod for a repair. In Garland, they had not only a fine helmsman, but also one of the mainstays at Hall Spars, a fellow who knows a fair bit about rig dynamics. They all worked into the night, affecting a repair with two men aloft, somehow avoiding the time-consuming task of pulling the mast. The next morning, incredibly, *Lolita* was ready for action.

Just before shoving off for Day 3's scheduled pair of windward/leewards, Savage called his crew together in the cockpit. "I am so proud of you," he said. "Of what you've accomplished. Of the way you just pulled yourselves together to get this boat ready. None of us wanted to go home. That's not why we came here. We came to race. Yesterday is history. Let's not worry about the enemy today. They don't exist. Let's focus on this boat. Let's go do what we do."

With that, a sky-high *Lolita* crew made way for the race course.

LIKE A FOOTBALL coach who excels at pre-game speeches, Frank Savage knows which buttons to push to motivate the troops. "He's just a great guy to sail with," said Garland, who's raced aboard *Lolita* on both sides of the Atlantic since 2003. "He never gets upset. Even after the collision, it was all positive. And he has a way with words. He's inspirational."

Savage is aware of, and takes pride in, his ability to inspire people. He sees many correlations between business and sailing: managerial savvy, team building, leadership. In lots of ways, these skills and qualities are the very essence of his being. After all, while growing up and going to school in Washington, D.C.—from elementary school to his master's degree at Johns Hopkins—he learned firsthand what it's like to follow the lead of an extraordinary person, his mother, Grace.

"She was an entrepreneur, never worked for anyone in her life," said Savage. "A very successful businesswoman, very international in her thinking. She had a plan for me, set me on a path. She's my greatest inspiration."

Surprisingly, Savage never set foot on a sailboat until the relatively advanced age of 40, nearly thirty years ago. He was on an airplane with his wife, Lolita, thumbing through a magazine with a photo of a boat heeling into the sunset.

"Doesn't that look great?" he wondered.

"Why don't you take a lesson?" she replied.

A week later he'd enrolled at the Long Island City branch of Offshore Sailing, a short distance from his home in Stamford, Connecticut. After a couple of days of classroom theory, the students were sent out in Solings. "We hit that first puff of breeze," said Savage, "the boat heeled over, and I fell in love. That's the only way I can describe it. I thought, 'This is *incredible*. I *love* this feeling.' I was lucky. It was an intense time in my life and

I found something that I really loved and could be absolutely committed to. It made me very happy. It still does."

He started racing aboard a friend's boat, eventually bought a Cal 33, then moved up to a Swan 46. One summer, en route to a cruise in Maine, he was cajoled into entering the non-spinnaker class at a Swan regatta in Newport, R.I., his first series in command. Savage thoroughly enjoyed the camaraderie though he failed to finish a single race. When it was over, he made a personal vow: "I am never going to be embarrassed like that again in my life."

Savage enlisted a knowledgeable sailor named Jeremy Maxwell—who would eventually become his crew boss and lieutenant—to help ramp up his boat and his program. The next year, he started winning races. One thing led to another. He had a chance to sail a Swan 56, then commissioned one for himself, which was launched in 2000. All his boats, by the way, have been named after the woman who nudged him onto the water in the first place: *Lolita*.

"Always, always, always," Savage laughed. "I've made a lot of stupid mistakes, but I'm not that stupid."

The last *Lolita* has enjoyed a stellar run with consistently impressive results, including multiple Swan Cup overall victories ("They're important because they give you bragging rights among your peers"), and that aforementioned overall title at Antigua in 2003.

"That was special," said Savage. "I think the people on the island were very happy to see a person of color win it all. The fact of the matter is that there are very few African-Americans who compete on a worldwide basis in racing. So I think that meant something to them."

And while Savage has no problem being a role model, be it to his own crew, his family, or even the islanders of Antigua, he also makes it clear that race has never played a factor of any kind in his sailing career. "Never," he said. "And this is a good thing for me, because I have had to deal with those issues in my life. This is what I love about this sport. Nobody cares what my color is. All anybody cares about is, 'Hey, what kind of breeze we got today?' That's because this is a *community*. Sailing has become a *community* to me."

FOR THE first race of Day 3, *Lolita* manages only an average start, but sailmaker and tactician Rob MacMillan makes up for it by nailing every shift, and the crew work is absolutely flawless. Sets, jibes, and douses are executed to quiet perfection, and the clean, efficient boat handling is rewarded with a second in the 12-boat Racing III division.

"We're back in the game," said Savage, shortly after crossing the finish line.

Among the *Lolita* regulars, sewerman Rod Clingman is one of the longest tenured, and between races he shares a few thoughts about sailing with Savage and his team. "It's been a great experience," he said. "I can't begin to tell you about the interesting people I've met. But the best thing about the program is there's just no ego involved."

Savage's son, Antoine, is also aboard, taking a rare break from his own burgeoning entrepreneurial career, and dad is obviously pleased about this rather special occasion. "You ready to get back in sailing shape?" he asks, as Antoine casts a wary eye at the primary winches. Then, quickly, it's back to action.

The afternoon race is marginally less successful, as *Lolita* registers a third (the spot she'll occupy at week's end in a tie with two other boats). Near the end, Savage takes the helm from Garland and there's some tricky steering in a couple of tight cross-ings before *Lolita* gets the horn.

"Nice job at the end, Frank," someone hails.

"It was easy," he replies. "I just follow you guys."

Back at the dock, however, as the crew tidies up the boat, Savage can't stop grinning. "Did you see them?" he asks. "They sailed *excellent*. They always do that."

He shook his head in wonder, and said it again: "They *always* do that."

Well, of course they do. It's the *Lolita* way.

The title of this next story could also describe my reaction when I was contacted out of the blue by *San Francisco* magazine—a publication I'd never laid eyes on—in the aftermath of local Bay Area celebrity Larry Ellison's nightmare participation in the deadly '98 Sydney-Hobart Race.  Ellison wouldn't grant me an interview, but someone sent me the transcript of a rare talk he did at the St. Francis Yacht Club that shaped much of my description of the events aboard *Sayonara*.  (The late Mark Rudiger, one of the sport's true gentlemen who is greatly missed, was also an indispensable source.)

In 2010, Ellison's BMW Oracle squad won the America's Cup.  But true to his word, he sold *Sayonara* not long after the tragic Hobart event and never again raced offshore.

# 24: Blown Away

## BILLIONAIRE LARRY ELLISON
## AND THE TRAGIC '98 HOBART RACE

THE COLOR OF HELL should be crimson, but all Larry Ellison could see was a storm-tossed ocean of blue. Barely hanging onto the helm of his state-of-the-art sailboat *Sayonara*, exhausted from two days of retching, the CEO of software giant Oracle gazed out at the violent seaway and was stunned by its awful magnificence. Just yards away, a section of "bulletproof" sail track began to peel away from the deck like a cheap zipper. Sails were flailing, action was required, men started hollering. Their words were lost in the screech of the wind.

*Sayonara* fell off a steep wave and Ellison's stomach plunged with her, abandoned in a weightless, 20-foot free fall. Boat and belly crashed to a halt at the bottom of the trough, and the long white deck was swept by a frothy wall of water. Soaked and weary, Ellison headed below and climbed into a bunk. For his condition, dry land was the only cure. It was hundreds of miles away.

Forty-eight hours earlier, on the Australian holiday Boxing Day (December 26, 1998), Ellison and his 22-man crew—a dream team of professional sailors—had set out from Sydney, Australia, in the company of 114 other boats to begin the 54th running of the annual Sydney to Hobart Yacht Race. Line honors for "first to finish" were just one of their goals. The other was to topple the course record of two days, fourteen hours, and seven minutes set in 1996 by the yacht *Morning Glory*, owned by Ellison's fierce Silicon Valley rival, Hasso Plattner. "Given suitable conditions, we could easily slice a half day off that," Ellison said prior to the race.

Before the week was out, the race would be front-page news worldwide: six sailors killed, fifty-five rescued. Ellison would be the subject of a *USA Today* cover story on thrill-seeking executives. The lead sentence: "The difference between God and software mogul Larry Ellison, the joke goes, is that the Almighty doesn't think he's Ellison." But there would be no walking on water this time.

As is often the case, the 630-nautical-mile race had begun with the threat of a weather front looming in from the west. It was nothing the veterans of the annual event hadn't heard before. "Just a spot of Hobart weather, mate," was the typical response. But the pre-race forecast of 35- to 45-knot winds turned out to be dangerously wrong. Less than 24 hours later, one shoreside station registered a gust of 71 knots—wind speeds over 80 miles per hour.

Roaring down the exposed coast of southeastern Australia, *Sayonara*, pressing hard, blew out three spinnakers. Once she was into the Bass Strait, the nasty stretch of water that separates the mainland from the island state of Tasmania, the gale arrived and matters started to deteriorate. Seated at the navigation table, drenched in sweat in the hot, clammy, unventilated cabin, Sausalito-based navigator Mark Rudiger pored over his charts in search of an escape route from the fury of the blow. Rudiger, whose navigation talents were central to Ellison's record-setting dreams, was surrounded by bunk-bound sailors, barfing noisily in buckets. Reduced by seasickness to part-time duty aboard his multimilliondollar, 80-foot thoroughbred, Ellison thought, *I've got probably the world's best professional crew, and we're at the limits of our ability to keep everything together and keep this boat racing. What happens on a 40-footer?*

Pandemonium. Two hundred miles to the north, a 40-foot sloop called *Business Post Naiad* was losing its battle with gargantuan waves. Despite the fact that 51-year-old Tasmanian Bruce Guy had secured some sponsorship money from Business Post, a division of the Australian post office department, there were no professional sailors aboard *Naiad*. Guy, a manager of a manufacturing business, was representative of most of the Sydney-to-Hobart boat owners. Though he'd been sailing more than 35 years, the '98 Hobart race was the first one in which he skippered his own boat. Most of his middle-aged crewmembers were yacht club buddies. One of the younger crewmen, 34-year-old locksmith Phil Skeggs, was a next-door neighbor whom Guy had taught to sail five years before.

*Business Post Naiad* had a good first day and, 24 hours into the race, was holding sixth place in her class. But early in the evening of December 27, as the 80-knot gale stacked up waves in excess of 30 feet, the boat rolled like a child's bathtub toy, her mast snapping in two places. Fearful that *Naiad* was about to split apart beneath them, the crew issued a Mayday and began motoring toward Eden, a small coastal fishing town where many boats were seeking shelter. Just before midnight, another huge wave grabbed *Naiad* and flipped her into the air. She dropped off the watery cliff upside down, the crew dangling by safety harnesses. When the boat crashed into the water, Skeggs, tethered to the submerged deck, could not free himself and drowned.

Several long minutes later, yet another monster wave tossed the helpless vessel right side up. Belowdecks, with food and gear and men flying past him, Guy was flung to the cabin floor. Crewmember Steve Walker lifted him, but Guy was badly exhausted and succumbed to a fatal heart attack. The others held on through an endless night until a rescue helicopter arrived at dawn.

With his hand welded to the control stick and his gaze steady on the liquid horizon, whirlybird pilot Dan Tyler didn't flinch as one giant swell after the next rolled under him and reduced the clearance between his fuselage and the wave tops to less than 20 feet. Rescue swimmer Murray Traynor was lowered into the roiling sea seven times to fasten lifelines to the surviving *Naiad* sailors, winching them to safety. The two bodies were later recovered.

IN 1979, AFTER HE won line honors in the disastrous Fastnet Race off England and Ireland, Atlanta media mogul Ted Turner stepped ashore full of spit and bombast. In stormy conditions similar to those that raged through the Sydney to Hobart, 15 sailors had been lost at sea. It remains the deadliest yacht race of all time. But when queried about the race, Turner was in no mood to discuss missing comrades. The worst moment, he told the *New York Times*, "was when I was told that some little boat was the winner. I had four hours of bitter disappointment before it was straightened out."

Turner's lust for victory was certainly not new to yacht racing, nor was the fact that the victor was the wealthiest skipper on the course. But in the '70s, the term "professional sailor" was seldom heard. In fact, when it came to yachting, Turner steadfastly refused to compensate his crews. His were high-profile campaigns to which outstanding sailors naturally gravitated. It was enough to be aboard, to win, to be a moth in the flame of Ted's burn toward the top.

But in the past decade, the win-at-all-costs mentality has become less about prestige and attitude and more about fiscal

Darwinism: survival of the richest. Owners like Ellison can now buy not only the fastest boats, but also the most talented crews to sail them. "The idea of giving somebody money to go race a sailboat is a fairly recent development," remarked John Rousmaniere, a noted sailing writer and historian. "When I was growing up, a 'pro' was the guy who took care of your dad's boat. He wasn't even allowed in the yacht club."

In the wake of sleek racing boats staffed by pro crews, overall participation in sailboat racing has declined. The schism between the haves and have-nots in elite races such as the Sydney to Hobart has never been greater, and the prospect of spending a boatload of dough to repeatedly take a thrashing at the hands of professionals soon loses its luster.

It was a forgone conclusion that Ellison would win the '98 Sydney to Hobart. "It was like a 500-horsepower car beating a 200-horsepower car," said San Francisco yacht racer Paul Cayard, CEO and skipper of AmericaOne, an America's Cup challenger. One of Ellison's original tutors, Cayard is among the highest-paid and most successful sailors in the world, those who can pull down hundreds of thousands of dollars a year.

Until recently, certain high-end racing rules forbade owners from paying their crews. Still, that did not stop some owners from being, well, creative. In the '80s, legendary San Francisco sailor Tom Blackaller, who also raced sports cars, was rumored to have received a new automobile engine from one patron grateful for his services. In the early '90s, international race rules abandoned the final pretense of purity. "It was stupid to have a rule that was being flagrantly violated," said John Burnham, editor of racing magazine *Sailing World*. "At that point the owners said, 'We're free to pay anyone on the boat.' "

The rule change expanded jobs for sailors, and owners went shopping. One of the first places they turned to was San Francisco, which has produced a pantheon of pros, including Cayard, Rudiger, and John Kostecki, who was just returned from Spain, where he had been training for his next assault on the Whitebread Round the World Race. Rob Moore, racing editor of the Bay Area's monthly sailing bible *Latitude 38*, reckons that San Francisco Bay, with its challenging currents and breezes, gives the hometown boys an edge. "If you can make it here, you can make it anywhere," he said.

In dockside parlance, pros such as Cayard and Rudiger are called "rock stars," simply because they are so damn cool. Actually, they are more like football stars—the quarterbacks and split ends. As a result, they are courted furiously by boat owners. Aboard *Sayonara*, the procurement of talent fell upon the shoulders of the boat's full-time captain, Billy Erkelens. He recruited Rudiger and the others and signed them to season contracts. Rudiger even has his own agent, Drue Moore, who also represents baseball slugger Sammy Sosa.

It's no surprise that Ellison, like George Steinbrenner or any other mainstream sports mogul, would want the premium talent. "He's put millions of dollars into his boat," said Rousmaniere. "So having guys like Rudiger aboard is an insurance policy to guarantee that he achieves a certain level of success. I'm sure he looks at it as a smart investment."

Indeed, when the going got tough in the Hobart race, the advantage of the rock stars' abilities became apparent. The pros aboard *Sayonara* were able to push forth and continue racing when dozens of lesser crews were fighting for their lives. It was no accident that they were miles and miles ahead of the hoi polloi when the storm made a mockery of the forecast.

AS THE STARTING gun sounded at the stroke of 1 P.M. on Saturday, December 26, Australian yachting journalist Rob Mundie took in the holiday spectacle. "It was a travel brochure Sydney scene with pristine blue skies reflected on the harbor," he said. "There was a refreshing northeasterly breeze bringing a sparkle to the harbor surface as thousands of spectators gathered to watch. It was a typical Sydney-to-Hobart start."

As *Sayonara* made a clean break from the field, Rudiger was struck by the similarity to the sheer natural beauty of San Francisco. Sliding south, he felt as if he'd just sailed under the Golden Gate Bridge and hung a turn for Santa Cruz. But Rudiger was not distracted for long. *Sayonara* was in a tight duel with the big Aussie yacht *Brindabella*.

Rudiger's onboard domain, the "nav" station, was tucked well aft and bathed in luminescence from an array of wind and boat speed instruments, two computers (one of which was used exclusively to download satellite weather images), radios, and a device that provided pinpoint position updates. His job, simply put, was to accumulate information and use it to find the fastest possible route from Sydney to Hobart.

Given the vagaries of wind and current, that course was not a straight line. An expert at interpreting data, Rudiger understood that what looked like a smudgy thumbprint on a satellite picture was really a treasure trove of information about air pressure and sea states and swirling breezes. It was knowing when the wind would advance or shift, hours *before* it occurred, not seconds after, that separated a seasoned pro from a weekend admiral.

Rudiger did not keep regular hours like the rest of the crew; aside from a ten-minute nap here and there, he stayed awake for three days. Everyone else was broken into teams under the command of watch captains.  The undisputed leader, Chris Dickson, was a native of New Zealand, a country renowned for its superior sailors.  The primary helmsman in what was essentially a five-man rotation, Dickson was a genius with a hair-trigger penchant for tantrums that would make John McEnroe blush.  Rudiger was the pragmatic yin to Dickson's emotional yang.

Although he was paying for everyone's fun, aboard *Sayonara* Ellison was not at his familiar apex of the organizational chart.  Instead, said Rudiger, he was more like the knowledge-able owner of a baseball team who enjoys coming down to the diamond and scrapping with the lads.  "We let him pitch and we let him catch," said Rudiger.  "Some owners don't want to be upstaged, but not Larry.  He knows where he can be and where not to be [when the boat's under way]."

Rudiger's first tactical call, a simple one, was to tap into the northerly wind flowing into the East Australia current, whose escalator effect added three or four knots to *Sayonara*'s speed.  With the north wind continuing to surge, *Sayonara* was holding a record-setting pace of 19 knots.  It was good, fast sailing, and *Sayonara*'s rock stars were definitely earning their paychecks.  No sooner did one spinnaker shred apart than they had another up and drawing.  Then, the fitting that secures the spinnaker pole to the mast failed and the pole went airborne, an unattended battering ram.  Had one of the sailors been standing alongside, it could've knocked his head off.  Securing it was a major fire drill.

Nine hours into the race, huddled over the nav station, Rudiger was alarmed by a fresh bit of information.  Scanning the digital barometer that records atmospheric pressure, he watched in amazement as the numbers started to plummet.  'It was a little like coming down the back side of Mount Everest," he said.  "It was one of the steepest drops I've ever seen."

In fact, a major low-pressure system that had evaded most of the sophisticated computer-generated weather models had piggy-backed onto the front and was on a collision course with the fleet. Rudiger caught a glimpse of the encroaching front in a crack of lightning. But then the gale was upon them, at the worst possible time, in the worst possible place. In the tens of thousands of ocean miles he'd logged, Rudiger had been assaulted by the standard offshore stew of honking winds, mighty currents, and potent frontal systems. But he'd never seen them converge so sneakily, so lethally, as now.

*Sayonara* sailed headlong into the tempest. The mercurial Dickson and his mates—including famous Kiwi sailor Brad Butterworth—showcased their brilliance at the helm. With surgical precision, Dickson feathered the wheel to avoid teeth-rattling collisions with the worst of the waves and, in the mightier gusts, angled the bow to spill wind from the sails and lighten the load on the huge carbon-fiber mast. If the mast crashed over the side, it could pierce the hull and sink the boat. The aura on deck assumed a desperate gravity. The priority was no longer winning but surviving.

That meant keeping the boat in one piece, an increasingly difficult proposition. But this was the pinnacle of professional sailboat racing, and *Sayonara*'s crew were effecting tricky repairs—jobs that would've been difficult for skilled tradesmen in a well-stocked boatyard—in appalling conditions. When the boom bent, two men quickly appeared with a hand drill and reinforced it with a steel plate. When the mainsail ripped, one group of sailors dropped it and replaced it with a storm trysail, while another went to work sewing the torn main. For every problem—and there were dozens of them—*Sayonara*'s crew had an answer.

*Sayonara* sailed into a brief calm as the eye of the storm passed over. The crew rehoisted the main and even set their biggest headsail. But the lull was a mirage. A wisp of wind appeared, and minutes later it was screaming at 45 knots. Phil Kieley, who runs Oracle's Sydney office, broke an ankle as the boat slammed down a titanic wave. (Kieley was one of the few non-pros on board, as was Rupert Murdoch's son, Lachlan.) One crew member was thrown into a huge winch and cracked his ribs; a third broke a thumb. One man was tossed halfway overboard without a harness and used his rock-climbing strength to pull himself back with one arm. The biggest scare came when no one could find Tasmanian sailor Graeme Freeman and briefly presumed he had been swept away; after a stem-to-stern search, he was discovered below snoozing under a sailbag.

Fueled by adrenaline, the rock stars kept working, dousing sail and coaxing the big, fragile boat onward. Off the coast of Tasmania, roughly 100 miles from the finish, Ellison, Dickson, and Rudiger conferred and decided to tack in closer to shore, away from the steepest waves and harshest gusts. It turned out to be a brilliant move, easing the strains on the hull and rigging and placing the boat in a perfect position to take advantage of a favorable wind shift. For *Sayonara,* the worst was over. Elsewhere, it was just beginning.

THE 52-FOOT *Winston Churchill*—built of wood and lead—was in many ways the antithesis of *Sayonara* and her carbon, Kevlar, and titanium components. Built in 1942 and a veteran of the inaugural Hobart race, the classic sloop had been lovingly restored by Richard Winning, whose family fortune had been amassed from selling the household appliances that Aussies call "white goods." Winning was the anti-Ellison. He didn't give a fig about records or line honors. "We look at [the race] as a bit of recreation," he'd said. "Gentlemen's ocean racing—that's our game." But even Rudiger had been impressed by the boat's robust construction, telling friends before the start that if things got really funky, there were worse places to be than aboard the good old *Winston Churchill.*

Through no fault of its seasoned nine-man crew, *Winston Churchill* was the last place anyone should have been. The faithful 25-ton woody had plied the waters off the coast of Australia for five decades. It took 25 minutes to bring her down. The wave that claimed her came out of nowhere, but as an instrument of destruction it was without peer. Slammed sideways down the face of the monster, *Winston Churchill* came to a halt, but three windows lining her aft cabin did not. In a blatant disregard of gravity, the powerful influx of water pinned one sailor, 51-year-old shipwright John "Steamer" Stanley, to the upper, windward side of the cabin. But he swam free and clambered topsides.

There, he was treated to the sight of more terrible mischief. Suspended in space, their feet dangling some two feet above the deck, were Winning and another crewman, John Dean. When the boat had been knocked on her sides, both sailors had been tangled in the rigging. When she finally eased back upright, their fouled harnesses had hung them from the lines. Stanley sorted out the mess.

Below, *Winston Churchill* was rapidly filling with water. Perhaps the boat had sprung a plank. Maybe the butt of the mast had busted loose and impaled the hull. It was all academic. What mattered was bailing the water, but it was a Catch-22. Electricity was needed to power the pumps, and the batteries required to start the engine were underwater. *Winston Churchill* was going down.

It was the second day of the race. A little after 5 p.m., Winning sounded a Mayday. He informed officials that his crew was taking to two life rafts. An old adage about life rafts says you never board one until you have to step up into it. Winning and three sailors waited until the deck was awash and then leaped into one raft. Five others—Dean, Stanley, Jim Lawler, Mike Bannister, and John "Gibbo" Gibson—scrambled into the other. They rigged a line between the two to keep them together. It broke immediately. The rafts careened off in opposite directions, toward opposite fates.

The four men in Winning's raft would be rescued just under 24 hours later, having survived two capsizes. The outcome for those in Stanley's raft wouldn't be known for over 30 hours. It started out badly. "A big wave hit us, we were pinned under the other guy's legs," said Stanley, "and that's when I broke my ankle." Then it got worse.

Stanley's raft, enclosed under a canopy, was unstable and soon took the first of dozens of rollovers. The sailors felt the contraption was safer when it was upside down, with them standing in the submerged canopy, so they abandoned the job of re-righting it and cut a hole in the floor for fresh air. Then, probably around 2:30 or 3:00 the next morning, "We were hit by this almighty wave," said Stanley.

"Suddenly the five of us were just crashing. It must have broken just as it hit us. When we finally stopped and I came up for air, I was hanging onto the outside of the raft. I yelled out, 'Who's here?' The only reply came from Gibbo. I looked back and there was white water for about 350 yards. I could see two people. I'm not sure who they were. I said to Gibbo, 'Mate, we're by ourselves here. We can't do anything for those boys. The wind is going to blow us faster than they can swim, and we can't go back.' We could only hope that they could hang on until day-break and be spotted by a search plane." They never were.

But Stanley's number wasn't up. He'd survived two hip replacements, the loss of a kidney, and a malignant melanoma, and this gale was not going to take him. Late that day he caught the attention of a passing plane with a pocket strobe light, and hours later a chopper was overhead. A rescue swimmer was low-ered into the water, and Gibbons was hoisted upstairs. When it was Stanley's turn, the pilot decided to deploy a ring rather than a man to winch him aloft.

"I must have tangled a rope from the life raft in with me and the ring," he said. "He started lifting me, and all of a sudden I looked down and said to myself, 'The life raft's coming with me.' I got to about 25 feet and thought, *Oh no, this is going to be dangerous*, so I just bailed out, straight back into the water. The next thing, the guy landed the ring about two feet away from me. I thought, *This guy is bloody brilliant*. I climbed back into it." Steamer Stanley was hauled clear of the breakers. He would live to sail another day.

Six sailors would not. In addition to those lost aboard *Business Post Naiad* and *Winston Churchill*, a British Olympian named Glyn Charles was killed when the boat he was steering rolled over and his safety harness failed; he was never seen again.

THE MOOD WAS somber when *Sayonara* coasted up to the dock in Hobart, the first boat home. The haunting sound of a bagpipe, echoing off the low-lying hills, provided the sound track. It could've been a dirge. Amazingly, despite the breakage of gear and sails, the boat was only five hours off the record.

There should've been more fatalities. Mundle, the Aussie journalist who later wrote a best seller about the race, believes it's a miracle that 30 or 40 sailors didn't perish. A larger disaster was averted by the heroism of countless military and civilian rescue teams. A total of 45 fixed-wing planes and helicopters conducted 500 hours of operations; altogether, 55 competitors were rescued. Of the 115 boats that started, just 44 made it to the finish line.

In the aftermath, the organizer of the race—the venerable Cruising Yacht Club of Australia (CYCA)—came under intense scrutiny, and many shoreside observers questioned the club's judgment for sending a thousand competitors into harm's way. Most sailors, including Rudiger, supported the CYCA and were loath to lay blame on what was essentially an unforeseen act of nature. *Brindabella* skipper George Snow, a Sydney-to-Hobart veteran who finished second to Ellison's first, spoke for most competitors: "It is a race for individuals, and individuals must make the decision whether they start or continue the race." Nevertheless, two independent inquiries—one launched by the coroner, the other by the CYCA—are currently under way.

There will no doubt be recommendations about boat designs and safety gear and abandon-ship procedures. But how does one regulate an act of nature? The storm that pummeled the competitors brought pro sailors with pillars for sea legs to their knees. Dozens of others had their destinies stripped from their control and are here to talk about their dance with doom only because heroic men and women went to sea and hauled their sodden, defenseless butts ashore.

Ultimately, the issue is control, and that, more than any-thing, is what Larry Ellison lusted for when he bought his dream team and steered into the blue ocean for a shot at the record books and a brief, illusory moment of immortality. He could buy the best boat and sails and talent, hut he could not serve up his Visa and purchase the perfect breeze to fuel his ambitions. When all is said and done, that is the essence, beauty, and irony of sailing. You can interact with the elements, but you can never hope to conquer them.

Of course, that minor inconvenience will never stop men like Ellison from trying.

**Larry Ellison's maxi-boat *Sayonara* makes her way up the Derwent River to the finish line of the tragic 1998 edition of the Sydney-Hobart Race.**

Erik Berzins

**The 39-foot rocketship, *Bien Roulée*, "hauls the mail" down the coast of Baja California in a race from Newport Beach to Cabo San Lucas.**

For this anthology, I almost included a companion piece about sailing north from Mexico, in the opposite direction than this downwind race from Newport Beach, California, to Cabo San Lucas, a trip that has its own nickname:  the Baja Bash.  But the mere thought of it made me seasick.

# 25: The Baja Express

## WHY CALIFORNIANS LOVE RACING TO MEXICO

THE DUKE. John Wayne. He talked...a little...slow...*the Duke*...
but beyond his laconic delivery stood the ultimate man of action. When one alights from a plane at the John Wayne Airport
in Orange County, California—as I did in the spring of 2008 to
sail the Corona del Mar (CDM)-Cabo San Lucas Race—your first
memorable encounter is with a 9-foot bronze effigy of the Hollywood hero, all done up in cowpoke duds and clearly ready to kick
some tail. As it turned out, it was an image I'd conjure repeatedly in the days that followed.

For much of his life, Wayne would call Orange County
home, something that Glenn Highland and Alan Andrews have
done since they were kids. Highland's now a retired CEO with
a house in Corona del Mar, and just around the corner from his
yacht designing neighbor, Andrews, whose impact on the sailing
world includes such West Coast rockets as *Magnitude 80*, *Medicine Man*, and *Locomotion*.

When Highland commissioned a new sailboat that he could
race to Mexico, or even Hawaii, as well as cruise to Catalina or
just daysail with friends, he called on Andrews to render the
design. Highland was adamant on several fronts: He wanted a
boat that was not beholden to any rating rule, that was light and
fast but with open and inviting accommodations for a racing
crew of six or a pair of couples on a weekend getaway.

The end result was *Bien Roulée*—very loosely translated,
it's a French idiom that suggests a "well-rounded" woman—a

39-foot carbon missile built by James Betts Enterprises in Ana-
cortes, Washington.  Displacing a mere 11,400 pounds, with a
carbon rig and all manner of related performance goodies, *BR*
was launched last fall but the boat's first offshore test would
be the CDM-Cabo Race, an 800-mile romp south of the border
hosted by the Balboa YC.

There's a long and storied tradition of racing from California to Mexico, and these days there are four prominent events
on the sailing calendar:  Long Beach YC's Long Beach-Cabo
Race, which was reinstated last November after a long hiatus but
drew just a handful of entries; San Diego Yacht Club's Vallarta
Race (a feeder for the annual week-long MEXORC Regatta), an
event from San Diego to Puerto Vallarta that drew 18 boats for
the April, 2008, running, but which is slightly longer (and often
with lighter breeze) than the Cabo races; the 125-mile Newport-
Ensenada Race, which routinely attracts hundreds of boats with
its easily managed distance; and the Newport Beach (or CDM)-
Cabo Race, hosted on alternate years by the Balboa and Newport
Harbor YCs, respectively.

For several reasons, the Cabo races—which are long but not
too long, contested in optimum spring conditions, and wrap up in
a hopping resort town with good berthing facilities—are currently
drawing the best fleets among the true offshore tests (though
more than one racer was overheard wishing that some of the various events would consolidate for even better turnouts).

For this year's CDM-Cabo competition, Highland, a rookie
ocean racer, and Andrews would both be aboard, along with
talented Southern California helmsman Chuck Clay; Andrews'
associate, bowman Erik Berzins; pitman Roman Villarreal, a
restaurateur by trade who'd also packed the galley with abundant
vittles (though much of it, alas, would go uneaten); and me.

On a Friday in late March, twenty-seven boats, including *BR*, the smallest boat in Class B, answered the starting gun off the Balboa Pier (ten more yachts, the Class A big boats and maxis, would roll a day later) in fairly typical Newport Beach conditions: a light southerly, flat water, and bright sunshine. Tit for tat, tack-by-tack, we collectively worked our way upwind and offshore toward the promise of stronger, veering breeze. About an hour in we were mightily headed and flopped over to starboard.

"Hopefully that's the last we'll see of port tack for the next 18 hours," said Andrews, and so it was.

The jib was soon furled, replaced by the masthead genoa, *BR* trucking along at the same speed as the true wind, about 9 knots. Up went a staysail, good for another half knot (little did we know, it would be days before it was doused). Near sunset, the wind had freed, and risen, sufficiently enough for the hoisting of the A3 asymmetric. *BR* surged forward in the fresh 20-knot nor'wester, instantly knocking off double-digit boat speeds. Villarreal, trimming the chute, said to no one in particular, "It's O.M.G. time," and when I asked what he meant, replied, "Oh. My. God."

The Duke might've put it another way: "Buckle up...Pilgrims. And hang on...to your hats."

THE FORECAST, frankly, had been too good to be true, which is why I scarcely believed a word of it. In the long term, rarely are things as wonderful (or awful) as the meteorologists say they will be. That said, Highland had secured the pre-race services of not one, but two, professional routers and their respective predictions had been virtually identical. Once offshore, some 25 to 35 miles from the coast, there would be heaps of northwest breeze, anywhere from 16–22 knots, right through the weekend and into the early part of the week, though winds would taper off in the latter stages of the trip.

Incredibly, the weathermen were only slightly off, and more remarkably, in our favor, for the breeze proved even sweeter, and more strapping, than advertised.

Your average race from Newport Beach to Cabo, according to veteran navigators, can be broken down into three distinct segments: the first half of the race, roughly 400 nautical miles, from the start to Cedros Island, near Turtle Bay; the central section, about 250 miles, from Cedros to Cabo San Lazaro, north of Bahía Magdalena; and the final piece to the puzzle, around 150 miles, from "Mag Bay" to Cabo Falso at the tip of Baja California, at the corner to Cabo San Lucas.

The first night of any ocean race is always surreal, but sometimes you get lucky and can ease into the at-sea routine. Not this time. The game was on from the get-go. *BR*, absolutely hauling the mail, seemed to understand this better than we did. Oh yes, there was a round-up or two (or three…you get the idea)—"Wind check!" hollered Clay—but there were also glorious spans when the helm went oh-so-light, and all was right in our 39-foot universe.

"I've sailed 29ers and 49ers," said Berzins. "But this is the first 39er."

Drivers changed on the hour, everyone upping the boat-speed ante. I topped off at 20.5 knots, then Villarreal registered a 21.5, and then Andrews and Clay bumped her up over 22. On it went through the night, the miles ticking steadily away.

We threw in the first jibe at 0830 on Saturday morning, an all-hands affair, and kept ramping down the coast. That afternoon, Highland fired off an email to the race office: "Remained an E-ticket ride all day off Mexico. Plenty of wind, big rough seas. Some jibes in 25 knots to get your attention along the way."

No one was enjoying it more than Andrews, the sailor known as "Light Bulb" for his switched-on ways. At dusk, at the wheel, he said, "I'm not even looking at the spinnaker," and what he meant was we were becoming a team, the trimmer and driver thinking and acting in unison, as one.

"You can just pick a path through the waves," he added, *BR* on a plane at 18-knots. "Even a one-footer can make a big difference. This is so much fun."

Yes, it was.


COOL. BLACK. Long. That was the second night at sea, made all the more challenging by the overcast sky and nary a single star by which to steer. As the breeze stabilized in the mid-teens, we jibed inshore onto port at 0230 on Sunday morning for better breeze, and back to starboard seven hours later on a long board that carried us past Cedros and on to the second half of the course.

During the day we changed down to the A2, which we carried through the afternoon, the staysail still set and along for the ride. At the wheel, sliding down the face of a 6-foot wave on another prolonged surf, Clay said, "I wish my brother were here. He could just sit there and watch. Not many people get to see this."

We could've used his bro' a short time later, when the breeze suddenly crested to 30 knots and we had a full-on fire drill swapping the A2 for the A3. The takedown was a nightmare, *BR* skidding sideways in the prolonged gust—with pace—a base runner sliding under the tag at home. But soon enough we were again a controlled, going concern and the third night at sea was another fast one, this time under welcome, starry skies, with our two best drivers, Andrews and Clay, doing the bulk of the heavy lifting.

On Monday, Highland filed another dispatch to HQ: "Challenging last 20 hours. Plenty of wind and seas... Have worn through (the covers on) all our spin sheets. Jury rigging many things but keeping the boat moving and laughing a lot at how crazy this all is. High boat speed 23.8, highest wind speed 33— but fantastic part has been how steady it has been at 15++."

The idea off Mag Bay is to stay well outside, away from the beach and wavering breeze, but the wind was still steady and we cut the usual stand-off waypoint, a tactic that caused a wee bit of trepidation until *Magnitude 80* passed us well inshore, en route to a new race record of 2d, 10h, 23m, 27s. We were obviously in very good company.

Of course, the sleigh ride had to end sometime, and it did, predictably, on the final approach to Cabo. By midnight Monday, the breeze had dropped into the single digits for the first time since the start over three days earlier. "We're racing the sun," said Andrews, meaning we'd best cross the finish line by sunrise, when the breeze faltered altogether, or we might be drifting around for a good while.

That would've been awful.

But our luck, and the breeze, held on, and though we had a few anxious moments keeping the boat moving after briefly parking off Cabo Falso, we crossed the finish line just after the 66-foot *Medicine Man* at almost the precise moment the tip of the orange sun broke the horizon on Tuesday morn.

Our time of 3 days, 17 hours—the 10th boat to finish— earned us a fifth in class in PHRF. We can only tip our hats to the J/125 *Reinrag2*, the winner in our division; the Calkins 50, *Sabrina*, the race's overall winner; and everyone else who topped us in the standings. We left everything we had on the race course, and the guys ahead of us surely did, too.

Looking back at our course track and comparing it to the competition, we quite possibly jibed a couple of times at less-than-optimum moments (a bit early here, a tad late there) and we seemed to be sailing hotter angles than boats like *Reinrag*, which suggests an A4 running chute would have been a useful addition to the sail inventory, but hindsight is always crystal clear. For a typical Cabo race, we were fine, but it was far from your typical Cabo race.

But in the meantime, we were in Mexico, land of tacos and tequila, pretty women and fine cigars. Thinking back on the Duke, it was a scene he'd have enjoyed, though he wouldn't have talked much about it.

And neither will I.

DanielForster.com

**A group of locals pay homage to the wing keel aboard**
***Australia II**—including the author, in the plaid*
**shirt!—shortly after winning the 1983 America's Cup.**

Here in my hometown of Newport, Rhode Island,
we're still taking this one hard. This piece was written
for the regional publication, *Newport Life*.

# 26: The Day the Cup Was Lost

## BLACK MONDAY FOR THE
## NEW YORK YACHT CLUB

TOM RICH was right in the thick of it.  Today, Rich is a successful local businessman, a boatbuilder who's called Newport home
for nearly 25 years.  And, like any long-time Newporter still registering a pulse, he recalls with precise detail the fateful events on
the glorious Indian Summer afternoon of September 26, 1983,
the day the New York Yacht Club—and, by extension, Newport—
lost the America's Cup.  Like the Kennedy assassination for those
of a certain era, that early autumn Monday remains vivid and
ingrained for anyone who lived in the City by the Sea during that
contentious, thrilling, final Cup season:  they clearly remember whom they were with, and what they were doing, when the
incomprehensible news came down.

Of course, Tommy Rich has a much different take than the
rest of us.  After all, he was one of 11 crewmembers aboard Dennis Conner's *Liberty*, the lean, red boat that put forth a gallant
effort, but ultimately failed.

It was the seventh, winner-take-all race in a best-of-seven
series versus *Australia II*, the so-called "little white pointer" that
owed its remarkable quickness and dexterity to what had been
the summer's worst-kept secret:  the radical wing keel affixed
to its underbody.  By this time, Conner, Rich, and everyone else
aboard the hundreds of vessels bobbing on Rhode Island Sound
knew that the Americans were at a severe disadvantage, that
*Australia II* was by far the faster, more maneuverable steed, and

that the New Yorkers' 132-year Cup winning streak, the longest in sports, was in serious jeopardy.

Still, something strange was happening on the water. The Americans had won the start and had extended their lead on the three subsequent legs. As they rounded the top mark, they held a 57-second advantage over the incredulous Aussies. Two-thirds of the deciding race was over. The Yanks, who'd won the first two races, then dropped the next three out of four, were back in the driver's seat. All they had to do was hold their lead on the final downwind leg under spinnaker, then back upwind to the finish line, and disaster would be averted. The Cup would remain in its rightful home, the planets aligned in their proper universe.

"We had a pretty good lead at that last weather mark," said Rich. But it proved tenuous. The Aussies, Rich felt, had started the Cup series at the base of a steep learning curve. "They hadn't been tested, they really didn't know how to sail their boat yet. It's how we took those first two," he said.

But now the Aussies knew exactly what they had and what to do with it, and while the Americans jibed back and forth toward the mark, adding considerable distance through the water, the crew on *Australia II* pointed their versatile vessel directly for the target, sailing "lower" and faster. At that point, Conner, Rich said, wondered aloud if anyone had any ideas. *Uh-oh*, Rich thought. *We're in trouble.*

ACROSS THE water, journalist Barbara Lloyd was watching the action from the press boat, *New Englander II*, which also served as a spectator craft. With good reason, Lloyd, then a columnist for *The Providence Journal* (before her long tenure with *The New York Times*), had mixed emotions about what she was seeing.

It had been a long, tiring summer for her and for the dozens of correspondents and photographers who'd been dispatched to Newport from newspapers, television stations, and magazines around the world. She was ready for a vacation. If the Americans were victorious—ho hum, they won again—it'd start as soon as she filed her last Cup story. However, with another Cup writer, Michael Levitt, Lloyd had a pending book contract contingent upon an Australian victory, a project with a short deadline: one month. For professional reasons, that was alluring, too. But when the Americans extended their lead to nearly a minute, she figured it was all out of her hands.

"I was greatly relieved," she said. "All the spectators were drinking, it was a big holiday for them. I never drank when I was working. But someone offered me a beer and I said, 'Yeah, give me that beer.' Then someone else said, 'Hey, know what? I think Dennis is behind.' And I looked out, and that was exactly what had happened."

As Lloyd put down her bottle—"I was in, like, shock"—about 10 miles away, in a bar on lower Thames Street, I was picking one up. ABC and CBS had sent small armies to town to telecast the scheduled deciding race on Saturday afternoon, which had ultimately been postponed because of light wind. Now, on what would come to be referred to as Black Monday, the networks were gone but WJAR-TV in Providence was broadcasting live, with aerial footage. After hearing about the late Aussie charge on Newport's local AM-radio station, WADK, I'd bee-lined it into Café Zelda in search of fellowship and fortification, and to bear slack-jawed witness to what was about to unfold. I wasn't alone.

AT TWENTY minutes past five, with star-crossed *Liberty* forty-one seconds in arrears and the sun already sinking in the western sky, *Australia II* crossed the finish line after her dramatic come-from-behind triumph and changed the America's Cup, and Newport, once and for all.

"It got real quiet [on *Liberty*]," said Rich. "That night is kind of a blur."

"I remember the town being as alive as you'd ever see it," said Lloyd, who went on to co-author the critically acclaimed account of the summer, *Upset: Australia Wins the America's Cup.* "And that was that, the beginning of a long thirty days."

For me, and countless others, it was only the start of a very long evening. I hopped aboard my friend Dan Spurr's dilapidated plywood launch, a leaky beast he called "the Red Rocket," and zoomed down to the Aussie docks for their arrival. The harbor was electric: horns blared, flares were ignited, there was screaming, shouting, crying, every form of emotion and nonsense imaginable.

Once *Australia II* was alongside the pier at Newport Offshore and safely secured in her slings, Alan Bond, the rich, rotund Aussie who'd bankrolled the campaign, acquiesced to the crowd's growing chant: "Show us the keel!" Like a preacher granting salvation, Bond lifted his palms skyward and *Australia II* followed, hoisted clear from the water without the drapes that usually covered her from prying eyes, the strange winged keel a rumor no longer. We paddled over to touch it, to perhaps gain knowledge of what had transpired, pilgrims searching for clarity. But they were just a set of big blue plates, and rather industrial-looking ones at that. It was impossible to fathom. These things had been our undoing? Here was the reason the Cup was gone?

THE AMERICAS CUP races arrived in Newport in 1930, when the New York YC abandoned the fickle, longstanding venue off Sandy Hook, New Jersey, in pursuit of finer breeze. Through three defenses, to 1937, the regatta was contested in magnificent J-Boats by barons called Vanderbilt and Sopwith and Lipton. A world at war put all that aside until 1958, when racing resumed in sleek 12-Meter sloops, and a new roster of Cup heroes—Mosbacher, Bavier, Ficker, Hood, Turner, Jobson, Conner—made their names on Rhode Island Sound.

Growing up on Aquidneck Island, I wasn't a sailor—not yet—but I loved those Cup summers in the '60s and '70s, loved walking down Thames St. on an August evening and hearing the accents—French, British, Italian, Australian—from all those drawn to our shores with hopes and dreams of whisking the Cup away. It seemed quaint, almost, that they'd come so far on such a futile exercise—after all, the Cup wasn't going anywhere, it was practically a birthright—but it made them all the more admirable. They were sportsmen in the truest sense of the word, and to my youthful eyes it made their hapless quest even nobler.

By 1983, however, I knew a thing or two about sailing, and shuffling down Thames Street in the wee morning hours of September 27—the first day of the new Newport—a few things were abundantly clear. First, there was one hell of a mess to clean up: they'd shut down lower Thames in the aftermath of the Australian triumph and the place had gone off; the empty beer cans were literally ankle deep. Second, that kooky keel had indeed been the centerpiece of a breakthrough 12-Meter, and you had to hand it to the Aussies: back then, as the Cup's original Deed of Gift stipulated, the race really was about "competition between foreign countries," and the Australians had proved that their sailors, yacht designers, and builders were more than a match for the Americans. Finally, Newport was at a crossroads, and that was most unsettling. What in heavens would happen next?

Brad Read, the executive director of the community sailing organization called Sail Newport, is unequivocal. "Losing the Cup," he says, "is the best thing for sailing in Newport that ever could've happened. It focused more attention on one-design sailing and fleet growth. Local fleets, like the J/24s and the Shields, just exploded. Kids sailing became huge. And I can make the argument that more big regattas and dramatic events happened after the Cup was gone than at any time previous to that."

Sail Newport was the brainchild of a band of local sailors and businessmen, a group that included Bart Dunbar, Robin Wallace, Dave Maguire, Tom Rich, and many others, and was originally launched as an event-management organization whose charge was to bring major regattas and races to local waters. And it was an immediate success, luring the Maxi-Boat Worlds to Newport in 1985. Today, while it still hosts and manages numerous events, Sail Newport's fundamental mission has expanded to the point that it's also what Read calls "a true public sailing organization" that has opened sailing, and access to local waters, to one and all.

Ironically, the New York YC, once viewed by many as sad Cup losers, has become a vibrant force in the local sailing scene. "They want to have big events, they want to host world championships, and they're willing to support these things with their volunteers, membership and money," said Read.

But if something was gained by the events of 1983, something was lost, as well.

"There was a huge vacuum afterwards," said Barbara Lloyd. "Summers are still crowded, but those people who came during the Cup really enriched the town. They weren't here for a day off a cruise ship; they came from all over the world and they lived here with us. They brought their families, they rented houses, they ate in the restaurants and drank in the bars. You were in the presence of a very international community, and they were here with a real purpose. There have been a lot of efforts to fill that gap, and Newport will always be a fabulous town because there is so much more than yachting here.

"But we'll never be able to duplicate what we had. And that's very unfortunate."

I WENT ON to cover a lot of America's Cup regattas after 1983, for sailing magazines and *The New York Times*. The best, in my opinion, were in 1987 and 2000. In the former, representing his hometown of San Diego, Dennis Conner went to Australia on a boat with a name that meant something—*Stars & Stripes*—and redeemed himself in the eyes of the world with a stirring victory. In the latter, a boatload of Kiwis defended the Cup on their home waters, a victory that galvanized the tiny, sailing-crazed nation.

Then, in 2003, a Swiss billionaire won it with a band of Kiwi mercenaries, an event that was devastating to the entire nation of New Zealand. Perhaps appropriately, he called his boat *Alinghi*, which has no meaning—he just liked the way it sounds. (The notorious regatta is covered in the final chapter of this book.) People tell me that the Cup was always about rich boys and their fabulous toys, but after 2003, the Cup lost its luster for me, and I haven't covered another one since.

Tom Rich, fresh out of college like a lot of the guys on board, made $7 a day in the summer of 1983, and that was for working on the boats, not sailing them...he did that for free, because he loved the sport. Don't fret for him, however; he's now one of the principals in Portsmouth's New England Boatworks, a going concern that's earned a formidable reputation amongst sailors. He's still working on the boats.

But in the immediate moments after the Cup was lost, almost by intuition, he went down below and grabbed the Ensign, the American flag, and unfurled it off *Liberty*'s transom. It fluttered in the breeze as the silent boat picked up a tow and returned to a changed town.

# 27: Where the Figawi?

## JOUSTING WITH TED KENNEDY

THE BIG, gray-haired dude behind the wheel looked remarkably familiar, of that there was little doubt. And in the clarity of hindsight, it couldn't possibly have been anyone else. But at that very instant, perhaps due to the heat of the moment, or the unfamiliar context in which the encounter took place, it took a long second to register that the man at the helm of the classic, beautiful blue schooner whose bow we were now crossing by a not-at-all considerable distance—and in a chartered bareboat no less, a vessel for which we harbored no true sense of attachment or sentiment—was in fact the senior Senator for the great Commonwealth of Massachusetts.

Yup. Ted Kennedy.

We were closing in on the finish line of the 36th annual Figawi Race from Hyannis—the long-time Kennedy family encampment on Cape Cod—to the outlying isle of Nantucket, on a glorious Saturday over Memorial Day weekend. The 22-mile contest across Nantucket Sound, to be honest, had been more of a cruise-in-company with a few thousand other kindred spirits in the 240-boat fleet. After a short beat upwind, we'd rounded the sole weather mark and cracked off to a tight reach for the finish just off the entrance to Great Harbor, where all sorts of nonsense and festivities awaited.

There was a definite *Sailing World* magazine bias to our crew: I was trimming main and playing connect-the-dots with the chartplotter, editor Dave Reed was on the jib and calling tactics, and senior editor and Figawi skipper Stu Streuli was on the helm. Stu's wife, Leslie, and our buddies Brian Cooney and Paul Faerber rounded out the team. We were sailing an immaculate, brand-spanking-new Beneteau 423 called *Summer Breeze* that we'd chartered back home in Newport.

We weren't alone. There were four other identical Beneteaus in our 14-boat, non-spinnaker class, which provided a nice little one-design element to the day's exercise. At the outset, Stu had made one thing perfectly clear. Especially on handicap, he didn't particularly care if we trailed the other boats in our division, which included an Ericson 38, a Baltic 37, a C&C 38, a Sabre 38, and an Alerion 33, all relatively quick steeds. But if we weren't the first Beneteau home, boat for boat, returning to Newport might not be an option.

For the first 21 miles, it was all going very much according to plan. We'd nailed the pursuit-style start. The sun was shining overhead, the 15-knot southwester was ideal, and we had the boat in a groove. The other Beneteaus were all properly astern.

And then that gorgeous 50-foot Concordia schooner from Hyannisport, *Mya*, came roaring up from behind, and we had one more obstacle to overcome before glory (such as it was) would be ours.

> So this guy goes to the house next door and says to his neighbor, "Gee, I think my wife is dead." And the neighbor says, "Really. That's awful! Why do you think that?" And the first guy says, "Well, the sex is the same but the dishes are piling up in the sink!"
> —Unknown Comic #1
> Figawi Annual Sunday Morning Joke-Telling Session

AS WE STEPPED on the launch in Newport for the ride out to the boat before heading to the regatta, a woman with a Nantucket sweatshirt was stepping off. I happened to mention we were headed in that direction and her companion asked about our plans.

"We're doing the Figawi," I said.

Her friend raised his eyebrows and chuckled knowingly. "Bring those rum-drinking shoes," he said.

To say the Figawi's reputation precedes itself would be an understatement.

The first Figawi, so the story goes, started in 1972 when a handful of friends and families decided that a fun race from Hyannis to Nantucket during Memorial Day weekend would be a swell way to spend a day and launch the sailing season, not to mention an inarguable means by which to settle the ongoing discussion of who owned the fastest boat. In this very grass-roots manner, a tradition was launched.

Figawi? The following anecdote may be apocryphal, but there's little doubt that Nantucket Sound and nearby Vineyard Sound can attract more than a small bit of fog. In the days before GPS put an end to navigational nightmares, it was not at all uncommon to become a bit wayward when transiting from the mainland to the island. And so when that first lost navigator, in his best Cape Cod accent, asked, "Where the Figawi?" the fledgling regatta also had a name.

By the late 1970s, word was spreading about this small, regional event, and the numbers began to grow. In 1978, organizers added a lay day and a race back to Hyannis, making it a 3-day affair. And the East Coast hailing ports from which sailors came to attend the Figawi continued to expand.

In the race program, Figawi board member Charlie McLaughlin summed up the welcoming feeling extended to every Figawi sailor:  "Your decision to join us in this event reflects an unusual level of intelligence, bonhomie, determination, and perseverance.  We are glad that you made it.  We hope that it's either the start of a long tradition or the next chapter of an even longer one.  And while we don't count heads, our guesstimate is that you have joined a rather non-exclusive club of some fifty thousand or more sailors who have tied up before you and taken home many great memories, most of which can be shared."

> I was at the Atlantic buffet last night and I was talking to this admiral, an elderly guy, and we were discussing our sex lives.  So I asked him, when was the last time for you?  And he says, "1955."  I say to him, "That's too bad."  And he looks at me and goes, "Not really.  It's only 2210."
>
> —Unknown Comic #2
> Figawi Annual Sunday Morning Joke-Telling Session

OF COURSE, as Charlie readily admits, some of those memories, depending on whom with which you're considering sharing them, are better kept within.  Certainly that's the case with Sunday morning's annual Joke-Telling Session, an event fueled by cheap mimosas and driven by a platoon of long-time Figawi regulars known as the Band of Angels.  They may be angels, but it's hard to tell which heaven they call home.

We've taken the liberty of publishing a few jokes, and to those who take offense, we apologize.  However, if you find these off-color, by all means, steer clear of the Figawi event tent on Sunday morning.  Way clear.  There are lots of churches open for business on Sundays in Nantucket.

One thing about the Joke-Telling Session, it's an equal opportunity offender. Being Nantucket, there are certainly more than a few filthy limericks aired out, but otherwise, the topics are wide-ranging and all-inclusive, and include men in prison, children's train sets, sex, priests, white people, black people, sex, Mexicans, Asians, Europeans, sperm whales, sex, the male anatomy, the female anatomy, sex, Genies who grant wishes, bodily functions, sex, doctor's visits, and, oh yes, sex.

Now there were a lot of things I really enjoyed over Figawi weekend. Heck, even the delivery out was a blast. You always feel like you're in the islands when the soundtrack over the radio is from WMVY (92.7 FM) on the Vineyard (even if the James Taylor tunes drive some of your crewmates crazy). Once out there, it was very hard not to get wrapped up in the ongoing discussion and debate over the proposed Cape Wind "wind farm" turbines on Nantucket Sound (and the local's vehement objection thereto). The sight of dozens and dozens of boats of all sizes and description motoring out to the starting line off Hyannis, and then parading back into the marina in Nantucket, was very, very cool. There's nothing more fun than renting bikes and tooling around Nantucket on its beautiful, winding bike paths. And the tent parties, overall, were hilarious.

When all was said and done, however, that Joke-Telling Session is the one thing that might really stand out.

Oh, yeah, that and Ted Kennedy.

A Greek guy and an Italian guy are arguing over who has the superior culture. All day long, back and forth, back and forth. The Greek says, "We built the Parthenon." The Italian says, "We built the Coliseum." The Greek says, "We gave birth to higher mathemat-

ics." The Italian says, "We forged the Roman Empire."
All day long, back and forth. Finally, the Greek guy
says, "We invented sex!" And the Italian says, "Yeah,
but we introduced it to women!"

—Unknown Comic #3
Figawi Annual Sunday Morning Joke-Telling Session

FIRST OFF, as the Senator himself might say, we need to
make one thing perfectly clear. Yes, there's no question that he's
had some well-chronicled misadventures in these waters, and
you may or may not necessarily care for his politics, but the man
definitely is a sailor, and a good one at that.

Approaching that finish line, we just needed to keep our
air clear and get across cleanly when Kennedy's *Mya* came rolling up to weather. Stu asked if we had room to cut ahead and
before he had a definite answer, the wheel was over and we were
clearly slicing over and past the schooner, with perhaps a boat
length to spare. Kennedy, regal behind the wheel, couldn't have
been more nonplussed. With a level gaze, he kept his perfectly
trimmed boat rolling right along. Midway through the maneuver, I glanced back, did a double take, and realized precisely with
whom we were dealing.

For the crew of *Summer Breeze*, it was our very first Figawi,
and we wouldn't require the Mt. Gay hats to commemorate it.

We had our souvenir.

*Herb McCormick*

**With Ted Kennedy's gorgeous schooner, *Mya*, in the background, skipper Stuart Streuli drives for the finish line of the often-hilarious Figawi race.**

A couple of years after writing this piece for *Sailing World* about jousting with Ted Kennedy off Nantucket, the illustrious politician succumbed to cancer and the wind farm project called Cape Wind, which is mentioned in this story, was finally granted approval after many contentious years. For better or worse, I'm convinced the latter would never have happened if Kennedy were still alive. Together, they marked the end of a singular era.

Bobby Grieser

**When Team New Zealand lost their mast on a windy day on the Hauraki Gulf, their hopes of defending the America's Cup toppled with it.**

For one publication or another, I covered every America's Cup from 1987, in Australia, to 2003, in New Zealand, which turned out to be not only a sporting event, but also a morality play. There sure was plenty of grist for the mill. Still, it turned out to be my last one, and later, when the event moved back into the courtrooms, I was happy to be done with it. But despite what many of my colleagues think, the announcement in 2010 that the next Cup will be contested in 72-foot catamarans, in my opinion, is pretty cool. There may be hope for the Auld Mug yet.

*Loyalty and Cyanide*

# 28: Loyalty and Cyanide

## HEROES AND VILLAINS AT THE AMERICA'S CUP

IN KEEPING with the party's circus theme, colorful clowns wielded tequila-filled squirt guns, and into one gaping mouth after another they happily dispensed a long, burning rivulet of gold. The big boat shed had been transformed into a concert hall, and live bands entertained hundreds of revelers. Out by the water, before the sparkling skyline of Auckland, New Zealand, a full-size merry-go-round and its partying passengers spun circles in the night. And on a nearby backstage, a pair of transvestites were, well, never mind.

The surreal scene was the syndicate headquarters of the Alinghi Challenge of Switzerland, which, hours earlier, on a brilliant early-March afternoon in 2003, had unceremoniously dispatched with a remarkably outclassed Team New Zealand defense effort in the series' fifth and final race to win the America's Cup by the startling score of five-zip. After a 152-year hiatus, the America's Cup was bound for Europe in the unlikely grasp of a new, landlocked defender. The Alinghi circus and its billionaire ringleader, pharmaceutical heir Ernesto Bertarelli, had indeed come to town and now the Cup was headed—in both literal and figurative terms—far, far away.

In the days that followed, Bertarelli announced the formation of an allegiance with vanquished American challenger Larry Ellison's Oracle BMW syndicate and San Francisco's Golden Gate Yacht Club, which in union would serve as the Challenger of Record for the 32nd Cup. Next, Alinghi unveiled a new protocol for the event designed to haul the Auld Mug, kicking and screaming, into the 21st century.  And then, his $80 million antipodal adventure having concluded in such excellent style, Bertarelli boarded a chartered plane in company with sailing's most prestigious if gaudy prize, and the Royal New Zealand Yacht Squadron's eight-year Cup stewardship was well and truly over.

But that was merely the final act in a maritime drama that had unfolded with countless subplots about boat design, sailing prowess, the specter of terrorism, and even national loyalty. For on that last count Bertarelli was hardly a lone accomplice in Alinghi's clinical Cup heist.  Leading his charge were a pair of expatriate Kiwis named Russell Coutts and Brad Butterworth, the modern-day Butch and Sundance of the America's Cup, the men who helped bring it to New Zealand, who defended it once for their homeland, and who in record-setting fashion would ultimately and controversially spirit it away.

When their work was done on March 2nd, Bertarelli threw his party, and the next morning, the country of New Zealand woke up with a raging hangover and a singular question with no easy answer:  How in the world did it happen?

WHEN RACING began a fortnight earlier, Team New Zealand (TNZ) seemed a confident bunch, and with just cause.  The primary source behind their outward optimism was their radical yacht, NZL-82.  The brainchild of a design team led by syndicate chief Tom Schnackenberg (aka "Schnack"), along the underbody of its stern counter the boat sported a much-ballyhooed hull appendage, or "Hula."  Also dubbed the "Kiwi clip-on" (sailing writers couldn't stop nicknaming the thing), the hula was essentially a second skin attached on centerline designed to probe a loophole in the International America's Cup Class (IACC) design rule, enhance waterline length and, ultimately, increase boat speed.

"Hula, hula, hula," went the waterfront chant. "New Zealand's gonna do ya."

But the Hula wasn't the only TNZ design innovation. In the overall theoretical scheme of things, equally important were the tall, unprecedented four-spreader rig and the remarkable, twenty-foot-long ballast bulb affixed to the keel which reportedly accounted for nearly 80 percent of the yacht's full-up 25 tons. In both its vast length and narrow, flat-bottomed cigar shape, it was far different than those employed by any of the current generation of IACC boats. Among other benefits, the bulb's mighty heft and purported stability allowed its designers to press on more sail area than Alinghi.

"There's no use being timid about these things," said the TNZ appendage designer, Nick Holroyd.

"We think we understand the design game," said Schnack on the eve of competition. "If we understand it as well as we think we do, we should have a little edge."

If history was any indication, there was no reason to doubt him. In the previous two America's Cups—their successful challenge against Dennis Conner's Stars & Stripes syndicate off San Diego in 1995, and their subsequent defense versus Italy's Prada Challenge in 2000—the Kiwis were undefeated (10-0) and in all ways dominant, thanks in no small part to their decided advantage in boat speed.

And as Conner once said, "The America's Cup is all about boat design; the only reason they race is to keep score."

Now, Schnack was essentially saying he and his team had taken that proven design prowess in the America's Cup arena and raised it to a new level. Coming from Schnack—a qualifed

nuclear physicist, one of the primary contributors to the burgeoning TNZ dynasty, the man Conner once called "the best
brain in yachting"—these were powerful words.

On the other hand, by virtue of their victorious 28-3 on-
the-water record in the Louis Vuitton challenger's series leading
up to the Cup, it was clear that Alinghi's yacht, SUI-64, was no
pushover. Though principal designer Rolf Vrolijk and his tech-
nicians hadn't necessarily pushed the design envelope to the
extent the Kiwis had, they'd created a fine all-around boat and
introduced some significant innovations, particularly in the rig
and sail plan. Alinghi was responsible for, among other things,
the square-topped, windsurfer-style mainsail that'd become the
standard cut of main for the other challengers as well as TNZ.

Still, going into the event, when it came to the matter of
yacht design there were few knowledgeable observers who believed that Alinghi could possibly have come up with the quicker
ride.

The TNZ sailing team could only hope this was true, for the
pressure on them was enormous. On the morning of February
15th, the first day of racing, in an editorial under the headline,
"Pray for a fair wind and a faster boat," the country's leading
newspaper, *The New Zealand Herald*, summed up the prevailing
national sentiment: "The new young (TNZ) crew, mostly un-
tested in the America's Cup, carry the hopes of every loyal New
Zealander as they set out to defeat the heroes of yesteryear... To
be honest, we don't really want a good match. We want to keep
the Cup."

Expectations were high and the stage was set for the re-
vamped hometown team to rise to fresh glory. Or, of course, to
suffer a terrible fall.

IT WAS A glorious day befitting the start of something big. The sky overhead was blue and clear and the beautiful Hauraki Gulf was flecked with whitecaps, the product of a puffy 20-25 knot southerly breeze gifted by the passage of an overnight front. Into the roiled sea steamed a massive spectator fleet estimated at nearly 3,000 vessels, the majority of which flew a black flag with the same one-word message as that displayed on the giant banner streaming from a helicopter aloft.

Loyal.

The title of a tune by popular Kiwi singer Dave Dobbyn, "Loyal" had not only become the TNZ theme song, it'd also become the catchword by which the very nature of the imminent competition was being defined.  To many, the protagonists were as clearly drawn as the good guys and bad guys in a spaghetti western.  On the one side you had Coutts and Butterworth and the small band of fellow New Zealand Cup veterans whose services Bertarelli had acquired to form the strong core of the international Alinghi team.

Or, in local parlance, the bloody traitors.

On the other you had 29-year-old TNZ skipper Dean Barker—Coutts's former understudy, to whom he'd graciously handed the wheel in the fifth and deciding race of the 2000 Cup against Prada—and his young, fresh-faced crew of sailors who, in the eyes of their supporters, had resisted the cash call of challenging overseas billionaires and remained true to the patriotic cause of defending the Cup for proud New Zealand.

The loyalists.

When the gun fired to start Race 1, however, finally they were all just sailors.  And it was seemingly time to discover which were the best.  But, as events quickly proved, that would have to wait for another day.

For the first race, beset by Kiwi gear failure, was little more than a TNZ comedy of errors, finished almost before it began. Just minutes into the inaugural upwind leg, over its cockpit rails NZL-82 began to ship truckloads of water, later estimated to be upwards of six tons. The alarming image of a Kiwi crewman up to his knees in aqua and bailing frantically with the plastic bucket that doubled as the onboard head—and failing to make the least bit of headway—would be a lasting one.

But that was just the first fallen domino. Minutes later, the outboard end of the slim carbon boom broke away, rendering the mainsail powerless. Then, the genoa's tack fitting exploded and the headsail peeled loose from the stay. An attempt to rehoist the sail up the damaged headstay track was an exercise in futility. Some twenty minutes into their second defense, the Kiwis unceremoniously retired from Race 1 and the Swiss yacht sailed the course unchallenged to take a 1-0 lead.

"Once the boom broke we knew it was going to be a struggle," said Barker. "It went from bad to worse."

Though he didn't know it at the time, the next day's loss would be even more painful. After trailing Alinghi up the first weather leg of Race 2, in an ideal, 12-knot northerly seabreeze the Kiwis overtook SUI-64 on the subsequent run and opened up a 34-second lead at the bottom mark.

"The Hula is a rocketship!" bellowed New Zealand television commentator Peter Lester. But it was wishful thinking; a favorable windshift and better breeze on the left side of the racecourse were the true reasons behind the successful come-from-behind maneuver.

Still, when the two boats rounded the buoy after the third and final beat, and hoisted spinnakers for the closing run to the finish, NZL-82 held what appeared to be a comfortable 26-second lead. It proved to be a mirage. Sailing under a flatter chute that more than compensated for the Kiwi's long waterline and extra sail area, in a devastating display of skill, speed, and power, Alinghi climbed over TNZ, jibed in front, and held on to win the race by a mere 7 seconds. The score: Alingi 2, TNZ 0.

"We're disappointed," said Barker, "but I think we can take a lot of positives out of today. We know we're competitive, so now it's up to us to make sure we don't make mistakes."

Two days later, in the moments leading up to the start of Race 3, they made a small one. But up against as formidable— and, sometimes, lucky—a tactician as Butterworth, it was fatal.

The third race was decided by a 20-degree wind shift that filled in literally moments after the start, and it was Butterworth who had Alinghi perfectly positioned on the course's right-hand flank to employ it. Ironically, Barker later explained that the TNZ weather team had recommended the right, but because of "confusion" onboard they set out for the left, in effect handing the race to the Alinghi, who never trailed. It was an admirable, if unsettling, admission, one that would soon lead to rumblings about the replacement of his schoolboy friend and tactician, Hamish Pepper. Once ahead, the Swiss sailed flawlessly, applying a taut cover around the remainder of the track to win by four-and-a-half boat lengths, or 23 seconds.

"Once again," wrote the observant British yachting journalist Tim Jeffrey, "the speed margin between Alinghi's SUI-64 and Team New Zealand's NZL-82 is infinitesimal, but the gulf between the teams is gigantic."

In four short days, the Kiwis had managed to lose in a variety of ways and found themselves in a deep hole. But as the days ahead would prove, there'd be no quick denouement to the 31st Cup.

ON THE SIXTH day of the exhausting ten-day layover between the third and fourth races of the match, Alinghi chief (and
onboard navigator) Ernesto Bertarelli lost it. "This," he declared,
"is a zoo."

Bertarelli's beef was with the Royal New Zealand Yacht
Squadon's principal race officer, Harold Bennett, who wound up
cancelling seven races during the span because of a pair of gales
and an endless string of zephyrs. "The average breeze on the
How-Wacky is a perfect 15 knots," noted *Washington Post* columnist Angus Phillips. "Half the time it blows 30, the other half it's
zero."

On several of the light, shifty days with the breeze ranging anywhere from 4-8 knots, the Alinghi afterguard reckoned
conditions were fine for racing. So, too, did many vocal members of the media. But Bennett wouldn't budge and, not surprisingly, he had Schnackenberg's full support. "If it becomes a coin
toss," said Schnack, after one light-air cancellation, "it's not the
America's Cup."

Only later did it become clear that TNZ's only chance of
winning a race might've been on a lucky shift on a fluky day.

But the Kiwis weren't going down without a fight, which
was evident when they announced a key crew change: French
match-racing ace and practice-boat helmsman Bertrand Pace
would come aboard NZ-82 as tactician in place of the rookie Cup
sailor Hamish Pepper, who did not survive the Race 3 loss.

Naturally, the TNZ backers didn't play the loyalty card when
it came to Pace or regular crewman and strategist Adam Beashel,
the youngest member of a famous Australian sailing clan. But
if an appreciation of irony was in short supply, simple common
sense had plain run out.

That was obvious when a Squadron member petitioned to have fellow "life members" Coutts and Butterworth, two of New Zealand's most accomplished sailors ever, expelled from its hallowed halls. Then came an extraordinary newspaper article about Coutts in the *Herald* entitled "Sailor of Fortune," which was not so much a profile as a character assassination.

"In many ways Russell Coutts and Switzerland have a lot in common," wrote reporter Jan Corbett. "They're both lovely to look at, in a conventional, angular, thin-lipped sort of way... They both have fashioned themselves as repositories for large amounts of money, often appearing in the same sentence as 'bank account'..." That was the opener. Then it got ugly.

For Corbett and others, the amusing game of "bashing Russell" helped fill the vacuum during the excruciating hiatus. Coutts's life story was certainly compelling: Having excelled as a junior sailor in his youth, he went on to win gold in the Finn class at the 1984 Los Angeles Olympics, became a world-champion match racer, and eventually earned the honor of driving Team New Zealand in back-to-back Cup-winning campaigns.

It was following his second Cup triumph, in 2000, that things became complicated. After dispatching with ease Italy's Prada Challenge, Coutts proclaimed that he planned to be at the forefront of a Kiwi dynasty that would retain the Cup for the next two decades. Then, some three months later—having cast his lot with Bertarelli and Alinghi for a reputed $5 million—he quit TNZ and brought Butterworth and four other veteran Kiwi Cup sailors with him. The Herald's front-page headline screamed, "We feel betrayed."

Three years later, on the eve of this Cup, Coutts revealed details of the complex trust under which the TNZ syndicate operated, and the difficult financial terms under which he, Butterworth, and Schnackenberg would've labored had they taken over the administrative reins from the group led by the late Sir Peter Blake. Blake's status as a legend whose reputation was beyond reproach—especially after being tragically slain in the Amazon in early 2002—didn't simplify an already sensitive situation.

In the end, however, given the opportunity (and the cash) presented to him by Bertarelli, the widespread practice of crewman and designers crossing nationality barriers, and the baggage he would've inherited had he stayed, few sailors begrudged Coutt's decision. It was quite another matter to many citizens in his homeland where, in many ways, his vast skills and unparalleled talent were never appreciated until he was gone.

It's a very old story.

But the Coutts affair wasn't the only toxic topic to emerge during the long, endless break. On February 25th, four days before racing recommenced, a letter containing cyanide and a threat of terrorism at the Cup races was delivered to the British embassy. It turned out to be an empty threat, but a disturbing reminder of the times in which we live.

For the Kiwis, more bad news was just around the corner.

WHEN TNZ and Alinghi reconvened for the long-awaited fourth race on March 1st, it was to a far different Hauraki Gulf than the one they'd encountered exactly two Saturdays before. Perhaps it was the low, bleak sky and lumpy seaway, or the discouraging showing by the hometown lads in the first three races, but on this summer weekend afternoon the scores and scores of spectator craft that'd stirred the waters on the opening day were absent.

Aussie journalist Bruce Montgomery, surveying the scene from the media vessel, counted fewer than a hundred boats in the starting area. For those resolute souls bobbing along under the Loyal flags, what they would soon witness would severely test their loyalty.

It wasn't a beautiful day, but it was dramatic. After three days of strong easterly winds there were significant swells of up to six feet coursing down the Gulf, and gusts registering in the upper 20-knot range continued to fuel the chop. Later, in yet another telling remark, Barker would say, "We certainly didn't expect to be racing in 28-29 knots during the Cup."

With a late hoist of their headsail just prior to the pre-start maneuverings, it started out poorly for the Kiwis. Alinghi jumped on their gaffe, easily won the start, and quickly consolidated on their early lead. After two legs Coutts and his mates held a slim but comfortable 17-second advantage.

As the Kiwis rounded the bottom mark and came hard on the wind for the second upwind beat, the scene aboard NZ-82 was deteriorating. Compared to SUI-64, the New Zealand boat appeared to be laboring, its fine, narrow bow often submarining through the waves while the Swiss boat, with its fuller forward section, lifted and knifed through the seas. Aloft, it was clear the Kiwi mainsail trimmer couldn't control the backwinding mainsail, while Alinghi's main was flat and efficient.

Worse still for the New Zealanders, the cockpit was once again awash and the bucket brigade in full bailing mode. Despite Schnack's denials, there were more than a few shoreside observers convinced that the Kiwis were purposely channeling water onboard in an effort to sink the Hula and maximize its capability. But even the conspiracy theorists had to admit this second serious dousing seemed extreme.

And then, perhaps at the worst possible moment, came a series of waves unlike any others. "We've got a flood of water," warned TNZ crewman Adam Beashel, his admonition caught by the onboard TV camera. "Bad wave. Bad wave." He wasn't kidding.

It happened quickly. When NZ-82 plowed down and into the third roller in the set, the loads on the hull and rig were enormous. Something had to give, and it did. With a sick, audible crack, TNZ's carbon-fiber spar buckled and toppled some twenty feet above deck. For all intents and purposes, so too did any hope of defending the Cup.

"This f------ boat!" screamed one frustrated Kiwi sailor, in an understandable if inelegant summation.

The dismasting post-mortem revealed that the stick had broken because of the failure of a custom tip cup at the outboard end of the second spreader, a fitting designed to tie together the discontinuous rod rigging employed on Cup boats. For the second time in four races, Alinghi circled the course alone to register its victory. As they approached the finish line under spinnaker, the sun now shining on its billowing sails, in the background a TNZ crewman took to the shattered rig with a circular saw.

It was another signature snapshot, for if the day had been an indictment of the Kiwi program, it was also a testament to the strength and preparedness of the Alinghi yacht. Now, all that was left was the inevitable.

In keeping with the timing of the series, and perhaps the spirit, racing was cancelled the next day with nary a whisper of air ruffling the still Gulf waters. It was Coutts's forty-first birthday, but he'd have to wait another day for his present.

On March 3rd, the stay of execution was over. On every count, Coutts, Butterworth and the Alinghi crew—which included two Americans, grinder John Barnitt and pitman Josh Belsky—sailed flawlessly. Alinghi hit the starting line perfectly and, as usual, Butterworth nailed the first wind shift. Soon after, he passed to Coutts the precise information he wanted to hear. "We're a little higher, a little quicker," he said.

Perhaps that was the biggest surprise of the match, but now there was no question about it: Alinghi not only had the better sailors but in all conditions, from moderate to heavy, they also had the far better weapon. Butterworth would later discuss the merits of SUI-64, particularly its ability to shift into an extra gear when necessary. "When Russell wants to put the accelerator down he can do that," he said. "I'm not sure the other guys can. It's a great all-around boat."

On the second-to-last run, as if to punctuate the reliability gap in their respective vessels, the Kiwis suffered one last breakdown, a spinnaker pole that shattered after striking the headstay. It was the final indignity. Alinghi won Race 5 by 45 seconds to finish their 5-0 sweep. Barker said, "They completed dominated us. They put together a faultless performance."

He was right. There was little else to say.

AT THE END, the editors of *The New Zealand Herald* rediscovered a welcome smidgen of their missing sense of humor. The Cup, they lamented, was off to "New Swit-zealand."

Indeed it was.

In defeat, the Kiwi's collective upper lip remained stiff. Schnack did concede that when it came to the innovative approach to NZ-82, perhaps they'd gone too far.

"We were very gung-ho in the design of the yacht, the rig, its appendages. We felt, and rightly so, that we were up against a formidable challenge," he said. "[But] we could afford to be more conservative in the design. We don't need to be the lightest here or there. The lesson is to be more conservative."

Amen.

But their boat, of course, was simply one part of the Kiwi's problem. Only in hindsight does the wide discrepancy in talent between the 2003 Cup finalists become clear. Perhaps the best and worst thing that ever happened to young Dean Barker was winning the final race in the 2000 Cup after Coutts handed him the wheel. On the one hand, it opened the door for him to take the helm of TNZ. On the other, it may have given him the false hope that he was ready to compete with his mentor on equal footing. He was not. And in fact, the exposed myth that the Kiwis had an endless well of Cup-caliber sailing talent from which to draw was one of the revelations of the 2003 Cup.

Still, one hopes that when the pain of losing the America's Cup lessens, New Zealanders will fondly remember and be justifiably proud of all the TNZ accomplishments. From their first Cup forays off Fremantle in their "plastic fantastic" 12-Meter to the renegade 1988 "Big Boat" challenge in San Diego to their devastating displays of sailing prowess in successfully challenging for and defending the trophy, they'd enjoyed one helluva ride. And the stunning transformation of the Viaduct Harbor in downtown Auckland will be a lasting legacy of those eventful years.

That said, had Coutts, Butterworth and friends not slipped away, the good times might still be rolling. When Coutts drove Alinghi across the finish line on March 2nd to win his third consecutive Cup, he'd proven not only that he's the world's top sailor but also the best ever to play the esoteric game of America's Cup. His fourteen individual race victories as a skipper surpasses by one the former record of thirteen held by none other than Mr. America's Cup, Dennis Conner. And, of course, the future is wide open.

As with John Lennon and Paul McCartney, the collaboration between Coutts, the deft driver, and Butterworth, the enlightened strategist, is one for the ages. Like the songwriters, their greatest moments have come as a pair, when each tapped into the other's unique talents to maximize their individual potential and create something special and unsurpassed.

For those Kiwis with a sense of history, it might all bring to mind one particularly wistful Beatles tune. For with Coutts, Butterworth, and, now, the America's Cup, gone from their shores, it'd be hard not to believe in, and long for...yesterday.

# Acknowledgments

FIRST OFF, my sincere thanks to all the folks whose stories I've told in the pages of this book. One of the great joys of nonfiction writing—particularly such an esoteric and enjoyable branch as marine journalism—is the opportunity to meet remarkable people and to delve deeply into their lives and times. I've done a bit of straight sports writing over the years, but the thing I love about sailing is that you often get to take part in the endeavor as an active participant, not merely as a reporter. And whether you go to sea with them or not, it's always a privilege to sit down with someone and ask them probing, and sometimes even uncomfortable questions. There wasn't a single person in this collection of tales who wasn't gracious, insightful, and incredibly accommodating. Thanks to everyone.

I've been lucky over the years to work with an extraordinary array of editors and publishers, starting with Murray and Barbara Davis, the founders of *Cruising World* magazine, and my first boss, *CW* executive editor Dale Nouse, a gruff ex-newspaperman who taught me the nuts and bolts of the craft, particularly how to "get off the stage." Sadly, all three are now gone...my gratitude lives on.

I got my start in the business at *Cruising World* (and later went to work for its sister magazine, *Sailing World*) and learned a ton from the rather astonishing list of editors and writers who became colleagues, mentors, and friends. Many of them had more than a little to do with the stories in this anthology. Special thanks go to Bernadette Bernon, Dan Spurr, Tim Murphy, Lynda Childress, Elaine Lembo, George Day, Noreen Barnhart, John Burnham, Gil Rogin, Danny Greene, Betsy Holman, Nim Marsh, Jeremy McGeary, Darrell Nicholson, Mark Pillsbury, Dave Reed, and Stuart Streuli; director of design Bill Roche, with whom I collaborated on countless stories over the years; and publisher Sally

Helme. My editors during my tenure at the *New York Times*, Susan Baker Adams and Neil Amdur, also deserve special recognition.

Over the years I was also fortunate to meet and even work with a wide group of writers whose style, techniques, and efforts greatly influenced mine, including Lin and Larry Pardey, Don Street, Jimmy Cornell, Steve Callahan, Alvah Simon, Barbara Lloyd, Angus Phillips, John Rousmaniere, Gary Jobson, Beth Leonard, Peter Nichols, Jonathan Raban, Derek Lundy, Kevin Patterson, George Vescey, Fatty Goodlander, Scott Bannerot, and the gang at *Latitude 38* (Andy, El Dee, JR, and especially Rob Moore). I've also been fortunate to roam the world with some of the best marine photographers in the field, including Billy Black, Bob Grieser, David Thoreson, Daniel Forster, and Dan Nerney.

I'd also especially like to thank Jim Morehouse of Paradise Cay, Inc. for his immediate, enthusiastic approval for this project and others, and Linda Morehouse for her advice and encouragement, and for pulling a ton of disparate design elements into a cohesive whole. And a tip of the cap to editors at the *Times*, *San Francisco* magazine, *Newport Life* magazine and *Rhode Island Monthly* magazine for permission to use previously published articles.

On a personal note, I'd be seriously remiss without thanking my sister Nina, Bob and Tommy; Carole and the Marshes of New South Wales, Australia; the Hennigans; Gail and Cubbie; Mark, Logan and DT; Cousin Furbio; PK and Terry; and Ski'in Ian, Dana and Abro.

Finally, to my daughter, Maggie: Thank you. You're the reason this book came together; I wanted to find and collect my favorite pieces (so far) so someday you'd have them all in one place. I love you. Now go do your homework.

—Herb McCormick
Newport, RI
March, 2011

# Story Credits

The Not-Quite Mellow Dude: *Sailing World*, July/August 2009

A Spaced Oddyssey? *Cruising World*, October 2009

Requiem for a Mariner: *Cruising World*, November 2006

His Old Man and the Sea: *Cruising World*, July 2003

Travels with Charlie: *Cruising World*, October 2004

The Master of Deviation: *Cruising World*, September 2008

Cruising at 80: *Cruising World*, June 2008

An Anchor Un-swallowed: *Cruising World*, April 2008

A Character's Assassination: *The New York Times*, August 6, 2000

Gone to the Sea: *Cruising World*, February 1993

*Rhode Island Monthly*, March 1993

Fathers and Daughters: *Cruising World*, December 2005

A Merry, Moveable Feast: *Cruising World*, December 2006

Across the Great Southern Ocean: *Cruising World*, August 1996

"Good Morning, Georgetown!": *Cruising World*, March 2010

Enthralled in the Land of Smiles: *Cruising World*, August 2006

Secrets Revealed: *Cruising World*, August 2005

In the Wake of 9/11: *The New York Times*, September 16, 2001

Stranger in a Strange Land: *Cruising World*, September 2001

Third Time Charmed: *Cruising World*, December 2008

Loaded for Bear: *Cruising World*, February 2006

Slidin' to the Island: *Cruising World*, March 2005

A Robust Spot of Yachting: *Sailing World*, June 2009

The Lolita Way: *Sailing World*, October 2008

Blown Away: *San Francisco* magazine, June 1999

The Baja Express: *Sailing World*, June 2008

The Day the Cup Was Lost: *Newport Life* magazine, "Best of 2007" issue

Where the Figawi? *Sailing World*, August 2009

Loyalty and Cyanide: *Cruising World*, May 2003

"This much-deserved anthology confirms what we already knew: Herb McCormick is a damn good storyteller. Every piece has a clever angle to get your attention, and he makes good use of the current vernacular—he knows who he's writing for. There might be a few more literary types out there, but he's the Jack London of contemporary sailing writers. He not only writes knowledgably about boats and weather, builders, and events, but he also penetrates his subjects to expose the ridiculous, the comic, and so insightfully, the tragic. The stories in this volume will enthrall sailors who just want to read about their favored pastime, but like the great South American novelists Herb studied at Williams College, he also exposes the human experience."

—Dan Spurr, former senior editor of *Cruising World*, editor of *Practical Sailor*, and presently editor-at-large of *Professional BoatBuilder* magazine. Author of *Yacht Style, Upgrading the Cruising Sailboat, Your First Sailboat, Steered by the Falling Stars*, and others.


"One of the most adventurous and inquisitive of boating writers, Herb McCormick has done (and written about) almost everything nautical, from the thrills of rounding Cape Horn to the simpler pleasures of cruising with the family. In Herb are combined the kid-in-the-candy-store's endearing amazement that all these things have come his way, and, at the same time, the good reporter's instinct to ask the tough questions—some of them about the sport's icons. *Gone to the Sea* is one good read.

 —John Rousmaniere, author *The Annapolis Book of Seamanship, Fastnet, Force 10*, and other books


"Over the last three decades, Herb McCormick has gone to sea in all kinds of vessels and his vivid reporting has allowed his many followers and fans to share his adventures. This anthology of his best writing is a perfect mix of racing stories and cruising tales, tragic failures and comic encounters, portraits of outstanding sailors and affectionate vignettes of his sailing friends. No other journalist can spin a better sea story than Herb McCormick and the proof is in your hands."

—Jimmy Cornell, author of *World Cruising Destinations, World Cruising Routes* and others.